I

# Facility Environmental Management Approaches

## Lessons from Industry for Department of Defense Facilities

Beth E. Lachman

Frank Camm

Susan A. Resetar

Prepared for the Office of the Secretary of Defense

National Defense Research Institute

RAND

The research described in this report was sponsored by the Office of the Secretary of Defense (OSD). The research was conducted in RAND's National Defense Research Institute, a federally funded research and development center supported by the OSD, the Joint Staff, the unified commands, and the defense agencies under Contract DASW01-01-C-0004.

**Library of Congress Cataloging-in-Publication Data**

Lachman, Beth E.
    Integrated facility environmental management approaches : lessons from
  industry for Department of Defense facilities / Beth E. Lachman, Frank Camm,
  Susan A. Resetar
      p. cm.
    "MR-1343."
    Includes bibliographical references.
    ISBN 0-8330-2995-9
    1. United States—Armed Forces—Facilities—Environmental aspects. 2.
  Environmental management—United States. I. Camm, Frank A.,
  II. Resetar, Susan A. III. Title.

  UA26.A2 L33 2001
  355.7'0973—dc21

                                                                    2001031853

RAND is a nonprofit institution that helps improve policy and decisionmaking through research and analysis. RAND® is a registered trademark. RAND's publications do not necessarily reflect the opinions or policies of its research sponsors.

Published 2001 by RAND
1700 Main Street, P.O. Box 2138, Santa Monica, CA 90407-2138
1200 South Hayes Street, Arlington, VA 22202-5050
201 North Craig Street, Suite 102, Pittsburgh, PA 15213
RAND URL: http://www.rand.org/
To order RAND documents or to obtain additional information,
contact Distribution Services: Telephone: (310) 451-7002;
Fax: (310) 451-6915; Email: order@rand.org

Many new innovative approaches to facilitywide environmental management are emerging throughout the private sector. Commercial facilities have found that such activities make good business sense, with benefits that include cost savings and improved operational flexibility. Department of Defense (DoD) installations have also started implementing and benefiting from such approaches. Leading commercial firms that have successfully implemented integrated approaches to facility environmental management can offer DoD useful insights.

This report documents a study that analyzed industry facilitywide environmental management to find implementation insights for DoD and its installations. This analysis integrates information about the broader evolving environmental policy context, literature about facility environmental management implementation, and two best-in-class facility cases studies, Procter & Gamble Paper Products Company Mehoopany, Pennsylvania, facility and the Walt Disney World Resort facility in Orlando, Florida.

This activity is part of a larger study for DoD that examined environmental management in four key areas: integrated facility management on installations, weapon system development and modification, depot-level logistics processes, and management of cleanup programs. The objective of this research was to help DoD redesign its environmental security program and related processes to meet its environmental obligations with greater economic efficiency to promote DoD's core national security goals. Related reports include Resetar, Camm, and Drezner (1998), Drezner and Camm (1999), Camm (2001), and Camm et al. (2001).

This report may be of interest to defense as well as other public and private sector installation managers, environment management professionals, and environmental policymakers.

The Office of the Deputy Under Secretary of Defense for Environmental Security sponsored this research. It was performed in the Acquisition and Technology Policy Center of RAND's National Defense Research Institute, a federally funded research and development center sponsored by the Office of the Secretary of Defense, the Joint Staff, the unified commands, and the defense agencies.

# CONTENTS

Preface . . . . . . . . . . . . . . . . . . . . . . . . . . . . . . . . . . . . . . . . . .    iii

Figures . . . . . . . . . . . . . . . . . . . . . . . . . . . . . . . . . . . . . . . . . .    xi

Tables . . . . . . . . . . . . . . . . . . . . . . . . . . . . . . . . . . . . . . . . . . .    xiii

Summary . . . . . . . . . . . . . . . . . . . . . . . . . . . . . . . . . . . . . . . . .    xv

Acknowledgments . . . . . . . . . . . . . . . . . . . . . . . . . . . . . . . . . . .    xxv

Abbreviations . . . . . . . . . . . . . . . . . . . . . . . . . . . . . . . . . . . . . .    xxvii

Chapter One
    INTRODUCTION . . . . . . . . . . . . . . . . . . . . . . . . . . . . . . .    1
    DoD's Facility Environmental Issues . . . . . . . . . . . . . . . . .    2
    Analytic Approach . . . . . . . . . . . . . . . . . . . . . . . . . . . . . . .    3
    The Case Studies . . . . . . . . . . . . . . . . . . . . . . . . . . . . . . . .    4
        WDWR's Similarities to a DoD Installation . . . . . . . . . .    5
        P&G Mehoopany's Similarities to a DoD
            Installation . . . . . . . . . . . . . . . . . . . . . . . . . . . . . . .    6
        Using the Case Study Information . . . . . . . . . . . . . . . .    7
    Report Roadmap . . . . . . . . . . . . . . . . . . . . . . . . . . . . . . . .    7

Chapter Two
    ENVIRONMENTAL POLICY CONTEXT . . . . . . . . . . . . . .    9
    Expanding Role of State and Local Governments . . . . . . .    10
    Proactive Environmental Performance Based on
        Collaboration . . . . . . . . . . . . . . . . . . . . . . . . . . . . . . .    11
    Evolving Two-Track Regulatory System . . . . . . . . . . . . . .    12

Chapter Three
PROACTIVE INTEGRATED ENVIRONMENTAL
MANAGEMENT APPROACHES . . . . . . . . . . . . . . . . . . . .    15
EMS and ISO 14001 Approaches  . . . . . . . . . . . . . . . . . .    17
  Total Quality Management Experience Led to the
    Development of ISO 14000 . . . . . . . . . . . . . . . . . . . .    18
  Industry Implementation of ISO 14001 . . . . . . . . . . . . .    20
  Benefits of EMS and ISO 14001 Approaches  . . . . . . . . .    22
  Potential Regulatory Benefits from EMS or ISO
    14001 Implementation . . . . . . . . . . . . . . . . . . . . . . .    23
Environmental Leadership and Project XL
    Experiments  . . . . . . . . . . . . . . . . . . . . . . . . . . . . . .    26
  Intel Corporation, Chandler, Arizona . . . . . . . . . . . . . .    29
  Weyerhaeuser Company, Oglethorpe, Georgia  . . . . . . .    30
  Imation, Camarillo, California  . . . . . . . . . . . . . . . . . .    32
  State Environmental Leadership Experiments . . . . . . . .    33
P2 and Pollution Avoidance Activities  . . . . . . . . . . . . . .    34
  Industry Facilitywide P2 Activities  . . . . . . . . . . . . . . .    36
  Government Laws and Incentive Programs for P2 . . . . .    40
Innovative Facility Permitting Activities . . . . . . . . . . . . .    46
  Industry Facilitywide Permitting Activities  . . . . . . . . . .    46
  States Encouraging Facilitywide Permitting
    Experiments  . . . . . . . . . . . . . . . . . . . . . . . . . . . . . .    49
Other Systems Approaches  . . . . . . . . . . . . . . . . . . . . . . .    52
  Evolving Toward Sustainability  . . . . . . . . . . . . . . . . . .    53
  Eco-Industrial Parks and Industrial Ecology . . . . . . . . .    56
  Ecosystem Management Approaches . . . . . . . . . . . . . . .    58
Integration of Different Approaches . . . . . . . . . . . . . . . . .    61

Chapter Four
SETTING ENVIRONMENTAL GOALS AND ALIGNING
ENVIRONMENTAL ACTIVITIES WITH THEM  . . . . . . . . .    65
A Brief Overview of Environmental Management at
    P&G Mehoopany and WDWR . . . . . . . . . . . . . . . . . .    67
  Environmental Management at P&G Mehoopany . . . . .    67
  Environmental Management at WDWR  . . . . . . . . . . . .    68
Developing a Proactive Set of Environmental Goals  . . . .    70
  Corporation and Facility Places Value on
    Environmental Stewardship . . . . . . . . . . . . . . . . . . . .    70
  The P&G Approach  . . . . . . . . . . . . . . . . . . . . . . . . . .    71
  The WDWR Approach  . . . . . . . . . . . . . . . . . . . . . . . .    74

Further Considerations in Developing Goals . . . . . . . . .    75
Aligning Activities Throughout an Organization with
    Its Environmental Goals . . . . . . . . . . . . . . . . . . . . .    77
Leadership Support for Environmental Management
    Throughout the Organization . . . . . . . . . . . . . . . . .    78
Coalitions with Other Internal Interests . . . . . . . . . . .    79
Environmental Champions with Flexibility and
    Day-to-Day Environmental Responsibility . . . . . . . .    81
Cross-Functional Teams Used for Specific
    Decisions, Projects, and Processes . . . . . . . . . . . . .    82
Responsibilities Defined Clearly Throughout the
    Company and Facility . . . . . . . . . . . . . . . . . . . . . . .    85
Decentralization to Promote Facility Innovation . . . . . .    86
Fostering Continuous Improvement Through
    Information Gathering and Sharing . . . . . . . . . . . . .    89
A Variety of Mechanisms for Internal Information
    Sharing . . . . . . . . . . . . . . . . . . . . . . . . . . . . . . . . .    91
The Keystone of Successful Change Management:
    Creative and Persistent Change Agents . . . . . . . . . .    94
Effective EMSs . . . . . . . . . . . . . . . . . . . . . . . . . . . . . .    96
Overview of P&G Mehoopany's EMS . . . . . . . . . . . . . .    97
Overview of WDWR's EMS . . . . . . . . . . . . . . . . . . . . .    98
Summary . . . . . . . . . . . . . . . . . . . . . . . . . . . . . . . . . .    99

Chapter Five
ENVIRONMENTAL ASSESSMENT, METRICS, AND
PRIORITY SETTING . . . . . . . . . . . . . . . . . . . . . . . . . .    101
Using Environmental Assessment, Metrics, and
    Accounting . . . . . . . . . . . . . . . . . . . . . . . . . . . . . .    101
Environmental Accounting . . . . . . . . . . . . . . . . . . . .    102
Supportive Organizational Context for Environmental
    Accounting and Assessments . . . . . . . . . . . . . . . . .    104
Quantitative and Qualitative Metrics Used to
    Stimulate Innovation . . . . . . . . . . . . . . . . . . . . . . .    106
Environmental Assessment and Prioritization Tools,
    Techniques, and Approaches . . . . . . . . . . . . . . . . .    111
Range of Tools and Techniques Customized for
    a Facility . . . . . . . . . . . . . . . . . . . . . . . . . . . . . . . .    112
Using Business Goals to Justify
    Environmental Actions . . . . . . . . . . . . . . . . . . . . . .    117
Facility P2 Assessments and Justifications . . . . . . . . . .    120

Chapter Six
    PROMOTING EFFECTIVE RELATIONSHIPS WITH
    RELEVANT STAKEHOLDERS ..................... 125
    Honest Environmental Reporting and Dialogues with
        Stakeholders ............................ 126
    Building Trust and Partnerships with Regulators ....... 129
        Taking Advantage of Evolving Regulatory
            Flexibility ............................ 131
        Educating and Training Regulators ............... 133
    Engaging the Surrounding Community, NGOs,
        General Public and Other Key Stakeholders ....... 134
        Employ Diverse Range of Communication
            Mechanisms Based on Facility and Stakeholder
            Needs ........................... 136
        Effectively Using Opinion Surveys ............... 139
        Use of Community Advisory Panels .............. 141

Chapter Seven
    TRAINING AND MOTIVATING ALL EMPLOYEES ....... 143
    Environmental Training for All Employees ............ 143
        Employees Are Empowered with Formal Training ..... 143
        General and Specialized Environmental Training
            Classes Customized for the Facility ............. 145
        Less-Formal Environmental Education Activities ..... 147
    Motivating All Employees ........................ 148
        Placing Appropriate Corporate Values on
            Environmental Issues ...................... 149
        Monetary Incentives and Environmental
            Accountability ........................... 150
        Special Incentives and Techniques for Average
            Employees ............................. 152
        Incentives at Mehoopany ...................... 152
        WDWR's Creative Motivational Incentives .......... 153
        Showing Business Cost Savings from Environmental
            Activities .............................. 156
        Manage Failures to Limit Disincentives for Risk
            Taking ............................... 158

Chapter Eight
    CONCLUSIONS................................ 161

Track and Participate in the Evolving Policy
  Development in Facility Environmental
   Management . . . . . . . . . . . . . . . . . . . . . . . . . . . . .  162
 The Expanding Roles of State and Local
  Governments . . . . . . . . . . . . . . . . . . . . . . . . . . . . . .  162
 Proactive Environmental Performance Based on
  Collaboration  . . . . . . . . . . . . . . . . . . . . . . . . . . . . .  163
 Evolving Two-Track Regulatory System  . . . . . . . . . . . .  164
 Fully Participate in Integrated Environmental
  Management Approaches and Experiments . . . . . . .  164
 Implement Environmental Management Systems that
  Align All DoD Environmental Activities with Core
   DoD Goals . . . . . . . . . . . . . . . . . . . . . . . . . . . . . . . .  166
 Promote and Creatively Use Environmental
  Assessment and Metrics . . . . . . . . . . . . . . . . . . . . . .  169
 Promote Effective Relationships with All Relevant
  Stakeholders  . . . . . . . . . . . . . . . . . . . . . . . . . . . . . .  171
 Train and Motivate All Employees About
  Environmental Issues  . . . . . . . . . . . . . . . . . . . . . . .  174
 Concluding Remarks . . . . . . . . . . . . . . . . . . . . . . . . . . .  176

Appendix A
PROCTOR & GAMBLE MEHOOPANY
ENVIRONMENTAL MANAGEMENT CASE STUDY . . . . . .  177

Appendix B
WALT DISNEY WORLD RESORT ENVIRONMENTAL
MANAGEMENT CASE STUDY . . . . . . . . . . . . . . . . . . . .  223

Bibliography . . . . . . . . . . . . . . . . . . . . . . . . . . . . . . . . . . . .  279

# FIGURES

3.1   The Relationships Among Sustainability Efforts . . . . .   63

5.1   P&G Mehoopany Waste Disposal Costs Versus
      Waste Revenue . . . . . . . . . . . . . . . . . . . . . . . . . . . . .   105

A.1   Waste Disposal Costs versus Waste Revenue . . . . . . .   188

# TABLES

5.1. Environmental Performance Measures— P&G Mehoopany .......................... 110
A.1. P&G's Core Values ......................... 180
A.2. P&G's Core Principles ...................... 181
A.3. P&G Mehoopany Environmental Summary Information .............................. 186
A.4. P&G's Environmental Quality Policy ............ 189
A.5. Comparison of P&G's Global EMS with ISO 14001: Performance Categories ...................... 191
A.6. Areas in Which P&G EMS Meets or Exceeds ISO 14001 ..................................... 192
A.7. Mehoopany Environmental Vision .............. 195
A.8. Environmental Performance Measures— P&G Mehoopany .......................... 206
A.9. Mehoopany Environmental Education ........... 218
B.1. Compelling Business Reasons for Environmentality at WDWR—Laser Printer Cartridges, 1995 ......... 257
B.2. Compelling Business Reasons for Environmentality at WDWR—Recycling Summary by Area, 1995 ...... 258

Integrated facilitywide environmental management approaches examine environmental issues across an entire facility, looking at potential interrelationships and then implementing holistic actions that minimize the total environmental impact. These approaches span across the boundaries of traditional environmental regulation on media and issues (e.g., air, water, land, hazardous waste, species). They not only examine various industrial, commercial, residential, natural resource, facility support, and other environmental sources on a facility but also the different processes, products, and business units.

Many innovative approaches to facilitywide environmental management are emerging in the private sector. Commercial facilities have found that such activities make good business sense, with benefits that include cost savings and improved operational flexibility.

DoD installations have also begun implementing and benefiting from such approaches. These facilitywide policies seek to adjust environmentally relevant processes in ways that enhance DoD's ability to pursue its core military mission while continuing to be an environmentally responsible public agency and setting a good example for others in the government and private sector. Like many of its commercial counterparts, DoD has had difficulty implementing its proactive policies in ways that affect decisions made throughout the organization. Leading commercial firms can offer DoD useful insights about how they have successfully implemented such integrated approaches to facility environmental management.

The Office of the Deputy Under Secretary of Defense for Environmental Security asked RAND to study how commercial firms, recognized as having the best environmental management practices in the country, have implemented these practices. This report provides implementation insights on commercial facilitywide environmental management that are relevant to DoD installations.

Activities often associated with implementing proactive environmental management, in DoD and elsewhere, include

- designing general environmental management systems (EMSs), including metrics, to ensure integration

- training and motivating people

- providing tools and information to support the environmental mission

- promoting effective relationships with relevant stakeholders

- determining the implications of future ISO 14000 implementation.[1]

RAND used interviews and a review of the secondary trade and academic literature to examine the methods that successful, proactive firms use to implement policies relevant to each of these elements. This report integrates information about the broader evolving environmental policy context, literature about facility environmental management implementation, and two case studies of best-in-class facilities, the Procter & Gamble (P&G) Paper Products Company's Mehoopany, Pennsylvania, facility and the Walt Disney World Resort (WDWR) entertainment facility in Orlando, Florida.

This report concludes that DoD should

- track and participate in the evolving policy development on facility environmental management

- fully participate in integrated environmental management approaches and experiments

---

[1]International Organization for Standardization (ISO) 14000 is a series of proposed international guidelines that could become standards for best environmental management practice and could shape DoD's regulatory environment in the future. The first element of the series, ISO 14001, was approved in 1996.

- implement EMSs that align all DoD environmental activities with core DoD values

- promote and creatively use environmental assessment and metrics

- promote effective relationships with all relevant external stakeholders

- train and motivate all DoD personnel about environmental issues.

Various DoD organizations are already trying to do many of these things. DoD can build on this experience and the much broader experience of commercial firms to extend and institutionalize its efforts. This report provides details on how to proceed in each of these areas.

## TRACK AND PARTICIPATE IN THE EVOLVING POLICY DEVELOPMENT IN FACILITY ENVIRONMENTAL MANAGEMENT

The U.S. environmental policy context has been changing for more than a decade now. Emphasis is shifting away from traditional centralized regulatory command and control toward more-flexible approaches that allow all stakeholders to collaborate in proactive ways. State and local governments have more authority and ability to customize regulatory programs and environmental approaches to the unique needs of a specific locale. In this emerging new setting, three closely related policy trends are especially important for DoD facilities:

- the national debate on an expanding role for state and local governments

- expanding opportunities to collaborate with specific state and local governments

- an evolving two-track regulatory system that offers proactive organizations greater regulatory flexibility and maintains traditional regulation for other organizations.

As state and local governments implement more-flexible regulatory programs, local facilities in DoD and elsewhere find it harder to track environmental issues and maintain internally consistent EMSs. The Office of the Secretary of Defense and the services can affect how such flexibility evolves by actively participating in national environmental policy debates and forums regarding this devolution process. They currently engage such organizations as the Environmental Council of the States and the National Pollution Prevention Roundtable, which are active in this new approach to regulation. Such efforts should expand as the environmental policy context continues to evolve.

At the same time, individual DoD installations should actively participate in state and local activities that develop specific new environmental laws and new incentive programs, such as Environmental Leadership experiments and pollution prevention incentive programs.

DoD should expand its engagement with the evolving two-track regulatory system as much as possible. Commercial exemplars, such as the facilities at P&G Mehoopany and WDWR, demonstrate the benefits that can flow from gaining regulators' trust. Significant opportunities exist to transfer lessons learned about this within DoD from its own exemplars to other bases. And as the evolving two-track regulatory system plays out at specific DoD facilities, DoD should bring this experience to bear in the ongoing national policy debate on environmental regulatory reinvention.

## FULLY PARTICIPATE IN INTEGRATED ENVIRONMENTAL MANAGEMENT APPROACHES AND EXPERIMENTS

Industry and federal, state, and local governments are trying to address environmental issues in a more integrated and holistic fashion at individual facilities. Such integrated approaches include using proactive EMSs and assessing them against or registering them to the ISO 14001 standard; environmental leadership experiments, such as Project XL; facilitywide pollution prevention planning and implementation activities; facilitywide permitting approaches; sustainability activities; and ecosystem management. Commercial facilities realize numerous benefits from such efforts, including cost savings, increased operational flexibility, improved facility image, and continuously improving environmental performance.

Some DoD facilities have participated in some of these efforts. DoD should continue to support and expand such participation, especially its ability to try multiple experiments and to find synergies in such efforts. It should transfer lessons learned from such experiments across facilities, especially across the military services. For instance, a more-assertive focus in this area would organize a DoD-wide conference that focuses specifically on integrated environmental management approaches at facilities. At such a conference, both innovative defense facilities and commercial facilities could provide lessons learned.

## IMPLEMENT EMSs THAT ALIGN ALL DoD ENVIRONMENTAL ACTIVITIES WITH CORE DoD GOALS

DoD facilities need to ensure that their EMSs promote and facilitate such innovative integrated facility approaches. Two things will help:

1. DoD should clarify environmental goals that are clearly linked to DoD's core goals: increasing military capability, managing resources efficiently, and complying with federal socioeconomic policy and public administrative laws that pertain to any federal agency. Each of these core goals plays an important role in installation management.

2. Once these environmental goals are clearly stated in terms of DoD's core goals, DoD should refine its EMSs to align all of its activities—environmental activities at individual installations and others—with these clearly stated organizationwide goals.

Commercial experience strongly suggests that such an effort will require a formal change in the management process to succeed. The basic elements of such a process are as relevant to integrated facility management as they are to implementing other changes in environmental management:

- Secure the support of the senior leadership.

- Build coalitions of those at a facility who must change to support implementation.

- Give a champion responsibility for day-to-day oversight at the facility.

- Use cross-functional teams on the facility to integrate relevant points of view.

- Assign clear roles and responsibilities for implementation.

- Decentralize execution to ensure proper integration in each part of the facility.

- Use ongoing information gathering and sharing for continuous improvement throughout the facility.

- Insert and sustain creative and persistent change agents throughout the facility.

- Develop an effective EMS.

Chapter Four discusses these in more detail.

## PROMOTE AND CREATIVELY USE ENVIRONMENTAL ASSESSMENT AND METRICS

Meaningful metrics provide the basis for assessing environmental performance and holding individual organizations accountable for that performance. To succeed, commercial facilities have found that they must hold their line activities accountable and provide metrics that help the activities understand how pursuing improved environmental performance contributes to their core missions. At commercial facilities, these core missions can typically be characterized in dollar terms—costs and net income. In DoD, the analogous currency is military capability and total ownership cost.

To develop such metrics, DoD should

- use DoD's core goals to justify environmental actions, as discussed above

- provide a supportive organizational context for environmental accounting and assessments; for example, extend current annual holistic facility environmental assessments, which focus on pollution prevention, to all facilities

- promote formal environmental accounting, but recognize its limitations; even the best accounting systems have difficulty capturing precise, complete measurements of how environmental performance might affect a line of business

- use a range of tools and techniques, quantitative and qualitative, customized to the key environmental aspects of an installation.

## PROMOTE EFFECTIVE RELATIONSHIPS WITH ALL RELEVANT EXTERNAL STAKEHOLDERS

Proactive commercial facilities identify and manage relationships with all relevant stakeholders, including regulators, the general public, suppliers, community and environmental groups, employees, the press, and others. Such stakeholder efforts take time and cost money, but they are a cost-effective investment necessary for implementing innovative integrated facility approaches.

To manage stakeholder relationships effectively, DoD should

- Maintain open relationships that support constructive engagement. Disney's experience with a proposed theme park in Northern Virginia, when compared with its experience at WDWR, provides specific evidence to support this point.

- Educate key stakeholders about the environmental challenges that a facility faces. Make sure that they understand what is unique about an installation. Defense facilities have many environmental issues not found in more common commercial facilities. A formal installation Environmental, Health, and Safety report, updated every year or two, can help.

- Tailor interaction to the needs of each stakeholder. Engage local stakeholders directly, especially on issues that they might perceive negatively. Build on DoD's experience to date with Remediation Advisory Boards (RABs). To address facilitywide environmental issues, conduct regular meetings with community leaders, public meetings, formal community advisory panels that participate in community environmental activities, meetings with the press, and meetings with facility's main environmental opponents, such as local environmental nongovernmental organizations.

- Sustain partnerships with regulators at all levels that build trust. Deal with them openly and constructively. Find nonconfrontational ways to educate their often junior staff, particularly on technical issues or options specific to a facility. Use these partnerships to seek flexibility.

- Reach beyond the environmental staff on a DoD facility to engage other appropriate DoD personnel in these interactions. Pick the right DoD personnel for the right stakeholders. Use the environmental staff to coordinate these efforts and ensure that they convey a uniform message.

- Periodically survey attitudes toward the facility, similar to P&G Mehoopany's Public Perception Survey of community stakeholders, to anticipate stakeholder opinions. Incorporate the findings proactively in facility environmental planning.

## TRAIN AND MOTIVATE ALL DoD PERSONNEL ABOUT ENVIRONMENTAL ISSUES

People implement all of the recommendations above. For these recommendations to succeed, people must understand them, their value to DoD, how the recommendations affect them personally, and what they as individuals can do to implement the recommendations effectively. Formal programs to train and motivate DoD employees increase the probability of success. These programs should

- Place appropriate values on environmental issues. Make them an integral part of DoD's core mission.

- To drive these goals home, publicly report progress against environmental goals to DoD personnel in terms relevant to DoD's core mission. Examples might be dollars saved or training hours achieved without environmental restriction.

- Train DoD personnel in (1) the importance of environmental issues to DoD, (2) what their responsibilities are, and (3) what they must do to exercise these responsibilities effectively.

- Train environmental and nonenvironmental personnel. Give environmental personnel more technical and deeper training, but ensure that nonenvironmental personnel understand how their actions affect environmental outcomes. Tailor training to the facilities and personnel in question.

- Promote less-formal events, such as Earth Day fairs and periodic open houses, that maintain awareness of environmental issues and help educate personnel about a facility's environmental challenges.

- Where possible, link measured performance to formal and informal incentives. Seek incentives that are compatible with DoD's usual management practices. For example, seek ways to link actions to personnel reviews and promotions. Use competitions and prizes for installations and individuals, even small ones that appeal to the average employee or service member. Ensure that these incentives promote DoD's true environmental goals.

Implementing integrated facility approaches to environmental management is not easy. In ongoing experiments, commercial facilities are making progress with such innovative approaches. Given the size, organizational structure, culture, and other unique aspects of DoD, it will inevitably have more difficulty implementing such approaches throughout its organization than leading commercial firms do. But DoD is already taking promising steps in many locations. The commercial lessons offered here can help DoD refine its approach and extend its successes to date to a broader set of facilities. Full coordination of its core military and environmental goals will take a long time, but DoD has started in the right direction.

# ACKNOWLEDGMENTS

Gary D. Vest, Principal Assistant Deputy Under Secretary of Defense (Environmental Security), suggested and supported RAND's study of proactive environmental management practices in commercial firms, of which this is one product. Patrick Meehan, Jr., Director of Program Integration for the Deputy Under Secretary of Defense (Environmental Security), was the program officer for this broader study. Both provided useful suggestions and feedback, as well as ready access to relevant staffs in the Office of the Secretary of Defense and the military departments.

Jeffrey Drezner was an equal partner with the authors in the design of the study underlying this report. He helped design the basic template used to structure the analysis presented here. Anny Wong provided a helpful in-depth review of this report.

The authors have benefited from discussions with and materials provided by representatives of industry, academia, government agencies, and nongovernmental organizations. The authors thank these many different people.

A special thanks goes to the staff and former staff at The Walt Disney World Resort and the Procter & Gamble Mehoopany facility who spoke with us, including Bob Boos, James C. Brogan, Bob Colburn, William Eberhardt, J. Andrew (Drew) Hadley, Bill Kivler, Ted McKim, Charles B. O'Hara, Armando Rodriguez, and Patty Smith.

Any errors of fact and judgment are those of the authors. Views and suggestions expressed here are not necessarily those of RAND or any of its sponsors.

| | |
|---|---|
| ABC | Activity-based costing |
| AFB | Air force base |
| BRT | The Business Roundtable |
| CAA | The Clean Air Act |
| CAAA | The Clean Air Act Amendments |
| Cal/EPA | California Environmental Protection Agency |
| CAP | Community advisory panel |
| Cast member | Employee (WDWR) |
| CBP | Chesapeake Bay Program |
| CERCLA | Comprehensive Environmental Response, Compensation, and Liability Act |
| CHEMS | Chemical Safety Management System (P&G Mehoopany) |
| COP | Comprehensive Operating Permit |
| CWA | The Clean Water Act |
| DEP | Department of Environmental Protection |
| DEQ | Department of Environmental Quality |
| DoD | Department of Defense |
| EAD | Environmental Affairs Division (WDWR) |

| | |
|---|---|
| ECE | Environmental Circle of Excellence (WDWR). Voluntary environmental team of cast members at a local property. |
| ECOS | Environmental Council of the States |
| EH&S | Environmental Health, and Safety |
| EI | Environmental Initiatives (WDWR). A cross-functional department that promotes and integrates environmental activities throughout the facility. |
| EIP | Eco-Industrial Parks |
| EISC | Environmental Initiatives Steering Committee at WDWR. |
| EMS | Environmental management system |
| EPA | Environmental Protection Agency. If used alone refers to the U.S. Environmental Protection Agency. |
| EPT | Environmental Product Team. A cross-functional team and environmental champion within the Process Services Module at P&G Mehoopany. It helps this unit deal proactively with environmental issues. |
| ERC | Emission reduction credit |
| ESH | Environmental, safety, and health |
| ETAG | Environmental Technical Advisory Group (WDWR). These interdisciplinary cross-functional groups provide specialized environmental expertise. |
| FTIR | Fourier transform infrared |
| GEMI | Global Environmental Management Initiative |
| HAP | Hazardous air pollutant |
| Integrated facility approaches | Approaches that address environmental issues by looking at the entire operating system as comprehensively and proactively as possible. |

| | |
|---|---|
| IPM | Integrated Pest Management |
| IRR | Internal rate of return |
| ISO | International Organization for Standardization |
| KEA | Key Element Assessment |
| MACT | Maximum achievable control technology |
| MEG | Mehoopany Environmental Group. A cross-functional department with primary environmental responsibility that promotes and integrates environmental activities throughout the P&G Mehoopany facility. |
| Module | What P&G Mehoopany calls their business units. |
| MRF | Material recovery facility. An on-site facility that separates and densifies recyclable materials [WDWR]. |
| NALGEP | National Association of Local Government Environmental Professionals |
| NEPPS | National Environmental Performance Partnership System |
| NGO | Nongovernmental organization |
| $NO_x$ | Nitrogen oxides |
| NPPR | National Pollution Prevention Roundtable |
| NSPS | New Source Performance Standards |
| P&G | Procter & Gamble Corporation |
| P&G Mehoopany | The Procter & Gamble Paper Products Company facility located in a rural valley along the Susquehanna River in Mehoopany, Pennsylvania. |
| P2 | Pollution prevention |
| P4 Project | Pollution Prevention in Permitting Pilot Project |
| PCSD | President's Council on Sustainable Development |
| PERC | Perchloroethylene |

| PID | Planning and Infrastructure Department [WDWR] |
| PPS | Public Perception Survey |
| Project XL | Project XL. This national U.S. EPA pilot program tests innovative ways to achieve better and more cost-effective public health and environmental protection. |
| PSM | Process Services Module |
| RCES | Reedy Creek Energy Services Inc. A service organization for energy and for water and waste resources at WDWR. |
| RCID | Reedy Creek Improvement District. The public entity that provides utilities to WDWR. |
| RCRA | Resource Conservation and Recovery Act |
| ROR | Rate of return |
| SARA | Superfund Amendments and Reauthorization Act of 1986 |
| SEES | At WDWR the Safety, Environment, Energy and Security Committee of the Contemporary Hotel. The hotel's Environmental Circle of Excellence. |
| SEM | Strategic Environmental Management |
| SFWMD | South Florida Water Management District |
| $SO_2$ | Sulfur dioxide |
| SVMG | Silicon Valley Manufacturing Group |
| TNRCC | Texas Natural Resources Conservation Commission |
| TQEM | Total quality environmental management |
| TQM | Total quality management |
| TRI | Toxic Release Inventory |
| U.S. EPA | U.S. Environmental Protection Agency |
| US F&WS | U.S. Fish and Wildlife Service |

| | |
|---|---|
| VOC | Volatile organic compound |
| WBCSD | World Business Council on Sustainable Development |
| WDI | Walt Disney Imagineering Division within Disney Company |
| WDWR | Walt Disney World Resort |
| WRI | World Resources Institute |
| XL | "eXcellence and Leadership"—see Project XL |

# Chapter One

# INTRODUCTION

Many innovative approaches to facility environmental management are emerging both throughout the private sector and within the Department of Defense (DoD). Leading commercial firms can offer DoD useful insights about how they have successfully implemented such approaches. This report documents how facilities with diverse activities have developed integrated ways of complying with current regulations and of preventing future pollution. The focus is on commercial efforts to implement integrated facility approaches to environmental management across the diverse and complex activities that are similar to those found on DoD bases.[1] Such activities include commercial, residential, industrial, and natural-resource management activities. This study addressed implications for DoD installations.

The Office of the Deputy Under Secretary of Defense for Environmental Security asked RAND to study the environmental management practices of commercial facilities recognized as having the best practices to draw lessons from them that DoD could use to improve its own. The project focused on environmental management in four

---

[1]*Integrated facility approaches* and *facilitywide approaches* both refer here to approaches that address environmental issues by looking at the entire facility as comprehensively and proactively as possible. *Integrated environmental management* refers to the broader concept of addressing environmental issues as comprehensively and proactively as possible across an entire system. Such a system may be an individual facility, several facilities, an entire company, or even a company policy. Thus, an integrated facility approach is one type of integrated environmental management approach. Note also that *base* and *installation* both refer to any DoD-owned facility, from a single building to a major post, and that *defense installation* refers to any DoD-owned facility, whether or not any military personnel are actually stationed there.

DoD policy areas: weapon system development and modification, depot-level logistics processes, integrated facility management on installations, and management of cleanup programs.

This report describes the analysis for the integrated facility management study.[2] In this study, we have been analyzing organizations that have been trying to address environmental issues in an integrated facilitywide fashion. We have focused on organizations that have successfully identified, implemented, and managed multimedia and/or integrated pollution prevention (P2)–type activities across their facilities and/or organizations. For this study, we identified and analyzed organizations that have proactive environmental management programs that include good ongoing assessment, measurement, and evaluation procedures and tools; motivated employees; and good mechanisms for sharing information and integration.

## DoD'S FACILITY ENVIRONMENTAL ISSUES

Defense installations are often more like towns than company facilities. Installation personnel have to deal with a wide range of industrial, commercial, residential, and conservation and/or natural-resource management activities. Environmental issues range from traditional industrial regulatory concerns (such as hazardous waste, remediation, and wastewater and air emissions) to other environmental issues (such as solid waste, water and energy conservation, recycling, and ecosystem management).

The following are special issues of concern for DoD implementation of facility environmental management approaches:

1. general environmental management systems (EMSs) and systems views to ensure integration

2. training and motivating people

3. assessment and priority setting, including providing tools and information to support the environmental mission

4. promoting effective relationships with relevant stakeholders.

---

[2]The analysis itself was conducted from 1996 to 1999. The reports for the other three studies have been or are being published: Resetar et al. (1998), Drezner and Camm (1999), Camm (2001); and Camm et al. (2001).

These items are based on DoD's need for and industry experience in implementing environmental management approaches. Through each of the industry case studies, we investigated these issues in each applicable substantive setting.

We should point out that DoD and defense installations have been very proactive in initiating many of the environmental approaches discussed in this report,[3] and we will briefly mention a few examples. However, because our research focused on private-sector industry practices and the lessons that might be drawn from them for defense installations, analyzing specific DoD efforts was outside the scope of this study.

## ANALYTIC APPROACH

The analysis began by developing an understanding of the defense context and determining the issues most important for DoD by

- meeting with numerous environmental policymakers and managers throughout the DoD, Army, Air Force, Navy, and Marines

- meeting with a range of operational managers and workers at two proactive defense installations: Vandenberg Air Force Base (AFB), California, and Aberdeen Proving Ground, Maryland

- reviewing numerous documents about environmental policy, procedures, and implementation practices at defense installations

- reviewing commercial environmental management practices to identify issues that were critical for DoD facilities.

This systematic review led to the focus and special issues of concern for this project described above. The review also helped us identify the type of commercial facilities and practices to analyze for DoD. For our industry analysis, we

- analyzed a range of facilities and the literature to identify insights for DoD

---

[3]For a brief summary of some of the proactive environmental projects that have been implemented throughout DoD and their respective points of contact, see Renew America (1995).

- conducted two in-depth case studies at two best-in-class facilities to address and understand implementation issues and insights for DoD facilities

- analyzed the broader context of evolving approaches in facility environmental management and the changing environmental policy context

- analyzed additional case studies from the literature.

Understanding the broader trends in federal, state, and local government policy (such as P2 laws and incentive programs) and industry's approach to environmental issues (such as sustainable development) plays an important role in understanding and successfully implementing integrated facility approaches to environmental management. The implications of such broader issues are discussed throughout this report, especially in Chapters Two and Three.

## THE CASE STUDIES

Ideally, we wanted to identify organizations that addressed a diverse and complex set of activities occurring on defense installations, such as industrial, commercial, residential, and conservation and natural-resource management activities; toxic substances and hazardous waste issues; and nontoxic substances and nonhazardous waste issues. Also, it was important to identify organizations that, like DoD, have multiple locations, widely distributed systems, and very large organizational structures. We also wanted to identify commercial organizations with strong environmental programs. Indicators of success included ongoing measurable environmental results, good relationships with stakeholders, and motivated employees. Finally, we needed to identify a specific commercial facility within that organization that had successfully implemented an integrated facility approach. It is difficult to identify private-sector organizations that both have a scale and scope of activities similar to those of defense installations and have taken an integrated approach to addressing the environmental issues of all these activities.

We chose the Walt Disney World Resort (WDWR) and the Procter & Gamble (P&G) Mehoopany facility as the two in-depth case studies because they have demonstrated environmental leadership; have innovative integrated facility approaches, effective EMSs, and important parallels in their operations with DoD installations; and have excelled in the areas of special concern for this study.

We spent a full day at the P&G Mehoopany facility and two days at WDWR interviewing various personnel about their EMS and practices.[4] We analyzed both EMSs. As part of this research, we also reviewed and examined the literature on industry practices as well as evolving environmental policy and its implications for EMS implementation. We also talked with other industry representatives, regulators and environmental policy leaders as part of this research. Our analysis of the two in-depth case studies, other industry examples, the broader evolving environmental policy context, and management practices were all used to develop the information presented in this report.

## WDWR's Similarities to a DoD Installation

WDWR's size, complexity, and diversity of activities and environmental management challenges are very much like those of a defense installation. Situated on 30,500 acres in central Florida, this very large Walt Disney Company operation includes four theme parks, 14 resort complexes, and four golf courses. WDWR receives over 100,000 visitors every day and has over 50,000 employees. As with many defense installations, managing WDWR is in many ways like managing a city or a county, although by a private company. Because of its size, the resort even has special county status within the state of Florida. The resort has its own landfill, infrastructure management and maintenance, sewage treatment plant, etc. WDWR is, in effect, a separate community, and operating and maintaining all the hotels, restaurants, theme parks, and other activities requires dealing with a diverse range of natural-resource, industrial, commercial, and residential environmental issues. WDWR has a proactive environmental program, which has achieved some significant environmental accomplishments, including a high rate of solid-

---

[4]The P&G Mehoopany plant interviews were conducted in October 1997, and those at WDWR in October 1996. Please note that these case studies are snapshots of the organization at these particular times. Since these interviews, the programs have most certainly evolved further, yet the lessons learned are still useful. Subsequent communications with P&G Mehoopany personnel have also indicated that, while some details may have changed, the messages are largely the same.

waste recycling and a zero-emissions wastewater treatment facility.[5] The management has been especially innovative and effective in its approaches to employee motivation and in relationships with regulators and other stakeholders, given the EMS challenges that such a large and diverse organization faces.

Some of the challenges of motivating employees about environmental issues are similar to those defense installations face. In particular, the resort's mission does not focus on environmental issues; its employees tend to be young, in their mid-20s on average; and employee turnover rates are high. As with many defense installations, WDWR is both large and a unique facility for its community, making it highly visible to both regulators and neighbors.

## P&G Mehoopany's Similarities to a DoD Installation

Being smaller and having fewer employees than WDWR, P&G Mehoopany is not quite as much like a defense installation, but it is relevant for other reasons. Located in a rural valley along the Susquehanna River in Mehoopany, Pennsylvania, the P&G Paper Products Company is the largest P&G plant in the world, with about 2,700 employees on 1,200 acres.[6] The P&G Mehoopany site produces tissues, towels, and diapers. Like many defense installations, P&G Mehoopany is the only large corporate facility in town and has high visibility with regulators and the community. The facility also deals with a diverse set of activities and environmental concerns regarding business, industrial, and natural-resource issues. The Mehoopany facility's diverse set of functional activities includes pulp production at a sulfite pulp mill,[7] water purification, drinking-water treatment, and wastewater treatment, as well as concerns about local logging practices and supply. The plant's diverse activities have significant potential environmental impact and great visibility in the community, a highly complex situation similar to what many defense installations face. The P&G Mehoopany plant has a strong, well-run, and

---

[5]Appendix B discusses WDWR's environmental accomplishments in more detail.

[6]Also, the terms *Mehoopany, the Mehoopany plant,* and *the Mehoopany facility* are used interchangeably to refer to the P&G Mehoopany plant.

[7]However, since the interviews, P&G Mehoopany has stopped producing its own pulp. Environmental practices and programs have remained in place to facilitate this transition.

efficient environmental program that has implemented innovative facilitywide approaches. The plant has achieved substantial reductions in air, water, and waste emissions and has also addressed natural resource issues, such as in sustainable forestry. For example, in 1996, Mehoopany's forestry group provided environmental and safety training to the facility's wood suppliers and trained 300 loggers in environmental practices. The group has won numerous government environmental awards, and Mehoopany has been recognized as a best-in-class P2 facility.[8] The facility's environmental program is built on a strong corporate EMS philosophy and ethic with a total quality environmental management (TQEM) approach. The facility's management is effective at integrating environmental issues into its business units, has good relationships with regulators and the community, and provides effective training and motivation to the employees in support of the environmental program.

## Using the Case Study Information

Integrated environmental management at facilities is a complex and evolving topic that involves many different dimensions in the actual implementation practices. Because the study focused on EMS implementation issues, it was important to provide detailed examples of how successful companies were able to achieve implementation. Therefore, this report provides specific examples about the details from the two in-depth case studies, as well as some other relevant industry examples and literature. To help set the context and provide even more details about the two in-depth case studies of implementation, the two appendices provide in-depth details about the P&G Mehoopany and WDWR facility environmental management case studies.[9]

## REPORT ROADMAP

Chapter Two describes the evolving environmental policy context. Chapter Three overviews different integrated environmental man-

---

[8]Appendix A describes P&G Mehoopany's environmental accomplishments in more detail.

[9]In subsequent discussions that involve both case studies, we will present the details for each study in alphabetical order: first P&G Mehoopany, then WDWR.

agement approaches and discusses the benefits to industry, especially regulatory related and operational benefits. Chapter Four
begins the discussion of significant factors in implementing an
effective facility EMS with the setting of environmental goals and
aligning environmental activities to meet them. The important role
of assessment and priority setting is described in Chapter Five.
Chapter Six discusses promoting effective relationships with relevant
stakeholders. Effective training and motivation of all employees
about environmental concerns are described in Chapter Seven. The
last chapter presents conclusions for DoD facility environmental
management.

# Chapter Two

# ENVIRONMENTAL POLICY CONTEXT

Historically, the U.S. environmental regulatory system has consisted of many federal, state, and local statutes and standards that were developed piecemeal to address a variety of environmental problems involving independent media, such as air, water, and hazardous waste. This system has also emphasized command-and-control approaches to addressing industrial pollution at the end of the pipe, after it has been produced. Over the last 25 years, this system of statutes has been very effective at improving environmental quality throughout the United States.

However, some environmental problems are worsening; continuing to make improvements in environmental quality and addressing new environmental threats in the future will require new approaches (President's Council on Sustainable Development [PCSD], 1996b, p. 26; Aspen Institute, 1996). Also, this fragmented command-and-control regulatory system has created a series of uncoordinated programs that focus on single media and have different standards, administrative requirements, and implementation practices. This regulatory structure has often resulted in inefficiencies in the implementation of such programs, in terms of the effects both on the regulated community and on public environmental quality. Currently, federal, state, and local governments are trying to address such problems by developing new and more-integrated and systems approaches to environmental performance.

This chapter describes three of the major trends within this new environmental policy context: the expanding role of state and local governments, proactive environmental performance based on collaboration, and an evolving two-track regulatory system. These trends are especially relevant for how industry has been implementing environmental management in its integrated facility approaches. The relevance of the trends will be explained throughout this document.

## EXPANDING ROLE OF STATE AND LOCAL GOVERNMENTS

States and local governments have played an important role in this regulatory process because they have often been responsible for interpreting, implementing, and enforcing environmental laws at the facility level and will likely continue to do so in the future. For instance, the U.S. Environmental Protection Agency (EPA) has delegated authority to state and local authorities for the management of many federal environmental programs, such as key parts of the Resource Conservation and Recovery Act (RCRA), the Clean Water Act (CWA), and the Clean Air Act (CAA). Mary A. Gade, former director of the Illinois EPA and former president of the Environmental Council of the States (ECOS) has said that "States already have responsibility for more than 700 delegated federal environmental programs." (Gade, 1996.) Many people feel that the regulatory and environmental policy role of state and local governments has expanded and will probably continue to expand. For example, a recent National Academy for Public Administration (1995, p. 2) study on EPA's role found that "EPA and Congress need to hand more responsibility and decisionmaking authority over to the states and localities." The former PCSD recognized the importance of the state and local government in addressing environmental problems:

> Many state governments have developed significant environmental management capacity. Indeed, many of the most creative and lasting solutions arise from collaborations involving federal, state, local, and tribal problems in places problems exist—from urban communities to watersheds. (PCSD, 1996b.)

The role of state and local governments is especially relevant for facility environmental management approaches because these government agencies have the most influence over facility activities. Specifically, state and local regulators are usually the ones that inspect and enforce environmental regulations at a particular facility.

## PROACTIVE ENVIRONMENTAL PERFORMANCE BASED ON COLLABORATION

A new type of relationship between industry and government has started in which everyone works together to address environmental performance preventatively.  Emphasis on building trust and on collaborations is increasing.  In the past, state and local environmental agencies primarily focused on enforcement, permitting, and other compliance functions required by federal, state, and local environmental laws.  During the late 1980s and into the 1990s, their activities expanded.  State and local governments have become more proactive in their environmental activities and in how they address environmental performance.  The adversarial role of state and local regulators has also started to change; state and local environmental agencies are now developing partnerships with the U.S. EPA, businesses, and other stakeholders to find and implement the best methods of improving environmental performance.  The EPA's role has started to change as well, emphasizing collaboration and cooperation among all stakeholders; EPA has over 40 voluntary programs at the federal and regional levels designed to work with industry and communities to improve environmental protection through voluntary commitments.[1]

State and local entities seek to work with businesses and other members of the community to improve environmental performance at lower cost.  For example, Illinois state regulators are trying to partner with businesses "to develop more cost-effective ways that business can comply with environmental laws" (Illinois EPA, 1996).  The regulators are also trying to utilize public environmental funding efficiently.  Many states and local governments have limited resources for managing environmental programs.  Many of these innovative experiments attempt to prioritize and streamline program activities, such as prioritizing which facilities require inspections when.  For example, many government agencies recognize that they can often lower their own operational costs and improve their efficiency and environmental effectiveness through such activities.

---

[1]For details on these programs, see U.S. EPA (1998b).  For more details on EPA's changing role, also see U.S. EPA (1999).

These activities include regulatory experiments and voluntary programs in partnership with many different stakeholders and in a wide range of environmental approaches and activities. Many states are providing compliance assistance and passing auditing laws to make it easier for industry to be in compliance. Regional, state, and local voluntary P2 programs, technical assistance activities, and state P2 planning laws are working to help businesses save money and reduce the amount of pollution that they generate. Facility and multimedia permitting and inspection programs are also being implemented to improve environmental performance and/or to reduce the regulatory burden on industry. The U.S. EPA and the states have jointly developed the National Environmental Performance Partnership System (NEPPS), which allows more state priority setting and flexibility in implementing EPA-delegated programs. Many states are exploring the potential regulatory benefits of industry's implementing EMSs, such as ISO 14001. Regional, state, and local government sustainable community, ecosystem, watershed, and other place-based management approaches are additional innovative means of improving environmental performance through partnerships with community stakeholders. Such federal, state, and local activities are helping to transform U.S. environmental policy and could change the nature of our future regulatory structure.

## EVOLVING TWO-TRACK REGULATORY SYSTEM

Such activities are helping to create a two-track regulatory system in which more-proactive and environmentally responsible businesses receive preferred treatment from regulators because they have demonstrated a commitment to the environment (Lachman, 1997a). Preferred treatment can include streamlining administrative requirements and the permitting process, easing inspection and enforcement policies, financial incentives, and waving some fines and penalties when companies promptly report violations. Many regulatory officials and environmental policy experts are starting to realize that a one-size-fits-all regulatory system is not currently appropriate and that facilities that have demonstrated superior environmental performance should be treated differently. For example, the Oregon Department of Environmental Quality (DEQ) recognizes that "our current regulations do not distinguish between companies that merely comply with environmental regulations and those that show exemplary commitment to managing for the environment." (Oregon DEQ, 1996.) Many of the more-proactive industry firms are taking advantage of such an evolving regulatory system and these evolving policy changes.[2]

Such policy trends are likely to continue. However, it should be noted that such dual-track systems are in their infancy. Many of these programs are still experimental. They have not yet been fully evaluated, and only a small number of private-sector companies have participated in and experienced the benefits of such experiments. It is unclear how successful and how widespread these approaches will be in the long term. A transitional regulatory system has been created, with an evolving series of alternatives for compliance within the existing regulatory structure. The alternatives available vary from location to location. Some analysts in the environmental policy community argue that such state and local experimental initiatives will have only marginal environmental and economic benefits and that they need to be made "bolder" to make any significant changes (Beardsley, 1996, p. 3). However, a diverse group of over 100 leaders from government, business, and environmental and other nongovernmental organizations (NGOs), who were brought together in a series of meetings about the 21st century (the Aspen Series) summed up the importance of such efforts: "Yet this transition stage, however tentative and incomplete, represents real promise. Important lessons are being learned that will accumulate in further improvement." (Aspen Institute, 1996.)

Many in the environmental policy community recognize that a new alternative system for environmental protection needs to develop, one that will take the regulatory system beyond traditional command-and-control approaches. Furthermore, many experts and recent studies strongly encourage the type of innovative state and local activities discussed here to help figure out how our regulatory system should evolve for the 21st century. For example, the two policy recommendations of the former PCSD are focused on regulatory policy: (1) to accelerate innovative approaches within the existing

---

[2]As was mentioned earlier, a two-track regulatory system benefits not only industry but also the regulators. Regulatory agencies can often improve the effectiveness and efficiency of their environmental programs by offering preferred treatment to superior environmental performers.

regulatory system, and (2) to create an alternative regulatory system. The former PCSD (1996b, p. 35) suggested a specific action:

> EPA and state agencies should accelerate efforts to conduct a series of demonstration projects to gain experience with policy tools and innovative approaches that could serve as basis for an alternative environmental management system.

The Aspen Series also suggested that an alternative path to the current regulatory system needs to be developed and encouraged the adoption, experimentation, and creative implementation of such an alternative at all levels of government (Aspen Institute, 1996). A recent U.S. EPA Science Advisory Board study also argues that more foresight and new approaches are needed to address future environmental problems that might be more far reaching than past environmental problems. In addition, over the last few years, EPA has been increasing its cooperative efforts with states and other key stakeholders; cooperation will be even more important as the United States deals with the environmental problems anticipated in the future (U.S. EPA, 1995a, pp. 5 and 18). EPA has listened to such input and is trying to improve the regulatory system through its "Reinventing Environmental Protection" efforts, which focus on better environmental information; strong partnerships; more-tailored, flexible approaches; getting to compliance and beyond; and lessening facilities' regulatory burden (U.S. EPA, 1999). This recognition of the need for regulatory change means that such activities and new experiments are likely to continue, offering unique opportunities for industry and defense facilities.

It is important to understand and appreciate this broader changing environmental policy context, which is helping to facilitate new approaches to environmental protection and changing the nature of environmental performance, regulations, and policy in the United States. How industry, DoD facilities, and communities deal with environmental issues is starting to change because of this process. Such national, state, and local regulatory and environmental policy changes and experimental approaches are fueling and facilitating industry activities, and this process is likely to continue and even accelerate in the future. Many of the more forward-thinking environmental companies are taking advantage of this changing policy process to implement proactive and integrated environmental management approaches at their facilities.

Chapter Three

# PROACTIVE INTEGRATED ENVIRONMENTAL
# MANAGEMENT APPROACHES

Many companies are taking more-integrated approaches to environmental issues, both across facilities and across entire companies. Having established integrated environmental management strategies and policies, many are starting to implement them. These companies are taking such approaches for a variety of reasons. In part, this is due to the changing policy climate, but there are also sound business reasons, such as cost savings, regulatory concerns, company image, and operational flexibility.

Integrated facility approaches address environmental issues by looking at the entire operating system as comprehensively and proactively as possible. Such approaches analyze, compare, prioritize, and address environmental concerns across traditional boundaries—such as different media and issues (air, water, land, hazardous waste, species, etc.)—and across the various functions (processes, products, business units, etc.) and activities (industrial, commercial, residential, natural resource, facility support, etc.) of the organization and/or facility. Such approaches integrate environmental issues into other business and operational concerns as much as possible. These approaches try to examine the various environmental issues across an entire facility and the potential interrelationships among the issues, then to implement actions that minimize the facility's environmental impact.

Such approaches are often difficult to implement because they cross traditional organizational structures, disciplines, ways of thinking, and other boundaries. Also, the complexity of analyzing and addressing such issues increases significantly across different types of functions, media, and activities. For example, comparing investments in reducing the air emissions of one process to those for the solid waste emissions of another and to those for the effects on species on facility grounds can be like comparing apples to oranges to bananas. Therefore, many of these approaches are still somewhat experimental and are evolving.  Some companies and some approaches have been more effective than others.  Some of these efforts have not been implemented long enough for us to understand their true effects.  Effectiveness often depends on the specific application, including the environmental issues addressed, corporate culture, etc.  We have tried to identify the successful applications of these approaches that are most applicable to DoD installations.

Companies are experimenting with a wide range of integrated facility approaches at individual facilities and across entire organizations. Since many of these approaches are difficult to implement, involve complex decisions, and are very recent, it is not possible to know how successful their implementation practices will be in the long term.  However, individual companies are making progress at improving environmental performance and reducing costs, as this report will illustrate later.  For discussion purposes, we have grouped these proactive integrated environmental management approaches into five categories:

- EMS and International Organization for Standardization (ISO) 14001 approaches
- Project XL and environmental leadership experiments
- P2 facility activities
- innovative facility permitting activities
- other systems approaches.[1]

These categories are not mutually exclusive; in fact, facilities often combine these approaches in their activities.  There is often synergy between many of these approaches.  Many of the more forward-looking environmental companies are trying to implement a variety of these activities and approaches within their organizations.  For

---

[1]Note that this list highlights the approaches most relevant for DoD facilities; it is not meant to be comprehensive, since there are so many innovative environmental management approaches.  For instance, other innovative programs include self-certification programs, emissions caps, and allowance trading systems.

instance, P&G Mehoopany has implemented an ISO 14001–type EMS and facilitywide P2 activities. Mehoopany tries to take a holistic systems approach in its environmental program and looks broadly across many different environmental issues.

The rest of this chapter gives an overview of each approach, provides best-in-class industry examples, and discusses how companies gain by implementing their own individual approaches. We have focused on examples that are the furthest along and most relevant for DoD facilities. This discussion also briefly mentions some more of the national, state, and local regulatory and environmental policy changes and some business quality management developments, because they play such a major role in fueling and facilitating such activities. Defense installations, like commercial facilities, have an opportunity to take advantage of the new attitude of collaboration and experimentation that many federal, state, and local regulators have adopted for addressing environmental performance.

The focus and implementation of such approaches are more integrated and comprehensive for some companies and some approaches than for others. Given the complexity, these efforts are often not completely comprehensive and integrated for all issues in the actual implementation because the tools and knowledge needed to be totally comprehensive do not yet exist. For example, a P2 facilitywide permit may currently cover an entire facility for air issues but not for other media. However, such a facilitywide approach to air issues can be an effective integrated facility activity and can provide useful insights for defense installations.

## EMS AND ISO 14001 APPROACHES

Most companies have some sort of EMS as an internal management information system to keep track of their environmental commitments and activities. To improve their management processes and environmental performance, many companies have been developing more-comprehensive and more-structured EMSs. ISO 14000—the environmental management standard ISO has developed for industry—has served as a catalyst for many of these efforts.

ISO 14000 consists of a series of voluntary business standards and guidance documents addressing EMSs, environmental labeling, environmental auditing, life-cycle assessment, and environmental performance evaluation. These environmental management standards and guidance documents help an organization set and meet policy goals through objectives and targets, organizational structures and accountability, and specific management controls and review functions, all with the oversight of top management. The documents focus on management rather than on performance, so ISO 14000 has established no environmental performance or compliance standards (U.S. EPA, 1995b).

Before describing the EMS approach, we will set the context by explaining how evolving management practices helped fuel such approaches in the environmental area.

## Total Quality Management Experience Led to the Development of ISO 14000

American companies learned the value of applying total quality management (TQM) tools during the 1980s. This led to the development of such approaches in the environmental area. At its heart, TQM can be thought of as a three-part technique (Levine and Luck, 1994; compare Womack and Jones, 1996):

- Identify your customers, including key stakeholders, and what each customer wants now and in the future.

- Identify the processes that ultimately serve each customer (stakeholder) and map their interrelationships.[2]

- Work continuously to remove "waste" from these processes to give your customers more of what they want.[3]

The development of ISO 9000, the internal industry quality management standards, expanded the use of formal TQM approaches. ISO developed its ISO 9000 family of auditing tools to define exactly what

---

[2]Examples include core product design and production processes; infrastructure support processes; remediation processes; and the associated material management, recycling, treatment, disposal, training, research and development, and compliance processes.

[3]TQM typically considers anything that does not add value to what a customer wants in the final product to be waste; this includes the emissions themselves and the activities required because emissions are quintessential forms of waste.

a firm has to do to implement TQM.[4] ISO certifies third-party auditors, who in turn apply standardized accounting methods to determine whether a firm has in fact changed its internal processes in a
way that implements TQM. As these third-party auditors looked over
their shoulders, firms began to achieve the desired outcomes. By the
early 1990s, ISO 9000 had demonstrated such success that many
industries required qualifying suppliers to use it. For example, the
U.S. automobile industry, already long known for its detailed quality
standards for suppliers, adjusted its old qualification standards to
use ISO 9000 as a baseline and built the QS9000 standards for supplier qualification on it (Johnson, 1995).

Meanwhile, other firms found that they could improve on ISO 9000
for their own internal activities. Although the third-party auditors
were available to certify compliance with ISO 9000, these firms found
that they could apply TQM concepts even more extensively with
even more-dramatic productivity results. Pioneers who successfully
improved their core processes began to see the connection between
reducing waste (broadly defined as anything that does not add value
for the final customer) and reducing emissions. Early applications of
TQM to emission reduction helped build the case for the new,
proactive corporate approaches to environmental management.
Since then, many other firms have applied TQM more broadly to
pursue a program of environmental management (for examples, see
Willig, 1994).

As firms discovered the usefulness of TQM for improving environmental management, they turned to the formal frameworks ISO 9000
program and the Baldrige Award criteria offer for help in refining
their programs.[5] About 20 major firms banded together in 1990 to
form the Global Environmental Management Institute (GEMI), with

---

[4]At the heart of ISO 9000 are three "quality systems" or "contractual models" approved
in 1987. The most comprehensive is ISO 9001, which covers design and development,
production, installation, and servicing of products. ISO 9002 covers production and
installation, and ISO 9003 covers final inspection and test. Other guidelines explain
the auditing approach itself and define how audits will occur. Many good references
are available; see, for example, Johnson (1993).

[5]Receiving the Baldrige Award is evidence that a firm has gone well beyond the basics
to become one of the best-quality firms in the United States. The specific details of the
Baldrige approach change each year. For the most up-to-date information available,
see the Baldrige links at http://www.quality.nist.gov.

the specific intention of formalizing the total quality environmental management (TQEM) concept. GEMI participants have all documented dramatic benefits from their own variations on TQEM. At about the same time, the Council of Great Lakes Industries began to develop its own quality-based implementation techniques. Building on the Baldrige Award criteria, the Council developed its own framework for TQEM in 1993, supporting it with a primer and case studies (Wever and Vorhauer, 1993). The resulting TQEM matrix provided a basis for detailed assessment of a firm's application of quality techniques to its environmental management program.[6]

Building on European efforts to apply TQM concepts to environmental management issues, the ISO began the development of a new family of audit-based guidelines, ISO 14000.[7] ISO members finally reached agreement on the first specific guideline from this family, ISO 14001, in 1996. More than 15 different guidelines and standards have been approved or are being developed in the ISO 14000 family of guidelines and standards.[8] Like ISO 9000, ISO 14000 calls for a detailed audit of the management processes an organization uses, in this case, to implement a formal EMS. Critics claim ISO 14001 is not as comprehensive as its ISO 9000 predecessors or as demanding as the major voluntary European environmental auditing systems based on ISO 9000. ISO 14001 does not require third-party auditing and does not commit a user to a proactive P2 program. Nonetheless, U.S. and foreign firms are using ISO 14001 as a useful framework for implementing a basic TQM approach to environmental management.

## Industry Implementation of ISO 14001

ISO 14001 describes the elements an EMS must have to ensure the incorporation of environmental concerns into business management. Implementation of this standard yields an EMS that will ensure that the organization's environmental policies are followed. The organization can also attain standard third-party certification or

---

[6]Wever (1996) details this approach, how to apply it, and how it compares with the other quality frameworks discussed here.

[7]Jackson (1997) discusses the European systems underlying the ISO 14000 series.

[8]For more information on the ISO14000 series, see ISO (1998) and http://www.iso.org/iso/en/iso9000-14000/iso14000/iso14000index.html.

can make a self-determination and a declaration that it complies with the standard. The ISO 14001 EMS has five main components:

- a policy and commitment to it
- a planning process
- implementation
- measurement and evaluation
- review and improvement.

The environmental policy must include a commitment to "continuous improvement" in meeting the goals and objectives set through the planning process.

Many companies are implementing ISO 14001–type approaches. By December 1997—14 months after the final publication of ISO 14001—2,400 organizations had registered worldwide, 85 of them in the United States. In terms of the numbers of facilities registered, the leading companies in the United States have been Ford, Lockheed Martin, Lucent Technologies, and Matsushita. IBM, United Technologies, 3M, Ford, and Digital Equipment have "declared their intentions to continue to register facilities in the U.S." Many other companies chose to implement ISO 14001–based EMSs at their facilities but did not officially register, partly because of the expense of registration and partly because of the lack of a clear competitive advantage to official registration. In fact, 2,500 organizations are implementing the standard, but most do not intend to go to full registration. Many companies, such as Monsanto, Compaq, John Deere, Georgia Pacific, and General Motors, do not see a need for third-party registration. But such companies have exploited what they consider to be value-added elements of ISO 14001, incorporating them into unique EMSs.

Experts believe that, by the end of 2001, a total of more than 20,000 domestic facilities will have become registered (Cascio and Hale, 1998). The automotive and electronics sectors have been the strongest industrial advocates, followed by chemicals, pharmaceuticals, aerospace, food and beverages, and petroleum. Support is worldwide, although the United States trails in actual registrations (Cascio and Hale, 1998). In general, firms see ISO 14001 as a useful tool whether they seek registration or not, in particular as a useful framework for assessing their own EMSs.

The P&G Mehoopany facility has implemented a TQEM-style EMS that is more advanced than ISO 14001 (see Appendix A). P&G, with the assistance of a third-party auditor, recently conducted a detailed assessment of its EMS, comparing it to the ISO 14001 standard. The conclusion was that P&G's existing EMS met the intent of ISO 14001 in every detail but one or two. In response, P&G adjusted its process to make the correspondence complete. Having done so, it sees no current reason to seek ISO 14001 certification. P&G considered self-certification but could not justify it economically. WDWR has not implemented an ISO 14001– or TQEM-type EMS, having a less-formal EMS. However, many of WDWR's policies and its implementation philosophy tend to fit into the ISO 14001–TQEM framework (see Chapter Four).

## Benefits of EMS and ISO 14001 Approaches

Implementing a formal and structured EMS, either officially ISO 14001 or a related approach, offers many advantages for a company, including the following:

- improving environmental performance
- ensuring environmental compliance
- saving costs
- potential regulatory benefits
- improving the company's image
- improving tracking, documentation, and management of environmental issues
- improving identification of P2 projects and other proactive environmental opportunities
- increasing internal visibility, awareness, and motivation for environmental issues.

NSF International studied the efforts of 18 organizations to develop and implement EMSs based on ISO 14001. These organizations reported a range of benefits: A 3M Corporation facility in Irvine, California, found that implementing the EMS brought a more "systematic approach to managing overall environmental compliance" and more "direct ownership of environmental compliance issues by facility operations." (Diamond, 1996, pp. 51, 53, 57–59, 88.)

An Allergan, Inc., pharmaceutical manufacturing facility in Texas felt its EMS provided a useful structured methodology for evaluating Environmental Health and Safety (EH&S) effects, policies, stakeholders' interests, facility-level targets and objectives, and legal requirements. The adoption of a formal EMS helped a Fluke Corporation facility integrate its environmental policy into the corporate culture and basic business practices. Pacific Gas and Electric Company found that formal EMS implementation helped ensure environmental compliance and reduced costs.

Similar comments came out in a U.S.–Asia Environmental Partnership survey of 30 major global companies about their corporate EMSs and their reactions to ISO 14001. Dwane W. Marshall, Director, Corporate Office of Environmental Affairs at Union Camp, went so far as to state that

> I cannot imagine that any manufacturer in the United States could sustain compliance with the myriad of regulations that govern our environmental conduct without some form of EMS. (U.S.–Asia Environmental Partnership, 1997, p. 86.)

Most of the 30 companies surveyed have implemented EMSs that they feel are more advanced than ISO 14001, and most of them did not see a competitive advantage from ISO 14001 certification. Some did see an advantage, however. For instance, Dr. R. Reisenweber, Vice President, Environmental Health, and Safety, Rockwell International, noted that ISO 14001 certification was a useful management tool for ensuring proactive environmental programs and that certification provides a competitive advantage (U.S.–Asia Environmental Partnership, 1997, p. 81).

As these examples illustrate, the implementation of a formal EMS can be the foundation for many of the other facility approaches. An EMS provides a useful framework for implementing integrated facilitywide approaches to environmental issues.

## Potential Regulatory Benefits from EMS or ISO 14001 Implementation

Another potential benefit of implementing a EMS or ISO 14001 certification is state and local regulatory benefits. Many states are developing pilot projects to explore how to use this voluntary industry standard to improve environmental performance while streamlining the compliance process. In the future, coordinating ISO 14001 certification with state requirements could provide companies with preferred treatment, such as reducing the numbers of permits, monitoring reports, and inspector visits. There is some controversy about regulatory use of the standard, especially because it is a business management system standard and not an environmental performance standard.[9] However, some state regulators hope to be able use this system to improve environmental performance, reduce the cost to companies of compliance, and save public resources.

A multistate working group on EMSs was formed a few years ago to help coordinate state efforts to explore ISO 14001 and EMS issues, specifically to coordinate information about EMS pilot projects.[10] The working group developed a guidance document to provide a framework for collecting information about the value of EMS implementation to regulatory agencies and others. This voluntary tool helps the states evaluate their own ISO 14001 and other EMS pilots. Pennsylvania, California, Massachusetts, Illinois, Minnesota, New Jersey, North Carolina, Texas, and Florida have been developing pilot programs to explore ISO 14001 implementation issues. For example, California is developing pilot projects to test how ISO 14001 programs will interact with specific performance requirements mandated by state regulations and laws. Issues the state hopes to address include how permits are issued, reporting and monitoring requirements, enforcement protection for self-disclosed violations, and information companies should be required to share to be deemed in compliance with state and local laws.

Based on the ISO 14001 concepts, Pennsylvania and its business community have developed an EMS group to explore ways to streamline regulation through the EMS framework. For example, the Pennsylvania Business EMS Group could devise ways to ease inspection and enforcement at facilities that have a validated EMS. Robert Barkanic, special assistant to the deputy secretary of Pennsylvania's

---

[9]For discussions of the pros and cons of regulatory use of ISO 14000 being, see Begley (1996) and Butner (1996).

[10]The states involved include Arizona, Pennsylvania, California, Massachusetts, Illinois, Minnesota, North Carolina, Oregon, Texas, and Wisconsin (NIST, 1998).

Department of Environmental Protection's (DEP's) Office of Air, Recycling, and Radiation Protection, presented the following vision for regulatory intervention based on EMS concepts:

> Long-term, the companies will never see us again. Getting there is the tough part. If they are demonstrating superior performance, it allows us to concentrate on the bad actors. It's a net environmental gain. (Begley, 1996.)

Pennsylvania's draft approach for improving its regulatory system—Strategic Environmental Management (SEM)—consists of tools business and government decisionmakers can use to increase "environmental performance in a post 'command and control' era" (Pennsylvania DEP, 1996). Pennsylvania DEP believes that SEM will help integrate an organization's environmental management objectives and its strategic goals to enhance its operational efficiency and effectiveness, help give it a competitive advantage, and help it identify cost-effective ways to maximize the facility's regulatory flexibility as the facility strives for zero emissions.

Pennsylvania DEP has defined the six key elements of SEM:  an appropriate EMS, P2 planning and activities, effective community involvement, environmental cost accounting, life-cycle cost assessment, and appropriate performance measures and indicators.  DEP has also defined what it considers appropriate for each of these elements.  For example, DEP requires the EMS to be backed by a corporate environmental policy that has strong support from top management; the resources must be available to implement that policy; compliance with all environmental regulations and statutes, goals, and targets for continuous improvement must be documented; the EMS must be audited periodically, with corrective actions taken as needed; there needs to be an active P2 program, and there must be appropriate community involvement.

SEM grew out of ISO 14001–types of ideas but has important differences, including a greater emphasis on P2, community involvement, and performance measures:

> DEP believes that organizations can further maximize environmental and economic benefits if they incorporate Strategic Environmental Management practices by further emphasizing pollution pre-

vention, community involvement and performance measures as part of the overall EMS.[11]

SEM is a regulatory flexibility initiative, which creates a "dual compliance track" for companies documenting performance beyond regulatory compliance (Pennsylvania DEP, 1996). The state has been developing and implementing partnerships and pilot projects with industry facilities to further explore, test, and develop the SEM approach.

## ENVIRONMENTAL LEADERSHIP AND PROJECT XL EXPERIMENTS

To demonstrate environmental leadership and better manage environment issues, some businesses have begun implementing innovative approaches. In addition, the U.S. EPA has developed initiatives that promote regulatory innovation by encouraging and rewarding exceptional environmental management and environmental leadership, which has facilitated industry activities. State and local government environmental experiments are also helping to facilitate environmental leadership in industry.

Project XL is a national pilot program that tests new ways of achieving better and more cost-effective public health and environmental protection.[12] This EPA pilot program began in 1995, as one of several Reinventing Environmental Regulation initiatives. XL projects are suppose to give the regulated community the opportunity to demonstrate excellence and leadership by developing projects in partnership with regulators and members of the general public that result in superior environmental performance when they have the flexibility to pursue alternatives to the current regulatory system. In return for regulatory flexibility from the EPA, the regulated entity in each project commits to achieving better environmental results than

---

[11]For the source of this quotation and to learn more details about how SEM differs from ISO 14001, see Pennsylvania DEP (1997) and the state's SEM Web site (http://www.dep.state.pa.us/dep/deputate/pollprev/tech_assistance/zero_emissions/sem/semhp.htm).

[12]XL stands for "excellence and leadership."

would have been attained simply through full compliance with regulations.

Through site-specific agreements with project sponsors, EPA is gathering data and project experience that will aid the redesign of current approaches to public health and environmental protection. Project XL sponsors can include private facilities, multiple facilities, industry sectors, federal facilities, communities, and states. Sponsors' pilot projects implement innovative strategies that produce superior environmental performance, provide flexibility, cost savings, or other benefits and promote greater accountability to stakeholders.

To choose among Project XL proposals, the U.S. EPA (1996) evaluates them according to whether they

- improve environmental results
- reduce costs and paperwork
- have stakeholder support
- test novel strategies, such as multimedia P2
- are transferable
- are appropriately feasible
- identify appropriate monitoring, reporting, and evaluation methods
- avoid shifting the burden of risk.

Project XL made a commitment to implement at least 50 pilot projects. Because of the limited scope, pilot projects should test new ideas that have the potential for wide application and that have broad environmental benefits. As of fall 2000, the 50 pilot experiments had been implemented and are being evaluated.[13]

Organizations that have facility pilots in the implementation and evaluation stage include the Berry Corporation, Weyerhaeuser, Intel Corporation, HADCO Corporation, Merck & Co. Inc., Imation, Anderson Corporation, Molex Incorporated, Massachusetts DEP, the Atlantic Steel Site of the Jacob Development Corporation, Exxon

---

[13]See http://www.epa.gov/projectxl/ for updated information.

Fairmont Coke Works Superfund Site, and Lucent Technologies. Defense installations are also actively participating in this program. For example, the approved pilot project at Vandenberg AFB will use the money that the facility would have spent complying with the administrative requirements of the CAAA to upgrade and retrofit equipment (e.g., boilers, space heaters). Other government facilities and entities with projects in the implementation and evaluation stages include Puget Sound Naval Shipyard, Elmendorf AFB, and Steele County, Minnesota.[14]

Not all of these efforts incorporate fully integrated facility approaches. However, many of them are trying to take integrated facility approaches and are very broad and proactive in their activities. For example, the Lucent Technologies Project XL pilot plans to use the implementation of ISO 14001 as a framework for developing specific facilitywide proposals to simplify permitting, recordkeeping, and reporting requirements, while driving continual improvement and P2 programs at several facilities within a region.

The benefits for participating companies and defense installations include regulatory flexibility, improved environmental performance, improved company image, and cost savings. These experiments require significant public involvement, which can increase costs. Also, because this is a high-visibility experimental program, these projects face more public scrutiny than many other such experiments. Because of such issues and the specific implementation criteria for this program, a large number of initially proposed pilots have not completed the program.[15] However, those that have been implemented achieve some of the aforementioned benefits. For example, the first Project XL pilot approved in July 1996 was for the Jack M. Berry Corporation, a citrus juice processor. In this project, Berry consolidated 23 federal, state, and local environmental permits into a single facilitywide Comprehensive Operating Permit (COP). This approach, which will improve environmental performance in a variety of areas, "is expected to save the company several million

---

[14]See http://www.epa.gov/ProjectXL/implement.htm for a full list of projects in implementation and evaluation and for more information on project status.

[15]See http://www.epa.gov/projectxl/inactive.htm for a current list of projects withdrawn or not accepted to the program.

dollars on the testing and administrative costs typically incurred over the five-year life of a permit" (U.S. EPA, 1997).

To further illustrate the focus of these integrated efforts and the benefits from such activities, the following subsections will discuss three Project XL examples in more detail. These examples also illustrate facilitywide approaches that try to address a variety of environmental issues across different media and activities. For example, Intel's Chandler, Arizona, facility addresses such diverse issues as air pollution, solid waste, water conservation, and employee vehicle miles traveled. For an even more-detailed discussion of facilitywide approaches trying to address a range of issues and activities, see the appendices.

## Intel Corporation, Chandler, Arizona

In November 1996, Intel agreed to implement an environmental master plan that includes a facilitywide cap on air emissions in place of the traditional individual limits for different emission sources at its new semiconductor manufacturing facility. In this Project XL agreement, Intel committed to

- maintaining a level of air emissions for oxides of nitrogen, sulfur dioxide, carbon monoxide, particulate matter, and volatile organic compounds that ensures that the current facility, and any other manufacturing facility built at the site, is a "minor" air emissions source, as defined by the CAA
- using state health-based guidelines to establish enforceable caps for emissions that affect the community adjacent to the facility and, in addition, voluntarily using these health-based standards to set emission levels to increase protection for those working in the facility
- reducing water consumption and the generation of solid, non-hazardous chemical, and hazardous waste
- establishing property-line setbacks that are 20 times greater than what local zoning authorities require
- reducing the vehicle miles that employees travel
- participating in equipment donation and training programs.

Environmental benefits from this project include reducing up to 60 percent of the solid waste and up to 70 percent of the nonhazardous chemical wastes the facility generates by the year 2000; recycling up to 65 percent of the fresh water used at the facility; and balancing limits on hazardous air pollutant emissions with health-based guidelines.[16]

The regulatory flexibility of this project will allow Intel to make operational changes without permit review, as long as permit limits are met and as long as the project includes multimedia performance-based permits that specify performance levels for each regulated pollutant to be used at the new facility.

The greatest benefit that Intel has gained from this project is the flexibility the streamlined permit gives, which allows accelerated product introduction, an important business advantage for Intel. Intel's design and manufacturing processes are designed for speed because of the nature of the technology development cycle and the competition within the microprocessor manufacturing industry. The company motto is "Quick or Dead": Speed in the permitting of new processes at a facility is critical for Intel. This regulatory flexibility leads to technological and strategic benefits. In addition, this "accelerated product introduction is likely to translate into a sizable economic benefit" (Boyd, Krupnick, and Mazurek, 1998, pp. 36–37).

## Weyerhaeuser Company, Oglethorpe, Georgia

Weyerhaeuser Company's project is a pulp manufacturing facility that is pursuing its long-term vision for a minimum (environmental) impact mill. At this facility, Weyerhaeuser is working to minimize the effects of its manufacturing processes on the Flint River and surrounding environment by addressing a wide range of environmental issues, including water use, chemical use, waste, energy, and forest management. For example, the company plans to

- cut its bleach plant effluent by 50 percent over a ten-year period
- reduce water use by about 1 million gallons a day

---

[16]The detailed statistics and commitments cited here are from the Project XL EPA Web site, http://www.epa.gov/projectxl/, which also contains the detailed minutes from stakeholder meetings during the project's development.

- cut the amount of solid wastes it generates by half within ten years
- reduce hazardous waste constituents
- improve forest management practices in over 300,000 acres of land by stabilizing the soil, creating streamside buffers, and safeguarding unique habitats
- devise a facilitywide plan to reduce energy use
- maintain criteria air pollutant emission at levels below the facilitywide emission caps.

As part of this experiment, Weyerhaeuser also is implementing ISO 14001 at the plant.[17]

Weyerhaeuser has been given the regulatory flexibility to consolidate routine reports into two reports per year and to use alternative means of meeting the requirements of new regulations that prescribe maximum achievable control technology (MACT). U.S. EPA also is waiving government review prior to certain physical modifications, provided emissions do not exceed stipulated levels. The management feels that this approach yields the following benefits (Risner, 1997):

- flexibility in the timing and nature of some reporting requirements
- ability to use alternative technologies to meet MACT air requirements, rather than the specified end-of-pipe controls
- preapproval of minor permit changes under CAA Title V
- permitting predictability for 15 years
- reduction of inefficiencies in the existing system
- alignment of environmental requirements with the company's business goals and local community interests
- a resulting significant savings in capital expenditures and annual operating expenses.

---

[17]See http://www.epa.gov/projectxl/weyer/ for the details and more information about what this project is trying to accomplish.

For instance, U.S. EPA and the Georgia Environmental Protection Division have already extended regulatory flexibility to the facility for environmental performance reporting, effluent permitting, hazardous air pollutant compliance, air quality permitting, and solid waste permitting (U.S. EPA, 1998a).

## Imation, Camarillo, California

Imation has proposed an emissions cap for hazardous air pollutants and criteria air pollutants as an Project XL experiment at its Camarillo manufacturing facility. This plant manufactures magnetic data-storage cartridges for the computer industry. Imation would also implement a simplified reporting system and an EMS verification process. This proposal would allow Imation to operate with more flexibility, reduce costs and paperwork, explore innovative approaches for environmental management, and increase environmental benefits.

Extra environmental benefits from the project come from the retiring or selling of volatile organic compound (VOC) emission reduction credits (ERCs) issued by the Ventura County Air Pollution Control District. As Imation acquires ERCs, they will be given to an existing committee made up of constituents from the business community, local environmental groups, and community groups. The committee will retire or sell the ERCs and invest the proceeds in projects intended to improve air quality in Ventura County. Specifically, Imation has proposed to

- set caps of 10 tons for individual hazardous air pollutants and 25 tons for total hazardous air pollutants
- establish a plantwide applicability limit for criteria air pollutants.
- adopt "prewiring" for future New Source Performance Standards (NSPS) sources to allow the facility to be exempt from the Title V permit modification process[18]

---

[18]The initial Title V permit would approve potential modifications at the facility. Imation could then make these changes in the future without going through a permit modification process.

- use extractive Fourier transform infrared (FTIR) spectrometry, a continuous emission monitoring system that allows the facility to speciate hazardous air pollutants[19]

- streamline the reporting process by consolidating other reporting requirements into the NSPS quarterly reports

- include an EMS in the monitoring and reporting process.[20]

Like Intel's project, this proposed project would reduce the environmental permitting time and administrative burden, which would enable the facility to bring new products to market faster and improve its ability to meet customer expectations.  This marketing advantage is significant and far outweighs the project development cost, which is estimated to be over $270,000 for purchase and installation of the FTIR monitoring system, plus the cost of implementing a comprehensive EMS.  Other cost savings would flow from the facility's much-simpler new-source review procedures (Krueger, 1997).

## State Environmental Leadership Experiments

Some states are also developing environmental leadership recognition and incentives, often using Project XL as a model.  For example, Illinois EPA issued a public review draft of a regulatory initiative in October 1996 that was modeled after the EPA Project XL program.  However, Illinois' effort has some differences, such as a specific emphasis on EMSs because Illinois state legislation established a voluntary pilot program to implement innovative EMS agreements with the regulated community.  According to Illinois EPA (1996), the law specifies that EMS agreements consist of "innovative environmental measures not otherwise recognized or allowed under existing laws and regulations of this State."  Illinois EPA hopes to implement about 15 to 25 pilot EMS agreement projects and to create a wide range of regulatory innovation experiences.

**Illinois.**  Illinois EPA requires that a pilot project demonstrate one or more of the following to implement innovative environmental measures:  reduce emissions, discharges, or wastes beyond regulatory

---

[19]This additional information will increase innovation in emission reductions.

[20]See http://www.epa.gov/projectxl/imation/ for more information.

requirements through P2 or some other appropriate method and/or achieve real environmental risk reduction or foster environmental compliance in a manner that is clearly superior to the existing regulatory system.

Under the Illinois initiative, there are two different ways to process a pilot project: through the U.S. EPA Project XL process or through the Illinois EPA process. Although there may be some flexibility about specifics, Illinois EPA requires the application for a pilot program to describe

1. the implementation of the EMS
2. suitable environmental performance plans
3. practices and procedures for performance assurance
4. suitable practices for productive stakeholder involvement.

**Oregon.** The Green Permits program is one example of Oregon's experiments with pilot projects for developing and testing regulatory flexibility and incentives for exceptional environmental management practices. This program is intended to "encourage and reward facilities which utilize innovative environmental management approaches and implement voluntary 'beyond compliance' activities" (Oregon Department of Environmental Quality [DEQ], 1996). Oregon is considering such potential incentives as streamlined monitoring and reporting requirements, expedited permits, longer permit renewal cycles, P2 technical assistance, awards and recognition, modified inspection procedures, and alternative enforcement responses to violations. The legislature created Green Permits in 1997 to promote such environmental leadership. One specific approach within Green Permits, the Environmental Management Incentives Project, focuses on industry EMS implementation. This project involves a multilevel system in which a company that has demonstrated superior environmental performance receives increasing regulatory benefits based on the level of performance (Oregon DEQ, 1998).

## P2 AND POLLUTION AVOIDANCE ACTIVITIES

Since the mid to late 1980s, many businesses have been implementing P2 activities to help improve environmental quality and save money.  A business may not define P2 exactly the same way EPA does.  EPA's official definition of P2 follows that of the Pollution Prevention Act of 1990 and Executive Order 12856—Federal Compliance with Right-to-Know Laws and Pollution Prevention Requirements (August 3, 1993):

> any practice which reduces the amount of hazardous substance, pollutant, or contaminant entering any waste stream or otherwise released into the environment (including fugitive emissions) prior to recycling, treatment, or disposal; and any practice which reduces the hazards to public health and the environment associated with the release of such substances, pollutants, or contaminants.

This definition focuses on activities prior to waste generation and refers to the use of materials, processes, or practices that eliminate or reduce the quantity or toxicity of wastes at the source.  Such activities include material substitution, improved process efficiency, preventive maintenance, improved housekeeping, and inventory control.  Aside from eliminating the discharge of harmful wastes, this definition also includes protecting natural resources through conservation and efficiency.  P2 also reduces the use of energy, water, and hazardous materials.

Many P2 practitioners within both government and private industry have adopted what is called an *environmental protection, waste-management*, or *environmental management* hierarchy.  This hierarchy presents options for managing waste and prioritizes them as follows:  source reduction, recycling, treatment, and disposal.  Whenever possible, individuals and organizations should first implement practices that reduce or eliminate wastes at the source, before they are generated.  Recycling comes next because it allows the reuse or regeneration of materials and wastes into usable products.  Treatment and disposal are considered last-resort options.

Definitions of the elements of this hierarchy may vary slightly from organization to organization, but these are the ones federal environmental regulations and EPA guidance documents use.  Individual state regulations also specifically define P2 and this hierarchy.  States often use EPA's definitions in their own P2 acts, although the legislation may change the interpretation slightly.

In practice, businesses and state and local governments have flexibility in what they label as P2 and in what they implement as P2 activities. For example, some businesses and some state and local governments consider recycling to be part of P2, although recycling is not technically part of the official definition. Another important gray area is avoiding environmental harm. Is an activity that helps reduce the loss of biodiversity, species, and/or habitat considered P2? Individuals and organizations differ in how they answer such questions, although the P2 activities of most businesses and many state and local governments do not currently include such a focus. However, regardless of the technical classification, many of the more-proactive facilities and companies whose land holdings and business activities can have a substantial impact on habitats, such as Georgia-Pacific and WDWR, include such activities in their facility approaches, even when not classifying them as P2. Regardless of the specific definition, industry has discovered the benefits of implementing P2 and the waste-management hierarchy.

Incentives for industry to implement more P2 practices include reduced operating costs, improved worker safety, reduced compliance costs, increased productivity, increased environmental protection, reduced exposure to future liability costs, and continuous improvement. P2 is often considered "business planning with environmental benefits" (Illinois Hazardous Waste Research and Information Center, 1993). Improving the company image is another benefit of engaging in such activities.

## Industry Facilitywide P2 Activities

P2 efforts that try to look across an entire facility, not just a single process, business line, or business unit, are examples of proactive facilitywide approaches to improving environmental performance. Many businesses have started taking such approaches. The Business Roundtable (BRT) conducted a study of best-in-class efforts to determine successful elements in implementing facility-level P2 programs.[21] BRT studied Intel's plant in Aloha, Oregon; DuPont's facil-

---

[21]BRT is an association of business executives who examine public issues that affect the economy and develop positions about what they consider to be sound public policy. For more information on the study, see BRT (1993).

ity in La Porte, Texas; 3M's plant in Columbia, Missouri; Martin Marietta's facility in Waterton, Colorado; and P&G's facility in Mehoopany, Pennsylvania. These facilities were chosen as best-in-class P2 facilities for benchmarking because they had significant results in reducing wastes and emissions and had a range of complexity regarding waste issues.[22] All these facilities have effectively implemented facilitywide P2 programs.

Facilitywide P2 programs differ by facility. However, companies usually conduct assessments of their facilities to identify P2 projects, then prioritize the ideas and develop a facilitywide P2 plan. Lastly, they implement P2 projects. Some plans are formal, others informal; for example, some include formal P2 teams, while others do not.

Ford Motor Company's assembly plant in Avon Lake, Ohio, illustrates P2 facility planning efforts. In 1996, this facility's significant P2 program accomplishments included

- reducing solvent use from 4,000 pounds per week to less than 100 pounds per week

- saving more than $225,000 by reusing shipping containers and increasing recycling of cardboard and wood

- reducing overall waste by 16 percent.

In 1997, the plant received a P2 award from the Ohio EPA for its efforts. This pattern of success began with establishment of a formal waste minimization and P2 team in 1994. The team analyzed plant processes; implemented specific measurement systems; and used surveys, benchmarks, and specific reduction goals to help identify, prioritize, and implement P2 projects as part of an ongoing P2 planning process (Ohio EPA, 1998).

BRT also studied "best practices" in P2 planning, examining company plans and activities that had been used to reduce pollution. BRT found that an effective P2 planning process requires three core competencies. The first is the ability to assess business and compliance needs; an essential part of this is assessing future conditions

_____

[22]They were also chosen because of such facility and diversity issues as facility size (larger than 500 employees) and the use of chemicals in manufacturing processes. For a full list of the selection criteria, see BRT (1993), p. 8.

and strategic issues. The second competency is an in-depth under-standing and analysis of the facility's manufacturing processes that includes effective use of such tools as process characterization, flow diagramming, materials accounting, and materials input-output analysis. The third competency is the ability to integrate P2 planning into business plans and processes (BRT, 1998, pp. 24–31).[23]

**P&G P2 Activities.** As a corporation, P&G emphasizes P2 as part of its environmental policy and program. One of the four basic guiding principles for implementing environmental policy at P&G Mehoopany is aggressive pursuit of P2, which includes trying to minimize waste, management costs, and lost material value. P&G Mehoopany uses a waste-management hierarchy that implements the three R's: Reduce, Reuse, and Recycle. Plant personnel try to prevent pollution at the source as much as possible.

At its Mehoopany facility, P&G has achieved substantial P2 results in a variety of areas, including air, water, and waste emissions. For example, overall site air emissions have been reduced 80 percent since plant start-up. The facility has won numerous P2-related awards, including a Pennsylvania DEP Pollution Prevention Recog-nition Award in 1996, and has been recognized as a best-in-class P2 facility. The plant has a very aggressive program for solid waste reduction and recovery. Mehoopany has traditionally recovered and sold or reused 90 to 92 percent of its waste streams. The absolute value of waste sold or reused has grown substantially. In fact, the plant had net earnings of over $2.5 million from waste in 1996–1997.

The Mehoopany facility has been very proactive, thorough, and strategic in implementing P2 projects. For instance, the facility reduced its use of chlorine and ammonium nitrogen, even though no current regulations forced it to do so. Mehoopany also made a strategic decision to favor incineration over land disposal, despite initial estimates of higher costs for incineration. Plant personnel decided to pursue use of a waste-to-energy facility because land dis-posal poses too many uncertainties, especially with respect to liabili-ties. Community concerns about plant odors have led the plant to invest $2.5 million in reducing odor. And because the community

---

[23]BRT (1998) and BRT (1993) provide excellent descriptions of the lessons learned about effective facility P2 planning and implementation.

still complains about odor at times, even though the problem has improved significantly over time, the plant is considering additional actions. No regulations even play here, although they could in the future. Mehoopany also changed its process of producing diapers by changing cutting patterns and the width of the paper rolls used, to reduce the amount of waste paper.

Mehoopany has gone beyond traditional P2 thinking by also working to avoid environmental harm to natural resources, an extension of the P2 philosophy and definition. The Mehoopany plant has promoted sustainable forestry to protect local forest health and to increase the safety of logging in these forests, even though P&G owns none of these forests. Mehoopany's staff has given technical training to its suppliers to improve their practices that affect environmental and safety performance. For example, in 1996, staff trained 300 loggers in such environmental practices as erosion control, harvesting strategies, and encouraging buffer strips around streams.

**WDWR P2 Activities.** WDWR's P2 efforts have focused on range of issues across the facility, including solid waste reduction, energy and water conservation, and reduction of chemical use. To illustrate the diversity of WDWR's effort, several different examples follow. WDWR has installed new closed-looped machines for dry cleaning that help cut down the use of perchloroethylene (PERC). Infrared sensors in many of the rest rooms and automatic irrigation controls reduce the amount of water used, by as much as 250 million gallons annually. WDWR reduced its napkin size by 25 percent, a source-reduction idea that saved material, waste, and money. The facility has an active Integrated Pest Management (IPM) program that includes using helpful insects, such as releasing ladybugs to help control aphids.

WDWR encourages recycling, reuse, and source reduction wherever possible. An on-site material recovery facility (MRF) separates and densifies recyclable materials, including paper, plastic, glass, steel, aluminum, and cardboard. The MRF handles more than 45 tons of material daily, representing an average recycling rate of more than 30 percent. Other used equipment and excess items are sold to staff or auctioned to the public. WDWR recycles about 73 percent (by weight) of its construction debris and landscape waste, about 56 percent of its overall waste. There is also an extensive composting facility. In 1996, around 3,000 tons of food waste were used as livestock feed. Sewage by-products, landscape waste, paper, degradable con-

struction debris, and ground wooden pallets are combined to produce 50,000 pounds of compost a day, some of which is used along
WDWR roadways. WDWR sells the excess fertilizer to the citrus
industry.

WDWR has a state-of-the-art wastewater treatment facility on site
that was an investment of over $100 million. This wastewater treat-
ment facility does not discharge directly into the environment.
Instead, all the plant's outputs are processed and reused in one of
three ways: Sludge is used as an input to the composting process;
some of the water is reused to recharge the ground water table; and
the rest of the water is reused for irrigation. WDWR has effectively
integrated different facility operations to develop this efficient system of reducing and reusing wastes. The resort has integrated such
operations as wastewater treatment, composting, material recovery,
landscaping, and disposal of solid and food wastes to develop a
comprehensive approach that exploits the synergies between such
activities.

**Benefits of P2 Activities for Industry.** Benefits from such facility P2
planning and implementation activities have included cost savings,
reduced waste generation, successful identification of P2 opportunities, and improved environmental management (Barwick et al., 1997,
p. 8). Specific cost savings include reduced operating costs, reduced
compliance costs, increased productivity, and reduced exposure to
future liability costs. For example, P2 efforts at Ford's Ohio assembly
plant yielded significant cost savings—over $400,000 (Ohio EPA,
1998). Other benefits include continuous improvement, increased
environmental protection, and improved company reputation. The
benefits also include improving company and stakeholder relationships. For example, all six facilities studied in BRT (1993) "felt their
pollution prevention accomplishments have a positive effect on their
company's image." The health and safety benefits include, in particular, improvements in worker safety, such as the reduction of
worker exposure to hazardous substances at Ford's Ohio assembly
plant.

## Government Laws and Incentive Programs for P2

U.S. EPA and state and local governments have encouraged and
facilitated such activities by promoting the prevention of pollution.
Almost every state government and many local governments have

created P2 offices, designated P2 staff, and/or trained environmental employees about P2 opportunities so they can help implement P2 programs.[24]  These P2 professionals work with industry, government officials, and community members to facilitate education, information sharing, and development and implementation of P2 activities. Both voluntary and regulatory programs are used to encourage and assist businesses in the development and application of practices and technologies that help prevent pollution.  Regional, state, and local P2 activities range from state P2 laws to voluntary programs for businesses to on-site technical assistance.

**P2 Legislation and Laws.**  At least 38 states have passed some type of P2 legislation (NPPR, 1996).  These laws often create P2 organizations with state funding, provide resources, officially designate P2 as the preferred means of achieving compliance with environmental law, and create official P2 technical assistance programs.  Many of these laws create mandatory or voluntary programs that require or encourage certain industries to develop P2 plans for an entire facility (*P2 planning* or *facility planning* laws).

About 20 states have P2 planning laws with mandatory reporting requirements for regulated community members that meet the designated criteria.[25]  Program requirements vary from state to state. Most require facilities that are large hazardous waste generators and/or toxic chemical users to conduct P2 planning and submit their plans, summaries of plans, and/or progress reports to the state. Implementation of the facility P2 plans is voluntary.  These laws try to motivate voluntary implementation of more source-reduction activities by helping individual facilities realize the business benefits of P2, which the P2 planning process will quantify.  Even though these laws create regulatory requirements, many of them, like New Jersey's Pollution Prevention Act and its associated planning process, are trying to define "a new approach, which emphasizes manage-

---

[24]For more information about the many different state P2 activities, see the National Pollution Prevention Roundtable's (NPPR's) P2 Yellow Pages (NPPR, 1995b; see also NPPR, 2000, for an updated, though abridged, Web edition).  For information about local government activities, see NPPR (1995a).

[25]The states include Arizona, California, Georgia, Louisiana, Maine, Massachusetts, Minnesota, Mississippi, New Jersey, New York, Ohio, Oregon, Rhode Island, South Carolina, South Dakota, Tennessee, Texas, Vermont, and Washington (NPPR, 1996).

ment systems, not command-and-control" (Dierks, White, and Shapiro, 1996).

One of the oldest and most comprehensive programs is Oregon's Toxics Use Reduction and Hazardous Waste Reduction Act, passed in 1989. This law is intended to achieve facilitywide changes that reduce, avoid, or eliminate the use of toxic substances and the generation of hazardous wastes by requiring affected parties to develop reduction plans and to monitor their progress on an ongoing basis. Large users of toxic chemicals and hazardous waste generators are required to develop P2 plans, although implementation of the plans is voluntary. Companies must submit the summary and annual progress reports on plan implementation to the state agency. Oregon DEQ provides information and on-site assistance for developing plans and implementing P2 activities. Because this program takes a regulatory approach and emphasizes business incentives for P2, it offers no governmental incentives. Oregon DEQ can review the plans and progress reports and, if it considers them inadequate, can issue a Notice of Deficiency requiring compliance. If compliance is still not met, DEQ can seek enforcement through judicial action or hold a public meeting revealing the findings (Oregon DEQ, 1993). However, as in many states implementing P2 planning laws, Oregon DEQ prefers to emphasize the benefits of compliance rather than rely on enforcement. Oregon claims that its program has successfully promoted industry source reduction and is evaluating options to improve its P2 planning efforts further (Marsh, 1996).

By taking such a facilitywide approach to P2 planning, these laws help encourage businesses to try to be more integrated and holistic in their approaches to P2.

**Voluntary P2 Programs.** In addition to the P2 laws described above, many states also have their own P2 staffs, technical assistance, and voluntary programs. Their objective is to improve environmental performance by helping businesses reduce their emissions and implement more P2 activities at their facilities in a cooperative, rather than punitive, manner. Such activities often include some formal or informal regulatory incentives and/or public recognition to encourage companies to participate and reduce emissions to voluntary program targets.

Texas has a large P2 program that incorporates voluntary P2 activities to complement its P2 planning law.  The Texas Natural Resources Conservation Commission's (TNRCC's) Office of Pollution Prevention and Recycling has a series of voluntary programs focused on P2 and conservation, recycling, small business technical assistance, and "Clean Texas 2000 Partnerships."  One example is the Clean Texas 2000 Partnerships program, a statewide program to educate the public about P2 and to develop, recognize, and inspire P2 activities in communities and industries.  In Clean Industries 2000, industrial facilities committed themselves to

- reducing Toxic Release Inventory chemicals and/or the generation of hazardous wastes by 50 percent or more by 2000
- implementing an internal environmental management program to ensure high levels of compliance with state and federal environmental standards
- forming a citizens' communication program
- participating in one or more community environmental projects each year.

A variety of industry facilities and defense facilities voluntarily participate in TNRCC's P2 programs.

Companies receive statewide recognition for their participation and successes in this program, as well as in many other voluntary P2 programs.[26]  Many states, including Kentucky, Ohio, Massachusetts, Minnesota, Vermont, and Maine, offer recognition and governor's awards for demonstrated success in P2.

Other incentives that state and local P2 organizations offer to businesses to implement P2 activities include P2 tax credits, loan programs, and grant programs to help industry, especially small businesses, invest in P2 technologies and practices.  Delaware and Oklahoma offer tax credits to firms investing in P2 practices.  Connecticut offers loans and lines of credit.  P2 grant programs in the City of San Francisco and in Indiana have successfully helped finan-

---

[26]Texas provides a range of voluntary P2 programs.  For more information on NPPR's programs, see TNRCC (1995).

cially strapped businesses research and develop P2 opportunities (NPPR, 1995a).

**P2 Activities Illustrative of Evolving Regulatory System.** These P2 activities provide specific examples of how the new collaborative, flexible, two-track regulatory system affects industry. The many different voluntary P2 programs show how many state and local governments are trying to work with industry, to be partners in source reduction. This collaborative relationship between government and industry affects how the regulators treat businesses. Businesses that are proactively participating in these programs may be treated differently by the community, by state and local regulators, and especially by other companies that participate in the voluntary programs. The community perceives these companies to be good corporate citizens. Regulators are more likely to trust them and see them as active partners in trying to help improve environmental performance and may even give such companies preferred treatment, such as conducting inspections less frequently.

Although preferred treatment is not always officially advertised, some state P2 legislation and state program documents outline such regulatory benefits. For example, the Illinois Toxic Pollution Prevention Act of 1989 describes such treatment: "Facilities which submit toxic pollution prevention innovation plans may receive preferred treatment in permitting or environmental law compliance problems." (NPPR, 1996.) Legislation in Arizona, Michigan, and Oklahoma outlines refunds or reductions of hazardous waste fees for P2 activities. Virginia legislation states that "waste generation planners may more easily comply with environmental laws." (NPPR, 1996.) Florida's Metro-Dade County Department of Environmental Resource Management has lowered fines or developed a more-lenient time schedule in enforcement settlement agreements in exchange for the implementation of P2 projects at the facility that had the regulatory violation (Metro-Dade County, undated). These examples also illustrate how important the relationship is between a facility and the regulators and community to receive preferred treatment. How facilities successfully manage such relationships for such benefits will be discussed in Chapter Six.

Many states whose programs have been around for several years, including California, Massachusetts, New Jersey, Oregon, Texas, and Washington, have been formally evaluating and updating their P2 planning processes and other activities.  State evaluations show different types of successes from these programs.  Waste and emissions have been reduced for certain chemicals, and industry participants and many individual companies have benefited from participation in these programs.  Industry has also cited some disadvantages, often related to new reporting requirements for P2 planning.[27]  Many states are using such evaluations to revise their programs.  Some of these states are using the findings to think more broadly about P2 and their state regulatory systems.  For instance, the P2 coordinators from the four Pacific Northwest states and EPA Region 10 have developed a regional strategy for advancing the regulatory integration of P2.  The strategy focuses on integrating P2-based approaches as a routine consideration in all environmental agency activities, including program objective and performance measures, and removing regulatory barriers to P2 activities.  Another major thrust is industry incentives, including regulatory benefits:

> Incentives such as streamlined reporting and/or monitoring requirements, regulatory flexibility, and adjusted fees will be available as incentives to send the "signal" that choosing prevention measures is the smart choice. (Ross & Associates, 1996.)

As these policies evolve, their effects on facility approaches may also evolve.  For example, NPPR's Facility P2 Planning Workgroup urges all state facility planning programs to require materials reporting.  In 1999, only Massachusetts and New Jersey required facilities to report materials accounting or process-level efficiency data (Barwick et al., 1997, p. 4).  Such a requirement would mean that more facilities would formally track materials usage, which most of industry does not support.  Businesses prefer voluntary P2 planning because they feel that the scope of mandated P2 planning is often limited and that the mandate creates "unnecessary administrative and reporting burdens" for facilities that are already effectively conducting P2 planning  (BRT, 1998, p. 2).[28]  Industry wants a flexible P2 planning process that includes "exit criteria" for facilities that have demonstrated a commitment to P2.  For example, Oregon and Washington allow a

---

[27]For a sample of these evaluations, see TNRCC (1995).  Also see Barwick et al. (1997) for details about other state studies.

[28]Both BRT (1998) and Barwick (1997) provide interesting overviews of industry and state government views about P2 planning.

facility's EMS to exempt it from P2 planning requirements (Barwick et al., 1997, p. 13).

In summary, given these government incentives and regulations and the overall evolving environmental policy context, many corporate facilities and DoD installations have been proactive about implementing P2 facility approaches and participating in government P2 programs. For example, Wright-Patterson AFB won a 1996 P2 award from the state of Ohio for the base's facilitywide P2 efforts (Ohio EPA, 1997).

## INNOVATIVE FACILITY PERMITTING ACTIVITIES

Innovative approaches to implementing facility environmental permits include experiments with facilitywide, multimedia, and P2 permitting. These permitting approaches try to integrate permits across media, source locations, and/or regulatory jurisdictions. Experiments conducted with regulators often include regulatory flexibility to streamline procedures and requirements, saving companies time and money. Many of these experiments began as unique projects driven by individual businesses, because their local regulators were open to new permitting approaches, while others are part of federal or state pilot programs, such as the Project XL permitting examples discussed earlier. Proactive companies seize the initiative to develop innovative permitting deals to help the environment and their bottom lines.

### Industry Facilitywide Permitting Activities

An Intel Corporation facility in Oregon has implemented an innovative P2-oriented permitting project, which addressed administrative inefficiencies. In 1993, the Oregon DEQ, EPA, and Intel formed a partnership to develop an experimental permit—the Pollution Prevention in Permitting Pilot Project (the "P4 Project")—under Title V of the CAA. This P4 project incorporates P2 and regulatory flexibility while improving environmental performance. A single Title V operating permit was developed for the Intel Aloha manufacturing facility. Under this experimental permit, Intel must manage air emissions by developing and implementing specific P2 activities. Intel shares its management plan with DEQ. The plan explains how, through P2, the facility will continuously reduce emissions from existing processes so that it stays within existing permit limits as production expands. The permit has given Intel the flexibility to change selected processes without updating the permit, as long as the facility meets certain air emission thresholds. This new facility-wide permit has saved Intel time and money. John Harland, Intel Corporation, Aloha, Oregon, has noted that Intel is "now encouraged and rewarded" for its P2 efforts besides being a "good corporate citizen" because of the benefits the company receives (Pacific Northwest Pollution Prevention Research Center, 1994). Specifically,

> the permit's flexibility provisions enabled the company to implement process changes and P2 projects without unnecessary delay, critical in an industry where continuous change is essential for remaining competitive and profitable. (Pacific Northwest Pollution Prevention Resource Center, 1999.)

This P4 approach has been used as a national model and has been applied at facilities in Arizona, Connecticut, Georgia, Massachusetts, New Mexico, Oklahoma, Texas, and Washington.[29]

WDWR has been creative in negotiating facility permits with regulators. The resort negotiated a unique 20-year comprehensive permit regarding wetlands and development at the facility. WDWR had been receiving individual permits for each development project, which required that wetlands lost to development be replaced by creating wetlands of equal size. This piecemeal permitting process made it difficult to understand the true environmental impact; in addition, small isolated pieces of wetlands in mitigation efforts often did not do very well. The process was also time-consuming and costly. It was often difficult for Disney to get agreement from the many different regulators for each of these permits. The regulators also wanted a more-comprehensive approach.

In 1991, Disney started gathering inputs from community groups and working with state and federal regulators to develop a unique,

---

[29]Such permits have been issued or are in the process of being drafted for Lasco Bathware, Yelm, Washington; Imation Enterprises, Weatherford, Oklahoma; Cytec Industries, Wallingford, Connecticut; Rio Grande Portland Cement, Tijeras, New Mexico; and Searle Chemical, Augusta, Georgia. The approach has also been adapted by Intel facilities in Arizona, Massachusetts, and Texas. For more details on these examples and more discussion of the costs and benefits of such efforts, see Pacific Northwest Pollution Prevention Resource Center (1999).

long-term comprehensive permit agreement.  After extensive negotiations, the company and Florida environmental officials "agreed on a large-scale off-site wetlands enhancement, restoration and preservation strategy."  Disney purchased 8,500 acres of ecologically sensitive land and gave it to The Nature Conservancy, along with some financial support, to manage as a wilderness preserve, which is now called the Disney Wilderness preserve.  The company modified its property development plans so that they would affect only 446 acres of wetlands.  Disney also placed permanent conservation easements on 7,500 acres of WDWR property, guaranteeing that the land will remain in its natural state.  In exchange, WDWR could develop other parts of its property without needing any additional approvals.  The total financial commitment was about $40 million (Disney, undated; Nature Conservancy, undated), but the company ended up saving money in the long run by avoiding permitting costs and potential delays of development.  If the traditional piecemeal permitting process had continued, Disney would probably not have been able to develop as much of the property, and the process would have been more time consuming and costly.

WDWR has also been assertive and creative about other permits, such as water permits.  Because of its construction and other dynamic activities, WDWR has many trailers and other facilities that require sanitary or potable water hookups that are often small.  Regulations require that a permit application be submitted and approved for each such hookup, which would be particularly time consuming for both DEP and WDWR.  So, after negotiations with WDWR, the Florida DEP gave WDWR the regulatory authority for an internal permitting system for small permit sources only.  WDWR Environmental Permits Department staff members created the system and serve as its managers and watchdogs.  In addition to managing the internal permit application process, staff members collect and review the data to make sure that all these small WDWR sources stay compliant.  DEP has reserved the right to review WDWR's paperwork and/or come inspect the system at any time.  The result is a win-win situation for both organizations.  DEP saves time and work, as does WDWR.  WDWR staff can process the permits faster than DEP's can, within a day and a half after an on-site facility applies for a permit instead of DEP's 30 days.  This timing can be critical for projects that need hookup approvals right away.

## States Encouraging Facilitywide Permitting Experiments

Our existing regulatory structure has been implemented as a piecemeal system, creating a series of uncoordinated, media-focused programs with different standards, administrative requirements, agency inspectors, and inspections. This fragmented regulatory structure has often resulted in inefficiencies for the regulated community, in environmental performance, and for the public regulators, especially when it comes to permitting requirements. Media-focused permits have often resulted in pollutants being shifted from one medium to another and eventually to the point of least regulation. Regulators have not been able to analyze environmental impacts from a facilitywide perspective because of the fragmented picture the media-focused system creates. Multiple-agency administrative requirements at different governmental levels, for different programs and media, have also resulted in excess expenses for both public agencies and industry, such as excess paperwork. States and local governments are trying to address such problems by developing more integrated and holistic approaches to environmental compliance. States are trying to address permitting requirements and inspections at a facility level instead of focusing on individual media issues.

Many different states are experimenting with multimedia, facilitywide, integrated, P2-oriented permits to help speed up and simplify a permitting process that can create a cumbersome burden on industry facilities. Such flexible regulatory approaches often replace many media permits with fewer or single facilitywide permits. These programs focus on one or more of the following goals: administrative efficiency, risk reduction, and P2. Administrative efficiency approaches attempt to streamline the regulatory approval process by reducing paperwork, integrating data management, shortening permit review and processing times, or implementing other administrative improvements. Risk-reduction permitting programs focus on reducing the multimedia environmental and health impacts of hazardous substances through improved treatment options or P2. P2 programs focus on reducing pollution at its source (Aderson and Herb, 1992). At least a dozen states are planning or already conducting permitting pilots, including California, Delaware, Oregon, Massachusetts, Maryland, New Jersey, New York, Pennsylvania, Virginia, and Minnesota.

California has been streamlining permitting experiments for both Title V of the CAA and at the multimedia facility level. California air quality standards are the strictest in the nation, and for any given source, federal, state, and local air quality requirements may overlap or even conflict. Since 1995, California air quality agencies, in collaboration with EPA, have been attempting to simplify and integrate overlapping, redundant, and/or conflicting requirements—including emission limits, monitoring, reporting and record keeping—into a single Title V requirement (Stromberg, 1996). In January 1997, California implemented a five-year pilot program to test replacing individual media and source permits with "facility compliance plans." This program will allow a new or expanding facility in a designated zone to substitute a facility compliance plan for any combination of state and local environmental permits. The California Environmental Protection Agency (Cal/EPA) and local environmental agencies will make sure that the facility compliance plans meet certain standards before allowing them to replace existing permitting requirements. Cal/EPA hopes that this consolidation program will save costs for both the industrial facilities and agencies involved in the experiment.[30]

The New Jersey Facility-Wide Permitting Program was one of the most aggressive multimedia permitting programs. This pilot program, which ran through most of the 1990s, allowed industrial facilities to replace many different media permits with a single facility permit. The program had two main goals: incorporating P2 into a multimedia permit process and increasing the administrative efficiency of the regulatory process. New Jersey believes that a facility-wide permit has "tremendous potential to create a regulatory approach which provides flexibility for facilities to implement cost-effective pollution prevention strategies" and provides testing for streamlining and integrating different permitting requirements for air, water, and waste (New Jersey DEP, undated).

Part of the flexibility is to allow facilities with facilitywide permits to change processes without lengthy preapprovals, as long as the changes do not lead to increases in the generation of hazardous waste or in the release of hazardous substances. In exchange for this

---

[30]"California Tests Replacing Permits with Compliance Plans," 1996.

flexibility, a facility must expand its P2 planning efforts, although actual implementation of the plans is voluntary. State officials believe facilities will voluntarily implement additional P2 projects because of the business benefits.

Under this program, New Jersey completed 12 facilitywide permits, which consolidated between 12 and 100 individual media permits into single facilitywide permits. The first facilitywide permit was issued for a Schering-Plough Corporation facility. This single permit, which replaced about 100 air and a couple of water permits, addresses releases of all environmental media, including air, water, and hazardous waste. To develop the permit, the facility first completed a plan that identified its P2 options, then updated the information for its current permits. The New Jersey DEP integrated the permitting information and developed a facilitywide permit proposal. Next, a public hearing was held to discuss the proposal; New Jersey DEP revised the permit; and the final facilitywide permit was issued. Although this process took longer than a standard permitting process, New Jersey DEP officials believe less time will be needed as they learn more about the new process.

Even in the early stages of this pilot, the initial participants felt they had benefited from it. One firm said that the facilitywide permit had simplified its compliance process. For example, the firm's five-year facilitywide permit combined 70 water and air permits and hazardous waste storage approvals, eliminating the need for frequent renewals of many different permits, and consolidated "a 3-drawer horizontal file cabinet filled with permits into one 4-inch binder." (U.S. General Accounting Office, 1996.) The company is also able to make some changes to production processes without engaging in a long preapproval process. More recently, ten of the 12 facilities in this pilot stated that the program's most significant benefit was increased operational flexibility (Minard, 2001).

To summarize, these many different permitting efforts emphasize a focus on P2, not just on compliance; planning and emissions calculations for the entire facility, not just individual processes; and benefits for facilities that achieve and maintain specified levels of performance. The benefits include the ability to change processes without revising permits, with lower administrative burdens and costs, and with the flexibility to pursue alternative technologies or means of meeting standards. These benefits accrue because of the production of "win-win" outcomes for regulators and corporations.

## OTHER SYSTEMS APPROACHES

Other systems approaches to environmental performance tend to emphasize place-based management for addressing the environmental problems across regions, states, watersheds, and communities throughout the United States.[31] These approaches include sustainable development, sustainable community, ecosystem management, eco-industrial park, and watershed management activities. These types of activities focus on integrated approaches to managing, creating, and preserving healthy environments in our cities, suburbs, towns, businesses, rural areas, and wildernesses over the long term. They also focus on the management of the environment in a specific place, which can be as small as a few city blocks or as large as hundreds of square miles spread within several states, such as the Chesapeake Bay watershed. Such approaches are initiated and facilitated by a range of stakeholders that include government, academia, businesses, private citizens, community groups, and other NGOs. Place-based approaches often involve collaboration and cooperation among these many different types of stakeholders.

While many of these innovative approaches are trying to be more holistic, we did not focus on them for this study for a number of reasons. First, many of these approaches being driven or implemented by a group of organizations (government, industry, and NGOs). Second, industry may not play a large enough role. Finally, many of these efforts are not very far along. These approaches do, however, have important implications for DoD in the broader context of changes in environmental policy, environmental activities, and potential future effects on DoD installations. And the effects could be either negative or positive.

One potential negative effect might be policies evolving out of such activities that could limit the ability of some defense facilities to pursue their own environmental activities or their defense missions. For instance, sustainability efforts focusing on sprawl could yield signifi-

_____

[31]*Place-based* refers to location-specific approaches.

cant community pressure for local policies that would affect Army attempts to relocate significant numbers of troops from one Army installation to another.  Prospective neighbors might apply such pressure because they feel that adding many more people would crowd the community.  On the other hand, DoD facilities might also be able to take advantage of some of these place-based activities.  For example, Eglin AFB participates in ecosystem management activities (discussed more later).

Because of such potential affects on DoD, which will probably become more significant for defense facilities in the future, we briefly discuss such activities below.

## Evolving Toward Sustainability

Many of the approaches build on sustainable development concepts. The most widely used definition for *sustainable development* is "development that meets the needs of the present without compromising the ability of future generations to meet their own needs" (World Commission on Environment and Development, 1987). However, each organization often has its own definition, especially for implementation.  Such definitions usually recognize sustainability as a process.

Many community place-based efforts use the term *sustainable community*, which emphasizes the community aspect of sustainable development.  Communities differ in how they interpret this term, although there are common elements.  Usually, the term refers to community efforts to address problems by taking a long-term systems approach to dealing with economic, social, and environmental concerns holistically.  Building consensus and fostering partnership among key stakeholders about community problems and solutions is also important to such efforts (Lachman, 1997b).

Hundreds of communities throughout the United States are developing sustainability projects and implementing more-sustainable practices because of the critical environmental and community problems they and our country as a whole face.  These communities recognize that many problems, such as urban sprawl, cut across many different segments of community and society.  These problems cannot easily be solved using traditional approaches or traditional elements within our society. Many people feel that, because such problems involve multiple disciplines, agencies, stakeholders, and sectors, it is better to address them through a new collaborative and holistic systems approach. The problems such efforts address cover a wide range of issues, depending on such local interests as urban sprawl, smart growth, new economic development, inner city and brownfield redevelopment, local small businesses, a strong local economy, environmental justice, ecosystem management, watershed management, land-use planning, recycling, agriculture, biodiversity, lifestyles, green buildings, energy conservation, and P2.

Likewise, many businesses are embracing sustainable development for their environmental visions. Many are also trying to implement it or at least to work toward "sustainability." A 1998 Arthur D. Little, Inc., study found that 96 percent of almost 500 companies surveyed thought that it is important to do something about sustainable development (Poltorzycki, 1998). However, company definitions also differ, especially for individual businesses and how they implement sustainability. For example, DuPont sees itself as transforming into a "sustainable growth" company that increases shareholder and society value while reducing its safety incidents and environmental footprint (DuPont, 1999). The term at 3M is *eco-efficiency*, defined as

> producing more with less resources and less impact on the environment [and] involves a number of performance elements, including reduction of the amount of material and energy put into product. (3M, 1998.)

Companies perceive potential financial and operational benefits from implementing more-sustainable practices: reducing costs and liabilities, increasing customer loyalty and market position, protecting businesses' right to operate, and developing new products.[32] Recognizing such benefits, many companies have become active in the international sustainable development agenda. The World Business Council on Sustainable Development (WBCSD) is a consortium of 150 international companies sharing a commitment to the environment and to the principles of economic growth and sustainable

---

[32]This list of benefits was based on hundreds of interviews and discussions with business people regarding sustainable development in a recent World Resources Institute (WRI) study; see Arnold and Day (1998).

development. These companies include such large corporations as AT&T, 3M, Arthur D. Little, DuPont, Dow Chemical, Eastman Kodak, General Motors, Nissan, Mitsubishi, NEC, Johnson & Johnson, P&G, Seiko Group, Shell International, Weyerhaeuser, Toyota, and AOL Time Warner.[33] The objectives of WBCSD are to secure a political and regulatory framework that will allow business to operate profitably while preserving the environment and to contribute to sustainable development through business leadership, policy development, demonstration of best environmental practices, and global outreach to all nations (WBCSD, undated). Such companies illustrate a growing international trend for businesses to view sustainable development as an important business issue, especially with respect to strategic planning and market competitiveness. For example, "3M believes that companies that contribute to sustainability by creating environmentally responsible products will be the most competitive" (3M, 1998).

Companies are also starting to become more directly involved in community sustainability issues, such as smart growth. For example, in the 1998 elections, 72 percent of the over 240 state and local ballot initiatives elections that were intended to manage sprawl passed (National Association of Local Government Environmental Professionals [NALGEP], 1999, p. 10). This shows that smart growth is an important issue throughout the United States, something businesses have begun to notice and are starting to see can affect their bottom lines. For instance, in a recent study about how businesses are actively promoting alternatives to sprawl, NALGEP (1999, p. 4) found that forward-thinking businesses are recognizing the costs and affects of sprawl. Specifically, business leaders

- recognize that sprawl threatens the quality of life in many communities and that quality of life directly affects economic prosperity
- recognize that urban sprawl threatens the health of central cities that is critical to the overall economic health of a metropolitan region

---

[33]See http://www.wbcsd.ch/aboutus/members.htm for a full list of WBCSD companies.

- are concerned that, in certain areas, sprawl is starting to make it more difficult to access, attract, and maintain a qualified workforce

- are taking advantage of economic efficiencies in redeveloping areas with established infrastructure, rather than building new infrastructure to develop in new, undeveloped locations

- are taking competitive advantage of smart growth practices.

This study also provides specific and diverse examples of how businesses are actively participating in smart growth activities. For instance, the Bank of America has invested significantly in revitalizing part of downtown Charlotte, North Carolina, and is a national leader in helping businesses overcome barriers in the redevelopment of urban brownfields. A very different example involves the Silicon Valley Manufacturing Group (SVMG), a trade association of over 130 of the largest employers in Northern California's Silicon Valley. Through their partnership in SVMG, these high-tech companies address traffic congestion, high housing costs, increased air pollution, and other sprawl-related problems that affect employees' and businesses' quality of life. For instance, SVMG has successfully engaged member companies to reduce air pollution and have worked to improve affordable housing options and multimodal transportation options for employees (NALGEP, 1999, pp. 48–49 and 78–79).[34]

## Eco-Industrial Parks and Industrial Ecology

Traditional industry involvement in such sustainability efforts, especially the community ones, is found in the development of eco-industrial parks:

> An eco-industrial park is a community of manufacturing and service businesses seeking enhanced environmental and economic performance through collaboration in managing environmental and resource issues, including energy, water, and materials. By working together, the community of businesses seeks a collective

---

[34]NALGEP (1999) also provides other excellent examples. For a good reference about growth management issues, see Porter (1997).

benefit that is greater than the sum of individual benefits each company would realize if it optimized its individual performance. (PCSD, 1996a, Appendix B4, p. 4.)

The main idea is to create synergies between various industries, agriculture, and communities to convert wastes into valuable products and feed stocks for other companies, at a profit. Such efforts are very recent and still evolving. Communities that are trying to develop eco-industrial parks include Chattanooga, Tennessee; Northampton County, Virginia; Brownsville, Texas; Burlington County, New Jersey; Skagit County, Washington; Tucson, Arizona; and Baltimore, Maryland. Companies get involved in such efforts because of the economic and community relationship benefits from working with neighboring companies. For example, some of the industrial by-products and wastes of the Chaparral Steel Company in Midlothian, Texas, have become profitable resources and inputs for neighboring industries. For example, the company's waste slag is being used at a neighboring cement plant. This arrangement has created a competitive advantage for Chaparral Steel, which has increased profits, saved natural resources, and reduced environmental pollution (PCSD, 1998, pp. 22–23).

Industry also enjoys regulatory benefits from such efforts, although regulations often are barriers to their implementation. Permitting procedures are a common regulatory barrier; they hinder the free flow of certain waste materials from one company's facility to another's adjacent facility, which uses the material as inputs. Resource Conservation and Recovery Act (RCRA) regulations are a main barrier to material exchange in eco-industrial park projects. But participating in these innovative efforts can help create regulatory flexibility. For example, at the New Jersey EcoComplex in Burlington County, New Jersey, "agreements are being constructed to ease regulatory burdens for businesses interested in joining the EcoComplex" (Lau, 1996, p. 18). Such regulatory flexibility is likely to continue as more eco-industrial park projects develop and evolve.

Eco-industrial parks and other such symbiotic industrial approaches are based on the concept of *industrial ecology*:

Industrial ecology is the study of a closed loop in which resources and energy flow into production processes, and excess materials are put back into the loop so that little or no waste is generated. Products used by consumers flow back into production loops through recycling to recover resources. Ideally the loops are closed within a factory, among industries in a region, and within national and global economies. (White House Office of Science and Technology Policy, 1994, p. 54.)

Industrial ecology came out of the academic and research communities, and such concepts are just starting to be implemented within industry, such as in eco-industrial parks.

Eco-industrial parks and industrial ecology approaches tend to focus on individual resource use and look across industry sectors and organizational boundaries more than do some of the other innovative approaches discussed. Also, such efforts tend to operate at a higher geographical level, rather than at a facility level. Although these approaches are in their infancy, they will have important implications for DoD installations as they evolve in the future. DoD should track such efforts and study opportunities for working more with other organizations, such as nearby companies, in analyzing and using their resource inputs and outputs.

## Ecosystem Management Approaches

Place-based management efforts related to natural resource management often focus on ecosystem management. Definitions of *ecosystem management* also differ, but the following is well accepted in the scientific community:

> Ecosystem management integrates scientific knowledge of ecological relationships within a complex sociopolitical and value framework toward the general goal of protecting native ecosystem integrity over the long term. (Grumbine, 1994.)

Some environmental managers, policymakers, and regulators are embracing ecosystem management concepts to address environmental protection and natural resource management in a more-integrated resource way and to be able to focus on entire systems.

A 1996 survey identified over 600 projects throughout the United States that are trying to implement ecosystem management approaches (Yaffee et al., 1996, p. 4). Many of these projects are collaborations of federal, state, and local governments; NGOs; and industry. For example, the Chesapeake Bay Program is a large ecosystem management effort that covers about 64,000 square miles of the Chesapeake Bay watershed across six states. A regional partnership involving Maryland, Virginia, Pennsylvania, and the District of Columbia; the Chesapeake Bay Commission, a tristate legislative body; and the U.S. EPA, the program establishes the policy direction for the bay and its living resources. The program works cooperatively with these and other partners, including other federal agencies, local governments, and industry, to improve and maintain the health of the Chesapeake Bay ecosystem.

Such efforts are often initiated and run by governments and/or NGOs. However, industry also participates, conducts, and benefits from ecosystem management approaches. The Western Private Lands Legacy, a Wyoming NGO, is developing and conducting a private, multiparty land-use planning and conflict-resolution effort. In this collaborative effort, ranchers use ecosystem information about local land to improve land-use decisions and conservation—which also helps in their business decisionmaking (see Geehan and Jenkins, 1996). Georgia-Pacific has used ecosystem management approaches in developing and implementing conservation and sustainable forestry practices. Its "Green Places" program was designed to identify and protect areas of company forests that have biological, historical, or physical significance. In addition, Georgia-Pacific has partnered with The Nature Conservancy to jointly manage 21,000 acres along the lower Roanoke River in North Carolina (Georgia-Pacific, 1997b).

DoD has also taken advantage of ecosystem management partnerships and approaches. For example, Eglin AFB has partnered with the Nature Conservancy for development and implementation of a base ecosystem management plan.[35] This installation consists of about 464,000 acres in the Florida Panhandle, mostly a sandhill vegetation ecosystem with prime habitat of old-growth stands of longleaf pine. The fire-evolved longleaf pine systems at Eglin are home to many endangered, threatened, and important species, such as the Red Cockaded Woodpecker (Hardesty et al., 1997). This planning

---

[35]See http://www.eglin.af.mil/46tw/46xp/46xpe/fact/ecosys.htm for more information about Eglin's ecosystem management activities.

activity allows Eglin to sustain base training and other military missions while protecting endangered species and the ecosystem. As noted earlier, this study does not focus on the many existing innovative DoD environmental management efforts but on the lessons that can be learned from private-sector experience. This DoD example was briefly discussed here because it illustrates the importance of the changing relationships of DoD facilities with outside entities. DoD's installation management and operations have traditionally been totally independent of outside organizations, especially with respect to environmental issues. However, defense facilities now need to be more responsive to neighbors, community, and the general public. Partnerships and public image have become more important as well. The significance of such issues will be discussed in Chapter Five.

Industry has found that such ecosystem management approaches can also bring regulatory benefits and that more regulators are encouraging such benefits for industry participating in these integrated efforts. In a 1995 state ecosystem management survey, the Council of State Governments found that many state natural-resource and environmental agencies feel that flexibility in regulations is an important component of ecosystem management approaches (Council of State Governments, 1995).

Florida is developing one of the most extensive statewide ecosystem management plans and comprehensive approaches to ecosystem management. The state is using ecosystem management concepts to promote long-term environmental stewardship among all its stakeholders. Florida's definition of a ecosystem management is very broad:

> an integrated, flexible approach to management of Florida's biological and physical environments—conducted through the use of tools such as planning, land acquisition, environmental education, regulation, economic incentives, and pollution prevention—designed to maintain, protect and improve the state's natural, managed, and human communities. (Florida DEP, 1995, p. 2.)

This approach has four main focus areas: place-based management, cultural change, improved foundations for ecosystem management, and commonsense regulations. *Cultural change* refers to integrating citizens' action into environmental protection programs. *Foundations* refers to science and technology, environmental education, monitoring, and other tools needed to make ecosystem-based decisions. *Commonsense regulations* focuses on improving environmental results by developing workable alternatives that give the regulated community incentives to voluntarily improve environmental protection beyond compliance. Implementing alternatives to the current regulatory process is a specific goal of Florida's ecosystem management implementation strategy. Such alternatives could be chosen in place of traditional regulation. Potential regulatory incentives being explored include longer-term permits, reduced permitting costs, faster processing for permits, technical assistance, incentives for redevelopment of urban areas, and making regulations more amenable to experimental use of new technologies (Florida DEP, 1995, pp. 18–23).

WDWR's innovative permitting activities have taken advantage of Florida's emphasis on ecosystem management approaches. The 20-year development permit example discussed earlier takes a more comprehensive approach to wetland mitigation, one that focuses on protecting an ecosystem. Despite the large expenses of purchasing the Walker Ranch property and donating it to The Nature Conservancy, WDWR ended up saving money in the long run because it gained valuable flexibility and was able to develop more property. The resort also benefited from improved relationships with regulators and other stakeholders and improved its environmental reputation within the local community and with guests. In addition, WDWR has begun ecosystem management of the property that it had set aside to be natural areas (these areas cover about one-third of the property). As part of this initiative, WDWR is looking at ways to enhance species habitats within its open areas and conservation areas.

## INTEGRATION OF DIFFERENT APPROACHES

Many of these approaches have overlaps and synergies. One important area of overlap is the use of incentives. Many government authorities and community and industry representatives recognize the importance of incentives to achieving compliance and improving environmental performance. These many different approaches emphasize incentives rather than penalties to encourage compliance and even going beyond compliance. For example, state and local environmental authorities' P2, innovative permitting, and environmental leadership activities emphasize incentives to encourage improved environmental performance. Similarly, U.S. EPA's Project XL focuses on voluntary experiments with benefits for participants that achieve superior environmental performance. Ecosystem management and sustainable community approaches often focus on voluntary collaboration and incentives to help motivate participants. In addition, firms use incentives to help motivate employees to participate in integrated facility management approaches, which will be discussed more in Chapter Seven.

Despite such overlaps, there is often a disconnect between some of the industry and technical approaches and the ecosystem management, community, and natural resource approaches. These disconnects often result from traditional disciplinary ways of thinking and orientation and from questions about who has primary authority in the efforts. Industry managers and engineers traditionally focus on technology and economic issues. Natural resource and land managers and biologists tend to focus on conservation and land management issues related to flora and fauna. This difference is the classic environmental education split between the "technology-technical" experts and the "bugs and bunnies" experts.

Figure 3.1 provides a context for the relationship between some of these activities and such disconnects. This oversimplified figure illustrates relationships between different activities related to sustainability and the ultimate goal of sustainable development and a sustainable earth.[36] First, the focus and interests of the traditional industry and technology experts are presented on the left side of the figure. At an operational level, such techniques and policies as P2, design for the environment (known as DfE), EMSs, and environmental technologies are implemented. Such tools are used in individual projects, such as company environmental projects and eco-industrial parks. Such efforts contribute to the development of broader concepts and efforts toward industrial ecology. Given the traditional interests and needs of manufacturing and industrial

---

[36]While *sustainable development* often means meeting current needs without compromising future needs, *sustainable earth* refers to the idealistic goal that sustainable development has been achieved everywhere on the earth.

RAND*MR1343-3.1*

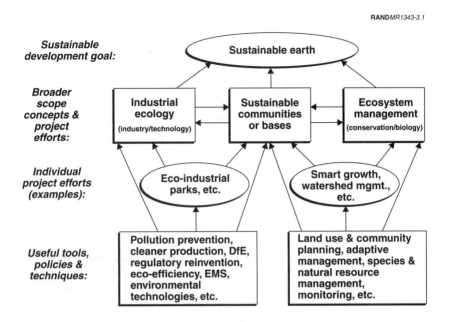

**Figure 3.1—The Relationships Among Sustainability Efforts**

facilities, it makes sense that they would mainly focus on technology issues. Next, on the right-hand side of this figure, are the traditional views of natural resource and land managers, who tend to focus on biological, land-use planning, and conservation issues. At an operational level, techniques and policies used here include land-use planning, adaptive management, and species and natural resource management. Individual project efforts focus on watershed management; smart-growth plans; and individual preserve, wilderness, and park management. Such efforts contribute to the development of broader concepts and efforts toward ecosystem management. Again, given the historical separation of such natural resource and land-use planning within local, state, and federal governments, this orientation was reasonable.

However, environmental approaches are changing. In practice, more interaction and integration are starting to take place across these areas than this figure suggests. However, such interactions are still not the norm, except in one main area: sustainable community activities. All these efforts have been found to integrate in different sustainable community activities.[37] At the community level, all of these concerns and issues regarding industry, technology, land management, and conservation come into play. Unlike most industries and most public natural resource management activities, U.S. communities include industrial, commercial, natural resource, and residential activities. To bridge the disconnect this figure illustrates, communities are trying to break out of traditional disciplinary, stovepipe, and media approaches for their sustainability efforts. As mentioned above, but is especially true for these sustainable community activities, such efforts are just beginning, and it is unclear how successful they will be over the long term.

Defense installations are often very much like communities in their functions and activities and could replace sustainable communities in this figure. DoD installation's environmental management activities have to balance and plan for industrial, commercial, natural resource, and residential activities. Therefore, like sustainable community activities, the EMSs of defense installations need to address multiple disciplines and media to integrate environmental concerns across traditional boundaries using systems approaches. Installations also can take advantage of the new innovative partnerships with industry, other parts of government (especially regulators), universities, and NGOs in such efforts. DoD environmental activities should take as much advantage as possible of all the aforementioned approaches and the underlying tools and policies that help facilitate implementation. The rest of this report focuses on specific ways industry facilities take advantage of such opportunities in implementing their EMSs. More important, the rest of this report identifies specific types of implementation practices that help facilitate successful facilitywide environmental management activities.

---

[37]For an introduction to such sustainable community activities and how some of these policies, tools, and efforts come into play, see Lachman (1997b).

# Chapter Four

# SETTING ENVIRONMENTAL GOALS AND ALIGNING ENVIRONMENTAL ACTIVITIES WITH THEM

To start moving from being reactive to being proactive about environmental policy, an organization must do two things:

1. Identify the environmental goals it wants to pursue. To succeed, the organization must understand how its environmental goals help it pursue its core goals—the goals that justify its existence.

2. Once it can state its environmental goals in terms of its core goals, create a mechanism for helping every part of the organization align its activities—environmental and otherwise—with these clearly stated organizationwide goals.

All the key elements of implementing proactive environmental management hang on these two major points.

This chapter first looks at how a proactive organization approaches the task of defining its environmental vision, principles, goals, targets, and so on. Such organizations typically recognize that environmental stewardship gives them the initiative to deal with the major environmental challenges that every large organization must face. By moving beyond compliance, an organization gains the flexibility and agility that are increasingly becoming the hallmark of modern best commercial practice. The chapter then explores the challenge of driving a new environmental vision into every part of a large organization, using a formal implementation paradigm that is becoming increasingly common in the best commercial firms.[1]

---

[1]For a succinct and widely used statement of this paradigm, see Kotter (1996).

This paradigm starts with leadership from the top, which then builds a coalition of all the players in the organization whose personnel must change their behavior in the workplace to implement change. Working with the coalition, the leadership assigns day-to-day responsibility for implementation to a formal champion. The champion works with the coalition to assemble cross-functional teams of relevant personnel and to assign clearly stated roles and responsibilities to these teams and their members. Together, the champion and these teams become active agents for change, working throughout the organization to affect relevant aspects of day-to-day operations. This effort will succeed only if the responsibility for and the authority to change are effectively decentralized and can operate effectively in the context of each local part of the organization that must change. Over time, the champion monitors these decentralized initiatives, tracks their progress against plans, and reports the status of the implementation to the senior leadership and the coalition for change. This reporting loop creates a mechanism that the organization can use as a catalyst for continuing change, change that will drive the organization to continue improving its environmental policy; practice; and, ultimately, performance.

Proactive organizations pursuing such changes benefit from effective EMSs. The chapter reviews how such organizations design and use EMSs. Almost every large organization has a sophisticated EMS of some kind in place today; compliance with today's complex web of environmental regulations is extremely difficult without one. Proactive firms design their EMSs to track not only compliance but also opportunities to benefit—while pursuing their core organizational goals—from environmental actions that go beyond compliance. Such EMSs work well only when they reflect an organization's broader core goals and help the organization integrate its environmental management with the management of its core business activities.

Organizational change moving toward more-progressive environmental management will benefit from an effective EMS, but effective implementation also requires a much broader set of supporting activities, such as the development of effective metrics and assessment tools, good working relationships with key stakeholders, and effective training and motivation for all employees. The following chapters examine each of these in detail. This chapter sets the stage for this broader effort by explaining the key first steps:  identifying relevant environmental goals and aligning all organizational activities to pursue these goals.

## A BRIEF OVERVIEW OF ENVIRONMENTAL MANAGEMENT AT P&G MEHOOPANY AND WDWR

It will be easier to discuss these issues if we first review the basic environmental management structures of each of the two sites our case studies focus on.  This brief digression identifies the key environmental players and organizations at each and defines acronyms that will appear repeatedly below.

### Environmental Management at P&G Mehoopany

Although P&G Mehoopany is a complex industrial site with many manufacturing and logistics activities, it has two overall plant managers.  The basic unit of business organization within the plant at Mehoopany is the *module*, an operationally focused business unit. The Process Services Module, for example, provides pulp mill, utility, and wastewater services for the whole site.  Mehoopany currently has about 23 modules.

The operations manager for each module is just as responsible for environmental results as for other core areas, such as safety and quality.  An operations manager delegates environmental responsibilities within the module.  The overall plant manager is ultimately responsible for implementing the facility's environmental standards and standard operating procedures at the facility.  The plant manager is very much aware and supportive of environmental issues.

The Mehoopany Environmental Group (MEG) is a staff support group of eight people with overall responsibility for environmental issues at the site.  The MEG leader is the site facility environmental manager and, as such, is responsible for understanding the applicable company and government requirements, evaluating the site's ability to meet them, and developing improvement plans.  The MEG leader and his staff oversee all environmental policy, management, operations, and training on site.  MEG reports directly to the plant manager.  The MEG staff works with the business modules, which retain responsibility for and control of resources on the line. The business units actually conduct the day-to-day environmental business of the site; so, in essence, MEG staff members are Mehoopany's environmental cheerleaders, working to build environmental ownership within each module. MEG must extract its policy and budget support from the business units.

The plant uses a flat ownership model with cross-functional teams. Crosscutting teams lie at the heart of much decisionmaking. In the environmental area, teams within Mehoopany bring together environmental people and engineers, integrate MEG with line modules, and integrate input from different paper product sites within P&G, including the corporate headquarters in Cincinnati, Ohio. Mehoopany uses cross-functional teams, such as the facilitywide Solid Waste Utilization Task Force and the Process Services Module Environmental Product Team (EPT), to facilitate environmental activities. For example, the members of the Solid Waste Utilization Task Force have different areas of expertise and come from diverse business units and focus on solid waste issues across the entire facility. The EPT is the environmental leader within the Process Services Module business unit and helps this unit deal proactively with environmental issues.

## Environmental Management at WDWR

WDWR has a decentralized organization in which independent business properties have management responsibility for the activities, and separate departments provide them functional support. There are about 20 different properties at WDWR, including Epcot, the Magic Kingdom, Disney MGM Studio, and the Animal Kingdom (these four are the theme parks) and each of the resort hotels (e.g., the Contemporary Hotel).[2] Each of these organizations has its own property manager. Functional support departments include such

---

[2]Organizationally, WDWR's properties also include All-Star Resorts, Blizzard Beach, Bonnet Creek, Caribbean Beach, Casting & Sun Trust, Disney University, Dixie Landings, Ft. Wilderness, the Grand Floridian Hotel, Facility Support, Magic Kingdom, Old Key West, Port & Dixie, Pleasure Island, Polynesian Hotel, Studio, Team Disney, Textile Services, Typhoon Lagoon, Downtown Disney, WDWR Warehouse, Wilderness Lodge, and Yacht & Beach.

traditional business support functions as legal, community relations, public affairs, and facility support.

The specific environmental organizational structure WDWR uses to carry out its mission has five formal environmental elements:

- Environmental Initiatives Department (EI)
- Environmental Initiatives Steering Committee
- Environmental Circles of Excellence (ECEs)
- Environmental Technical Advisory Groups (ETAGs)
- Departments with Environmental Responsibility.

EI is a cross-functional department that promotes and integrates environmental activities throughout WDWR properties. EI has main responsibility for internal and external communication, and awareness for WDWR's environmental activities. The Environmental Initiatives Steering Committee consists of cast members from different departments and properties at WDWR. This committee develops a WDWR action plan and priorities and establishes guidelines for WDWR's "Environmentality" program, discussed below.

ECEs are voluntary environmental organizations of cast members at a local property that help address environmental issues in their areas. The ECEs establish priorities and localized action plans and help motivate cast members to implement these plans.

ETAGs are interdisciplinary, cross-functional groups that provide specialized environmental expertise throughout WDWR. They recommend policy for their specialized areas. WDWR has about a dozen ETAGs, including "The Green Team," "Water Management," and "Alternative Fuels."

The main departments with environmental responsibility include WDWR community relations, WDWR public affairs, WDWR news and media information, the Environmental Affairs Division (EAD), Reedy Creek Energy Services Inc. (RCES), Walt Disney Imagineering (WDI), the Disney University, Epcot Science and Technology, and other WDWR operational areas. EAD is basically responsible for environmental compliance and is the main engineering support for most WDWR environmental issues. This division handles most of WDWR's compliance issues. RCES provides the operations and maintenance and design for Reedy Creek Improvement District

(RCID), the public entity that provides utilities to WDWR. RCES is a service organization for energy and for water and waste resources. RCES is a subsidiary of the Walt Disney Company. WDI is the R&D part of Disney, which conducts some environmental research and handles property development issues. All these different departments, as well as individual properties, help support WDWR's Environmentality activities.

## DEVELOPING A PROACTIVE SET OF ENVIRONMENTAL GOALS

### Corporation and Facility Places Value on Environmental Stewardship

Companies that are forward thinking about environmental issues and management value sustainable development and environmental stewardship as part of the organization's business. *Environmental stewardship* is recognizing the importance of maintaining and enhancing the quality of the land and natural environment for future generations. Companies that embrace this concept are taking a long-term view of their effects on society. Firms that truly embrace environmental stewardship principles are departing from traditional views of private-property rights and ownership. A firm that accepts these principles will not, despite owning a piece of land, simply do as it wishes with that land. Such firms do so not simply for regulatory reasons (such as the effects of air or water emissions on the surrounding community) but because of a perception that the obligation to maintain the piece of property for future generations and for society is of greater importance. Firms are using such rationales for take proactive approaches to environmental protection, recognizing and trying to calculate the costs and consequences of corporate activities in the long as well as the short term.

Environmental stewardship is also a strategic planning issue and offers the organization a competitive advantage. For example, DuPont's business vision and strategic planning process incorporate environmental and sustainability issues. DuPont has even developed a company symbol that depicts the interlocking values of society, environment, and shareholders, values that are to be fully integrated into all business visions and strategies (DuPont, 1999). Intel's 1998 EHS performance report states that the company's environmental progress results were "driven by our commitment to long-range strategic goals" instead of focusing solely on compliance (Intel, 1999).

Environmental stewardship means more than having environmental propaganda in the company annual report and company public relations materials.  Environmental stewardship is realized through (1) the development of a strong environmental vision, policy, and principles that are effectively implemented throughout the company and (2) honest and practical leadership support for environmental concerns.  Such environmental policies and visions of stewardship need to be supported by specific implementation procedures.

Progressive facilities have environmental policies and principles that are actually implemented throughout the organization in business terms.  Company headquarters often develop a forward-looking overall corporate environmental vision, mission, policy, goals, and principles.  Both P&G and Disney have strong environmental visions, policies, and principles at the corporate level.

## The P&G Approach

P&G's overall environmental quality policy was designed to facilitate the improvement of the environmental quality of its products, packaging, and operations around the world.  That policy (P&G, undated b) is to

- ensure P&G's products, packaging, and operations are safe for its employees, the consumer, and the environment
- reduce, or prevent, the environmental impact of P&G's products and packaging through their design, manufacture, distribution, use, and disposal, whenever possible
- meet or exceed the requirements of all environmental laws and regulations
- assess company environmental technology and programs continuously and monitor progress toward environmental goals
- provide P&G's consumers, customers, employees, communities, public interest groups, and others with relevant and appropriate factual information about the environmental quality of its products, packaging, and operations

- ensure that every employee understands and is responsible and accountable for incorporating environmental quality considerations in daily business activities
- have operating policies, programs, and resources in place to implement the company's environmental quality policy.

The P&G Mehoopany facility built on this policy to create its own unique environmental vision, principles, and operating plans. The environmental vision is as follows:

> We are visionaries and broad in our approach to environmental protection. Today's actions move us toward greater knowledge, better technologies, and more reliable systems, all ingredients to our products—a safe and clean environment for our employees, community, and future generations, and full public acceptance of our operations. (Mehoopany Environmental Group, 1995.[3])

The implementation of this facility vision includes an emphasis on environmental stewardship, P2, and continuous improvement. For instance, P&G Mehoopany beneficially uses many unavoidable solid wastes and is moving toward its goal of eliminating landfill use. The facility also manages total wood resources by working with wood suppliers to promote environmental protection, sustainability, ecosystem health, and long-term availability.

P&G Mehoopany's environmental program has four main driving ideas, which the facility has made visible to all. At every level, managers and employees check their everyday decisions against these (P&G Mehoopany, 1997b):

1. Good corporate principles and values include ownership, integrity, and trust. *Ownership* focuses on total business ownership of environmental aspects and personal responsibility and accountability. *Integrity* means doing what is right and obeying the letter and spirit of the law. *Trust* refers to respecting the customers and treating them "as we want to be treated"—a customer-focused culture.

2. Environmental success and business success are absolutely linked. Environmental performance is viewed as a business strat-

---

[3]For the full vision statement, see Appendix A.

egy.  Business and environmental staff are partners linked in site direction setting.  Environmental costs are internalized as much as possible into the business units.  P&G Mehoopany has a consistent strategy of "zero loss/total quality approach."

3. Broad policy ownership by all employees is key to success. Employees network across the site to address environmental issues.  The operation takes ownership of its environmental issues.  Training, awareness-building, and recognition are important parts of this process, as are environmental teams.

4. The site takes an environmental systems approach.  P&G's fundamental structure, both within the company as a whole and at Mehoopany, uses a good, broad EMS framework with a site "system ownership" focus.  P&G Mehoopany focuses on systems that maintain ownership and that develop and implement solutions for environmental issues using a systems approach.

Four other environmental principles also guide the staff's implementation of environmental policy:

1. complying with all environmental laws and regulations

2. protecting the environment as much as possible—"doing the right thing," going beyond laws and regulations, and considering risk reduction as an important goal in its own right

3. working in partnership with internal and external customers, including the regulators, the neighbors, the community, and the environment itself (the river, forests, etc.)

4. pursuing P2 aggressively, including minimizing waste, management costs, and loss of material value.

These principles enabled P&G Mehoopany to make a significant attack on odors at its facility, even though odor is not a compliance issue.  Community concerns led Mehoopany to invest $2.5 million to reduce odor without any formal economic justification.  And because the community still sometimes complains about odor at times, even though it has improved significantly over time, the plant is considering additional actions.  No regulatory actions play here, although they could in the future.

## The WDWR Approach

WDWR's approach to environmental management tends to be less structured and more informal because the organization and its culture are very decentralized, relaxed, and not as structured. Even though WDWR's approach is less formal, it is proactive and focuses on guests and continuous improvement.

The Disney Corporation defines its environmental program, philosophy, and policy in terms of a single word, *Environmentality*, which it defines as follows:

> Environmentality is an attitude and a commitment to our environment, where we, as the Walt Disney organization, actively seek ways to be friendlier to our planet. We're committed to making smart choices now to preserve our world for the future. We encourage environmental awareness among our Cast, our Guests, and the community. (WDWR, undated.)

To implement this approach, WDWR has defined its facility Environmentality vision as follows:

> The Walt Disney World Resort is a "Green Property" where Environmentality is communicated to all guests, cast members, and community by what we say and what we do. We strive to be a model for the world. (WDWR, 1996.)

More specifically, WDWR has defined Environmentality in business terms for all the WDWR properties, so that employees will understand how it is important to their business. According to WDWR (1996), the principles of Environmentality are

- going beyond what the law requires
- improving services to guests
- meeting cast expectations
- achieving positive operational results
- doing good business
- keeping a mentality of doing what is right for the environment.

WDWR's commitment to environmental activities focuses on P2 activities and continuous improvement. As the points above make clear, it pursues these from a clear business perspective. The Walt

Disney organization integrates its environmental and business visions when it talks about "making smart choices now to preserve our world for the future." WDWR's cultural flexibility, forward-thinking principles, and vision of being an environmental leader have allowed it to develop innovative, facility-unique projects, such as the 20-year development permit discussed earlier. As another example, WDWR invested over $100 million to build and run a state-of-the-art, zero-emissions wastewater treatment facility.

## Further Considerations in Developing Goals

Proactive companies state specific environmental goals in simple terms that help individual decisionmakers relate them to broader corporate goals with little ambiguity. For example, the goal of ensuring compliance with all current laws is simpler to state and use than any goal about the importance of P2. Any goal referencing P2 must provide a way of thinking about what a manager should be willing to sacrifice with regard to the core interests of the firm to invest in P2 that goes beyond compliance. A common "win-win" answer is that P2 is appropriate when full environmental accounting reveals that P2 is cost-effective for the firm. Chapter Five addresses this perspective in more detail.

An important part of developing environmental goals and policy is identifying the company's key stakeholders and clarifying its goals and policies with respect to each stakeholder. The stakeholders that commercial firms most often mentioned were customers, employees, shareholders, and the external community, including regulators. For example, P&G's Mehoopany's stakeholders include all consumers, as well as its customers, employees, shareholders, communities, suppliers, environmental and other public interest groups, press, and regulators. Mehoopany even considers nature itself to be a key stakeholder.[4] WDWR's stakeholders include similar groups: guests, employees (cast members), shareholders, community members, environmental groups, local press, and regulators.

---

[4]Mehoopany had an employee contest to develop an environmental motto for the facility: "treating nature as a customer." This is a restatement of P&G's view of itself as a consumer products company for whom the customer is always at center stage. The motto effectively turns the spotlight to a new customer—the environment itself. This motto came from an employee with a deep appreciation of P&G's culture.

These different stakeholders expect different things from a company's environmental policy and activities. For instance, customers may demand "greener" products; regulators may offer incentives for becoming more proactive; employees and local communities may become increasingly fearful of the effects of chemicals used in a plant; and shareholders may grow intolerant of the growing risk they associate with potential future regulation. The more deeply the firm can integrate the environmental concerns of its stakeholders into its normal management practices through an effective environmental policy, effective goals, and implementation of the goals, the greater the firm's opportunity to achieve a cost-effective accommodation. Chapter Six addresses these issues in greater detail.

Having an environmental ethic, philosophy, and/or sense of social responsibility is often part of the corporate culture for the commercial firms recognized as environmental leaders. For example, in 1975, Sam Johnson, then chairman of SC Johnson Wax, stopped the company's use of chlorofluorocarbons (CFCs) long before CFCs were shown conclusively to be a problem, explaining as follows:

> When we set aside the obvious business benefits of being an environmentally responsible company, we are left with the simple human truth that we cannot lead lives of dignity and worth when natural resources that sustain us are threatened or destroyed. We must act responsibly and we must act now. (Wever, 1996, p. 39.)

This sense of environmental duty was integrated into the company's operations.

By the same token, proactive companies' philosophies include the integration of environmental issues with other high-priority business items. For example, Lockheed Martin's executive officer, Peter B. Teets, has said that

> it is imperative that ESH consideration be integrated directly into our business, just as quality and customer satisfaction are now "built in" to our product and services. . . . We cannot afford to allow ESH consideration to remain separate from our core business activities as we strive for greater efficiency and continuous performance improvement. (Lockheed Martin, undated.)

Individual facilities often set policies and principles for themselves that allow them to customize their environmental management programs to meet unique local and facility needs. This flexibility and initiative at the facility level are especially important to an organization's ability to implement an integrated approach to environmental management, as P&G Mehoopany and WDWR have. This brings us to the question of implementation.

## ALIGNING ACTIVITIES THROUGHOUT AN ORGANIZATION WITH ITS ENVIRONMENTAL GOALS

Stating clear goals is hard enough; realizing them is harder still. The best commercial firms have learned that realizing proactive environmental goals requires a commitment to formal implementation strategies designed to drive fundamental organizational change. The following are the factors relevant to preparing for, executing, and supporting implementation:

- Prepare for and execute the implementation
  - Secure the support of the senior leadership
  - Build coalitions of those who must change to support implementation
  - Give a champion responsibility for day-to-day oversight
  - Use cross-functional teams to integrate relevant points of view
  - Assign clear roles and responsibilities for implementation
  - Decentralize execution to ensure proper integration at the local level
  - Use ongoing information gathering and sharing to start continuous improvement
  - Facilitate creative and persistent change agents
  - Develop an effective EMS
- Support the implementation
  - Develop effective metrics and assessment tools
  - Manage effective relationships with relevant stakeholders
  - Train and motivate those who must change to enable change.

The remainder of this chapter now turns to the factors relevant to preparing for and conducting implementation, discussing each factor outlined above in detail.  Later chapters will address the additional factors needed to support the implementation.

## Leadership Support for Environmental Management Throughout the Organization

Effective preparation for and execution of major organizational changes must ultimately start at the top.  In proactive commercial companies, the senior corporate leadership and the senior facility management value environmental activities and enable innovative environmental leadership and implementation at the facility level. The member companies of the WBCSD recognize this need for high-level corporate support in their work on trade and environmental regulation:  "A crucial step is to make environmental management a priority within each company's structure, taking that responsibility right up to the Chief Executive."  (World Business Council for Sustainable Development, undated.)

Senior corporate leaders have taken responsibility for improving environmental management and promoting it as a matter of the highest concern within their companies by

- making environmental performance part of the corporate vision statement or placing it on a short list of high-level corporate goals
- integrating environmental functions with health and safety functions
- making the senior management position responsible for environmental, health, and safety functions a high-ranking corporate executive position that high-quality managers might strive for throughout their careers
- most important, personally participating in the development and promulgation of corporate environmental goals and the periodic review of corporate performance in terms of the goals.

All these actions bring environmental concerns closer to the core interests of the firm and thereby raise their credibility in the eyes of all employees.  An example of senior leadership taking such action comes from Eastman Kodak.  There, the corporate health, safety and environment committee is chaired by one of the three members of Kodak's CEO department, and part of senior managers' pay is based on environmental performance (U.S.–Asia Environmental Partnership, 1997, p. 52). Both P&G Mehoopany and WDWR have high-level corporate support and leadership for their environmental programs.

Support from the facility manager is especially important to effective facilitywide environmental management approaches. At proactive plants, the facility manager values environmental concerns and supports them through facility goals, policy, and individual decisions and actions. He or she also allows environmental projects and activities to compete with other facility interests, even when the exact economic returns are difficult to project. This particular kind of support is especially important because it is often difficult to quantify some of the more innovative environmental activities and their benefits in traditional economic terms.

Both P&G Mehoopany and WDWR had leadership support for environmental management throughout their organizations. P&G Mehoopany's plant manager actively supports the facility's environmental program. WDWR's Environmental Initiatives Department (EID) provides leadership for all partners in Environmentality. EID consists of five cast members who are responsible for communication with all levels at WDWR. Individual business units are also supportive. In 1996, the operations manager for WDWR's Contemporary Hotel, for example, was an innovative and environmentally conscious manager who personally spearheaded many environmental initiatives, such as supporting the hotel staff's ECE.[5]

## Coalitions with Other Internal Interests

Progressive companies build coalitions among interest groups in the facility and firm to give environmental concerns appropriate weight in corporate decisionmaking. Such facilities have environmental managers who identify potential allies with similar or synergistic interests and exploit the existing organizational resources and programs to integrate environmental concerns throughout the organization (Brown and Larson, 1998, p. 5). Coalition-building is easier when environmental managers can state their goals in terms relevant

---

[5]See Appendix B for details on other activities that he helped initiate.

to others in the firm.  When a firm's customers seek "green" products, marketing is a natural ally for the environmental function.
When environmental emissions account for a significant portion of
operating costs, those responsible for cutting operating costs,
through reengineering, quality programs, or other methods, are natural allies.

Broader coalitions make it easier to see environmental concerns as
being compatible with core organizational concerns, thereby raising
the legitimacy of environmental concerns throughout the organization.  Greater legitimacy should make these concerns more successful in intracorporate negotiations and should draw more-effective
corporate personnel to activities responsible for environmental
decisionmaking.  Environmental managers at both P&G Mehoopany
and WDWR have effectively used allies and coalitions.

**Coalition Activities at P&G Mehoopany.**  At P&G Mehoopany, MEG
staff members work effectively with individual business units to
show that environmental success and business success are absolutely linked.  For instance, the staff has shown that waste prevention
adds to manufacturing quality and reliability.  In turn, facility staff
members have recognized that management considers environmental performance to be a business strategy.  The business and environmental staffs are partners linked in setting the site's direction.

Internalizing environmental costs as much as possible into the business units has helped build joint interests between the environmental and operational units.  As a result, individual operations
managers, such as the Process Services Module manager, support
proactive environmental management.

**Coalition Activities at WDWR.**  At WDWR, one of EI's main jobs is to
help build and facilitate cooperative activities across properties.  The
department's experience with encouraging guests to recycle cans
illustrates successful coalition-building around particular interests.
EI has been working with the various properties—especially the
theme parks—and WDI to provide recycling containers for guest use.
WDWR had been doing recycling backstage.  Because guests could
not see this activity, they kept asking why the theme parks and other
properties did not recycle.

EI wanted to solve this problem by providing generic containers for
recycling at all WDWR properties.  But because everything, even

trash cans, is themed for each park, WDI wanted recycling containers to be themed as well.  So, WDI and EI worked together to develop a basic type of recycling bin that has a different theme for each park. These bins, for cans and bottles only, are strategically located next to regular trash cans.  They have been successful, with minimal contamination.

## Environmental Champions with Flexibility and Day-to-Day Environmental Responsibility

Members of the senior leadership, and the coalition leaders they work with, cannot spend all their time on any one issue.  They must appoint executives and managers who can work full time on environmental issues and act in the leadership's name on a day-to-day basis.  These champions are held accountable for the success of the organization's environmental program.  Their primary job is to protect and promote broad corporate goals as the specialists responsible for implementation, who spell out the day-to-day details of the corporate environmental policy.  That is, even as environmental goals become more important to the firm, they do not become all important; champions must find and maintain the right balance in terms of day-to-day decisions.  For example, all six facilities in BRT (1993) used a champion, facilitator, or focal-point person to lead the P2 program.  An example is the waste-management team leader at the DuPont facility in La Porte, Texas (BRT, 1993, p. 19).

Such champions are often more likely to succeed if they have traditional management experience in the company and are not purely environmental specialists—and perhaps not environmental specialists at all.  They must be experienced enough as managers to ensure that they can induce others with specialized skills to perform for them.  While they inevitably become advocates for the specific proposals their subordinates develop, champions must find ways to temper the proposals and then promote them in ways that reflect the broader goals of the organization.

Effective champions know the corporation and the cultures at their individual facilities and use this knowledge to their advantage.  All six facility P2 teams in BRT (1993) knew the cultures at their facilities and designed their P2 programs accordingly (BRT, 1993, p. 28).

As the linchpins in the middle of this integration process, the firm's environmental champions must succeed for integration to be effective. Success depends on a firm's ability to draw high-quality, experienced general managers into these positions. That means the positions must have the status of being desirable steps on a promotion path within the firm.

## Cross-Functional Teams Used for Specific Decisions, Projects, and Processes

At the level of specific decisions, projects, or processes, cross-functional teams provide a way to bring an environmental perspective and expertise into corporate decisions and to temper the environmental perspective with broader corporate concerns.

Such teams are especially important for cross-cutting and facility-wide issues, such as P2. As described in Chapter Three, Ford Motor Company's assembly plant in Avon Lake, Ohio, successfully used a P2 team. The Southwire Company plant in Starkville, Mississippi, used a combination of diversely skilled teams to identify and implement facilitywide P2 projects. This facility had an employee waste-minimization team in each department and a high-level corrective action team (which included the environmental coordinator and plant manager) (Georgia Department of Natural Resources, 1997). BRT (1993) found that all six facilities used cross-functional teams effectively for P2. For example, DuPont's La Porte, Texas, facility had a waste minimization team with five subteams: information and metrics, planning and implementation, outreach, facility opportunity, and training and recognition. Intel's Aloha, Oregon, facility had manufacturing and R&D cross-functional P2 teams (BRT, 1993, p. 23). Both P&G Mehoopany and WDWR have also used cross-functional teams effectively.

**Cross-Functional Teams at P&G Mehoopany.** At P&G Mehoopany, cross-cutting teams lie at the heart of much environmental decisionmaking. Teams tend to be small (with six or so members), with members who are senior. Team members represent not only their own organizations but are also able to make decisions on their behalf. Some teams go on for years; others address a simple issue and disband. Their lifespans depend on their demonstrated utility. The teams do not actually make decisions but feed information and recommendations to a single decisionmaker who has ultimate responsibility.

As already mentioned, MEG is a long-lived environmental team that helps integrate all environmental issues across the facility. Other, more-focused teams are also important. For example, teams developed the basic approaches that led to recent reductions in nitrogen oxides ($NO_x$) and chlorine at Mehoopany; the general plant manager ultimately made the specific decision in each case. The basic idea is to encourage bottom-up initiative by encouraging the teams to formulate concepts for senior review. This approach promotes employee empowerment and helps Mehoopany develop more junior talent that will grow into the leadership of the future. While this occurs, the current leadership retains ultimate responsibility.

Sector teams across different P&G facilities provide the strongest links between P&G Mehoopany and the rest of P&G on environmental policy.[6] An example is the North American paper team. Key corporate environment policies and activities have arisen from such sector teams. An example is the Designing Waste Out initiative, which started within a couple of the sector teams and spread to the whole company because it succeeded in those sectors.

The Solid Waste Utilization Task Force, a Mehoopany facilitywide team, has been instrumental in P&G Mehoopany's success in reducing the amount of its solid waste and increasing cost savings in this area. The task force develops strategy and priorities for waste minimization, and team members represent key business units, energy, MEG, and finance. Half the members come from the plant floor. An important effort has been helping to implement the "three R's" (reduce, reuse, and recycle) throughout the plant. The group has been instrumental in helping develop and implement P2 ideas for solid waste and helped develop the corporatewide Designing Waste Out initiative.

The EPT in Mehoopany's Process Services Module business unit helps the unit deal proactively with environmental issues. With the help of MEG staff, the EPT has developed an aggressive environmen-

---

[6]*Sector teams* focus on a specific sector of the company, such as paper. These teams provide information between different facilities that focus on the same business sector.

tal improvement plan (discussed more in Chapter Five) and has even created its own vision. It currently meets monthly or as needed. Regular members come from each of the operating departments, the Process Technology Group within the module, and MEG and include the module's reliability leader.

**Cross-Functional Teams at WDWR.** Cross-functional teams are also very important at WDWR, given its size, complexity, diversity of activities, and decentralized management structure. WDWR uses interdisciplinary, cross-functional groups across business units to provide specialized environmental expertise. EI facilitates environmental information-sharing throughout the properties and other business units. WDWR also has about a dozen ETAGs, which include Water Management, Green Team, Recycling Committee, Alternative Fuels, Wildflower Roundtable, Compost/Organic Fertilizer Committee, Natural Habitat Group, and the Pest Management Advisory Committee.

In its ECEs, WDWR has given special attention to empowering team members to set their own agendas and to implement their ideas. For example, the staff of the Contemporary Hotel generates the ideas and prioritizes them, and the operations manager gives the staff the resources to execute the ideas. One project the staff developed was purchasing two-sided copy machines and implementing two-sided copying practices at the hotel to minimize paper usage.

**Additional Considerations in the Use of Cross-Functional Teams.** Simply placing a functional interest on a team does not mean the team will reflect the interests of that functional area. The legitimacy of environmental concerns relative to broad corporate interests must be clearly established before team members will take an environmental member seriously. For example, P&G Mehoopany's Solid Waste Utilization Task Force made sure that waste revenues and costs are directly costed back to the appropriate business unit so that the plant can see the actual environmental costs. At WDWR, EI sits down with the property managers and explains the business benefits of implementing the activities, including financial advantages and customer satisfaction.

Cross-functional teams are most effective when their members are authorized to make decisions in their functions' names, rather than just representing their functions' positions. This typically means that the environmental specialists serving on such teams should have broad capabilities within their environmental specialties. Such capabilities are most effective when the environmental function allows effective training over the course of an individual's career. That is, heavy use of cross-functional teams should not be so time consuming for participants that they cannot develop competence in the functions they are supposed to bring to a team.

Teams work best when governed by consensus; with experience, team members tend to develop skills that support consensus decisionmaking. But to the extent that teams require leaders or that leaders need to intervene to manage a failure to reach consensus, they usually come from a broad management background, not a functional specialty, such as environment. For example, in their best remediation management practices, Olin and DuPont facilities both used cross-functional teams that included leaders with business management backgrounds (Drezner and Camm, 1999). WDWR's ECE at the Contemporary Hotel had the business experience, leadership, and guidance of the operations manager.

## Responsibilities Defined Clearly Throughout the Company and Facility

An effective approach to environmental management assigns responsibilities clearly so that specific individuals or teams feel the effects of environmental decisions on the organization as a whole and can be held accountable for promoting the goals of the organization as a whole over the long term.

It is tempting to reflect the goal of full integration in such a statement as "environmental management is everyone's responsibility." Proactive firms find that anything that is everyone's responsibility is no one's responsibility; it easily falls through the cracks. Successful integration requires a clear assignment of responsibilities throughout the facility. For example, firms may hold a centralized organization responsible for remediating closed disposal sites but charge operating divisions for any remediation associated with disposal after a set date. Firms may charge operating divisions for compliance costs associated with their operations rather than covering these from corporate overhead.

At each level in the firm, general management is responsible for successful implementation of its EMS but delegates day-to-day responsibility to a champion, whom general management monitors on a regular basis. The champion "owns" environmental management, but does not manage the production activities, where compliance and many P2 activities actually occur. The champion informs the supervisors about such activities so that the supervisors can remain accountable for all aspects of production, including the environmental elements. While assigning responsibility clearly, this approach allows multiple channels of communication between the leadership and the field. These channels and the authority associated with them must be adjusted repeatedly in response to actual performance to get the balance between environmental and core concerns that the leadership seeks.

Both P&G Mehoopany and WDWR assign environmental responsibilities to their core business activities and then have environmental organizations and technical cross-functional teams ensure that these core business activities have access to the technical environmental expertise required to execute these responsibilities as well as possible. At P&G Mehoopany, the operations manager for each module is responsible for environmental results and delegates environmental responsibilities within the module. MEG facilitates and integrates environmental action within and across each of the modules. At WDWR, each property and functional area has associated environmental responsibilities, and EI is the environmental team that facilities Environmentality activities across the facility.

## Decentralization to Promote Facility Innovation

Efforts to integrate environmental concerns across the organization naturally raise questions about how centralized environmental activities should be. Effective commercial firms choose an appropriate balance of centralization and decentralization. Facility approaches are effective when the organization is decentralized enough to allow facilities to innovate.

Decentralization is especially important to allow facilities to take integrated and holistic environmental approaches. Much of what a facility does in terms of innovative environmental activities depends on the unique local circumstances, including specific facility operations, facility environmental effects, community concerns, and the relationship with regulators. Facilities need to have the authority and flexibility to customize their environmental programs to their own unique needs.

In addition, as was discussed at length in Chapter Three, proactive integrated environmental approaches tend to be experimental and nontraditional (e.g., cutting across media and traditional organizations), are often difficult, are customized to a site, and evolve over time. Such approaches are still in their developmental infancy. Fostering experimentation and innovation requires flexibility and empowerment at the local level.

A proactive company's culture allows flexibility and often fosters the ability of individuals to seize the initiative and act as environmental change agents throughout the facility. Facilities have both corporate cultures and facility cultures. Effective decentralization gives the individual facility more control and authority, which in turn increases the ability of the leadership and culture to affect the integration of environmental issues throughout the facility. A facility is also more likely to implement change when it has ownership.

One of the key findings of BRT (1993) was "that each facility had the flexibility to implement pollution prevention based on what would work best within their individual cultures" and the "importance of allowing facilities the flexibility to implement programs based on what is appropriate for their business and/or culture." This flexibility is necessary for integrating P2 within business processes and for facilitating innovation and change (BRT, 1993, p. 10).

Effective decentralization is important for another reason. To promote integration with core business activities, companies seek to decentralize environmental activities to the same extent that they decentralize their core business activities. Here, core activity managers take responsibility for environmental issues relevant to their own activities. To allow this, proactive companies typically decentralize management of environmental activities relevant to the products produced at particular sites. Such decentralized management recognizes variations both in product-level priorities and in regulatory environments across the firm. To reflect the variations, these companies attribute the costs associated with site-specific environmental activities to the appropriate products, weigh and manage compliance and P2 options locally, and manage the relevant permitting processes locally.

Both P&G and Disney have decentralized authority and flexibility that enable Mehoopany and WDWR to innovate to meet facility needs. Both facilities experiment with many different environmental approaches in many different areas, resulting in very diverse sets of environmental activities. The facilities try to look broadly, creatively, and facilitywide as much as possible to address a range of issues. Both look across media, such as air, waste, water, and natural resources, and try to be multidisciplinary and to break out of traditional stovepipe organizations and ways of thinking.

**Local Initiatives at P&G Mehoopany.**    We have already discussed many of Mehoopany's diverse environmental activities and so will mention only a few here. P&G tries proactively to minimize air, water, and waste emissions. P&G Mehoopany has reduced odors, even without a compliance requirement, because of community concerns regarding odors. The plant creatively reuses and treats waste as a marketable product, addresses natural resource issues, and tries to treat nature as a customer. For example, Mehoopany has developed special programs locally to work with suppliers in sustainable forestry practices. A member of MEG's staff has even participated on the Pennsylvania Governor's Twenty-First Century Environmental Commission to help think strategically about how environmental issues should evolve in Pennsylvania in the 21st century.[7]

**Local Initiatives at WDWR.**    WDWR has taken advantage of a decentralized organization to customize, diversify, and innovate in its environmental approaches.   As noted above, WDWR has a very decentralized culture.   Individual property and department managers have the responsibility for environmental activities. Together, this structure and a culture that encourages creativity help promote innovation in diverse areas across WDWR. For example, the pest management group raises ladybugs, butterflies, and other insects as part of its IPM program, while the Land Pavilion at Epcot Center helps raise such insects and researches IPM.

---

[7]See Pennsylvania 21st Century Environmental Commission (1998) for more details.

WDWR has also made this process fun and educational for guests.  At the Contemporary Hotel, a costumed cast member called Dr. L. Bug gathers children in the back of the hotel to release ladybugs to help control aphids.  This activity could only work in the specific setting where it occurs.[8]  More conventionally, the Contemporary Hotel has developed ways for its restaurant and hotel employees to recycle 59 percent of the hotel's waste stream, including 100 percent by weight of its food waste.  RCES, WDWR's service organization for energy and for water and waste resources, had a full-time recycling administrator who worked with the Contemporary Hotel (and other WDWR properties) to emphasize recycling because of the cost savings to the hotel.

## Fostering Continuous Improvement Through Information Gathering and Sharing

With the support of the senior leadership and an effective coalition, a champion can work with cross-functional teams to drive change designed to improve the environmental performance of specific parts of the organization.  Once an organization learns how to implement a proactive approach to environmental management, it can build on this capability to improve its performance over time.  In fact, a proactive approach does not arise in a single bound.  Rather, the approach involves so many parts of the organization in such basic ways that a proactive approach more often emerges, in a more and more fully realized form, over time as an organization learns how to pull all the pieces together.

As being proactive becomes a normal part of day-to-day planning and management, this approach supports an ongoing effort to learn from the facility's own experience and the experience of others facing similar challenges.  Proactive facilities use partnering, information sharing, and benchmarking to sustain their learning efforts.  Such facilities learn about the environmental performance of other organizations, report the results to the senior leadership, and use the results to sustain senior-level support for continuing improvement in environmental performance.  This process includes learning from

---

[8]See the appendices for more details about both P&G Mehoopany's and WDWR's diverse environmental approaches.

other facilities within their own organization; from corporate headquarters; from other businesses; from information clearing-houses (such as P2 and technical assistance ones); from state regulators; from the literature, research, and trade press; and from other individuals and organizations outside their company.

**Importance of Benchmarking and Continuous Learning.** Over the last 15 years, proactive firms have turned increasingly to benchmarking to improve their performance. Benchmarking means different things to different firms. It can range from broad insights about another company's performance level to very detailed studies in which the company's specialists on a particular task compare notes with their counterparts in another firm and develop specific ways to adapt observed practices for application at home. But the key to benchmarking is a recognition that other firms may have discovered solutions that one particular firm has not even dreamed of. And as innovation proceeds, other firms are likely to discover new solutions faster than any one firm does.

Benchmarking to discover such solutions is as important to environmental management as it is to any other aspect of management. In some ways, benchmarking offers higher payoffs in environmental management because it is often possible to learn a great deal from the environmental management practices of firms in other industries—firms that are not competitors and hence are more likely to share sensitive information about innovative programs. Over the long run, repeated benchmarking offers standards against which firms can judge themselves, allowing them to adjust the goals for their own facilities repeatedly to yield continuous improvement. Innovative firms have set up such organizations as GEMI to do precisely this in the field of environmental management (see GEMI, 1994). Such consulting groups as A. D. Little, Arthur Andersen, and the American Productivity and Quality Center maintain more-or-less formal databases on best environmental management practices that they continually update to serve customers of their consulting practices.[9]

---

[9]See, for example, Blumenfeld and Montrone (1995), pp. 79–90; the Global Best Practices links at http://www.arthurandersen.com; and the International Benchmarking Clearinghouse links at http://www.apqc.org.

Numerous other specific examples exist of industry environmental benchmarking studies and information sharing within and across facilities and companies. For instance, Lockheed Martin held a conference on best practices in October 1998 for Environment, Safety and Health (ESH) leaders from across the corporation. The participants shared information and transferred lessons they had learned about best ESH practices (Lockheed Martin, 1999). P&G Mehoopany was one of the participants in the BRT (1993) study, a classic example of an effort to look across companies to determine successful elements in implementing facility-level P2 programs.

**Continuous Learning at P&G Mehoopany.** At P&G Mehoopany, benchmarking and information sharing are important both across facilities and within the facility. Several examples have already appeared in the cross-functional team discussion. In conducting their facility annual environmental audits, P&G facilities learn from each other. The environmental audit team's members come from the plant being audited, corporate headquarters, and other plants. Mehoopany's environmental manager has been involved in audits at plants in Toronto and in California. He has learned a great deal from these that he can apply at home. In addition, MEG staff members participate in national environmental conferences, such as the NPPR, to learn from other organizations' environmental activities.

**Continuous Learning at WDWR.** Benchmarking and information gathering and sharing are key to a diverse, decentralized, complex, and large organization like WDWR. EI works to transfer lessons learned from one property to another, regularly exchanges information and ideas with Disneyland, and benchmarks other companies and talks with other studios. For example, one EI staff member shares information with the San Diego Zoo and Busch Gardens about best environmental practices. In fact, one of WDWR's long-term environmental goals is to maintain a benchmark database of outstanding programs outside WDWR.

## A Variety of Mechanisms for Internal Information Sharing

Industry facilities whose EMSs have more-effective and integrated facility approaches have developed a range of effective mechanisms for internal information-sharing across different parts of the organization, including different business units and corporate headquarters. Sharing the latest information among all employees is important for integrating environmental issues throughout the facility and into core business processes. Such internal communications serve three purposes:

1. They convey a message to the organization as a whole that the senior leadership is committed to effective environmental management. This occurs when the firm makes a new commitment to environmental management and it is repeated over time to verify continuing support.

2. They convey the achievements of environmental management to the senior leadership, helping to keep the leaders accountable for the firm's overall environmental performance and allowing them to make any needed adjustments to ensure that the environmental management program actually being implemented continues to reflect corporatewide goals. Not incidentally, such communications maintain the awareness of senior managers contributing to their continuing willingness to support environmental management efforts in the broader context of their responsibilities.

3. They convey information on both successes and failures between business units to maintain the momentum of change and to support learning across the organization. Note that failures can threaten a program, especially early in its life, if the firm does not react to them constructively. Communication about failures is most successful when coupled with a constructive corporate response.

The mechanisms proactive facilities use for internal communications include both formal and less-formal approaches. Formal mechanisms include regular meetings, cross-functional teams, sharing metrics, reports, and newsletters. As already discussed, cross-functional teams, in which staff from different business units and levels of management and operational staff meet to discuss key environmental issues, are an effective means of sharing information across different units. Literature, such as facility environmental reports and environmental newsletters, is also often used to help share information throughout a facility. Less-formal activities include facilitywide and community events, such as environmental open houses, community environmental activities, and Earth Day fairs for company employees and their families.[10]

BRT (1993) found that all six facilities studied increased P2 awareness and facilitated key information exchanges through effective communications. The techniques used varied because they were customized to individual company and facility needs and cultures. The Intel facility in Aloha, Oregon, used newsletters and magazines to increase awareness about the facility's P2 activities. The 3M facility in Columbia, Missouri, had best-practice meetings and published P2 success stories. In addition, the corporation helped information flow across different facilities by publishing an annual compendium of P2 projects. The DuPont facility in La Porte, Texas, sent electronic mail to facility employees about P2 progress, shared metrics on a monthly basis, and published P2 success stories (BRT, 1993).

**Diverse Mechanisms Used at P&G Mehoopany.** P&G uses a range of formal and informal mechanisms to facilitate communication across its modules, facility, and corporation. Formal mechanisms include the use of teams, company documentation, newsletters, staff environmental meetings, training classes, e-mail, and an internal home page. The cross-cutting teams that lie at the heart of much of P&G's environmental decisionmaking are also extremely effective for internal information sharing. For instance, the Solid Waste Utilization Task Force facilitates information-sharing about solid waste across the plant. Because environmental staff from different P&G facilities and P&G environmental headquarters participate in the annual environmental audits, they are an excellent means of transferring environmental information across facilities.

Many informal communications also take place. For instance, MEG routinely shares its experiences and information with facility modules at Mehoopany and with the environmental staffs of other P&G facilities and corporate headquarters. Facility environmental open houses, plant tours, Earth Day fairs, newspaper articles, company environmental newsletters, and informational brochures are effective ways to help share information among staff.

---

[10]Such mechanisms often help improve relationships with the general public as well, which is discussed in Chapter Six.

**Diverse Mechanisms Used at WDWR.** WDWR also uses a range of formal and informal mechanisms to facilitate communication across its decentralized organization. Cross-functional teams are used extensively for environmental communications. The ETAG, for example, is an interdisciplinary cross-functional team that provides specialized environmental expertise and communication. One such ETAG is the Energy Star Team, which specializes in energy conservation. At WDWR, information is shared between properties and other functional areas through an environmental bulletin board and e-mail.

EI actively and constantly communicates and facilitates communication throughout WDWR, regularly communicating with staff in other areas. EI also routinely keeps the Disney Corporate Vice President for Environmental Policy informed about what is going on at WDWR, and he in turn shares information about other parts of Disney. EI and Disneyland also often communicate directly to exchange information about their programs, as do other parts of WDWR that also have environmental responsibilities. For example, EAD staff members talk frequently with Disneyland compliance staff members. EI also shares information with employees through the facility's monthly newspaper, *Eyes and Ears,* and by holding Earth Day fairs. Such mechanisms will be discussed more in Chapter Seven.

WDWR also fosters frequent informal communication. For example, the operations manager at the Contemporary Hotel informally networks and shares his environmental information, acting as an environmental resource for anyone at WDWR who wants to hear about what he knows. He also schedules meetings with theme park representatives for them to visit the hotel to see what it has done and to exchange ideas.

## The Keystone of Successful Change Management: Creative and Persistent Change Agents

Successful environmental management means motivating managers and other employees to be creative and persistent agents of change. Most firms have not traditionally paid explicit attention to environmental concerns while executing core activities. And the standard relationship between a firm and its regulators has not created a great deal of room for mutually beneficial discussion, much less negotiation. Any effort at change creates resistance. Alternatives to the status quo can threaten people show have a vested interest in the current way of doing business. Even some environmental specialists can find a more-proactive approach that raises the visibility of environmental management very threatening, if they have become experts on managing end-of-pipe solutions and traditional regulation.

A proactive EHS manager "is an agent of organizational change—selling the benefits of responsible and proactive EHS behavior, and devising strategies to implement such actions." In addition to technical expertise, a manager trying to sell such new ideas needs to understand accounting, business strategy, marketing, finance, community organizing, staff training, and management consulting (Brown and Larson, 1998, pp. 1–8[11]).

This is the case with both P&G Mehoopany and WDWR. Both facilities effectively promote the development of innovative and creative environmental change agents. In fact, P&G's overall corporate culture tries to promote change agents. One of the corporation's principles focuses on innovation as a key to success: "we challenge convention and reinvent the way we do business to better win in the market place." P&G Mehoopany effectively uses this corporate culture and the focus on change agents in the environmental area. WDWR's culture also facilities creativity and gives employees the flexibility to initiate such creative projects. EI is, simply stated, an organization of environmental change agents. The 20-year development permit effort is a classic example of allowing a change agent to develop, negotiate, and implement a new approach.

Alternatives may need time and effort to work as well as the status quo does or to achieve as much acceptance among customers. Proactive facilities seek ways to overcome these problems at the front line of change itself, one manager at a time. A creative manager is necessary, but creativity is not sufficient. Creativity can provide cost-effective alternatives to the status quo; persistence and motivation

---

[11]This article also presents a good discussion of three keys to institutional transformation—political opportunities, mobilizing structures, and framing processes—and how EHS managers can use them to create change.

are necessary to see those alternatives through to ultimate adoption.[12]

## Effective EMSs

As noted earlier, almost every large organization maintains a sophisticated EMS, simply to ensure that the organization complies with the complex set of regulations it faces. By itself, this stance is reactive. A proactive stance requires an EMS that tracks not only compliance but also all the activities discussed above.

Implementation of such systems varies from one proactive company to another, although they tend to fit within an ISO 14001, TQM, or TQEM framework.[13] Such approaches help guide a firm through the necessary elements of an effective EMS. An organization that implements the ISO 14001 standard will have an EMS that ensures policies are followed and will demonstrate this to others. Then the organization can decide whether to obtain third-party certification or to make a self-determination and declaration with the standard.

Such proactive industry EMS structures have five key components:

1. Policy and commitment. A proactive EMS structure includes a forward-looking environmental policy with a commitment to continuous improvement and P2 and communicates this policy throughout the organization.

2. Planning process. The planning process incorporates specific environmental goals, objectives, and legal requirements and includes a systematic, broad-based process to identify, evaluate, and prioritize environmental "aspects" or "impacts" that need improvement.

3. Implementation. An effective implementation process is embodied in a clear organizational structure with clearly defined resources, roles, and responsibilities. The process also includes

[12]For an excellent example of the kind of behavior desired, see Berube et al. (1992), pp. 189–207.

[13]That is not to say that many American firms plan to use third-party auditors to be certified to ISO 14001; few do. But many use the specification as a useful benchmark to improve their own internally developed EMSs because it is currently the dominant model used to implement TQEM.

appropriate skills training, awareness programs, two-way communication at all levels, documentation, and specified procedures.

4. Measurement and evaluation.  Monitoring performance and making corrections are important parts of the EMS, processes that includes record keeping and periodic audits of the management system (these are not traditional compliance audits).

5. Management review.  The EMS includes a management review process that reassesses the policy and system and changes them as needed to promote continuous improvement.

Adoption of a proactive EMS begins with the establishment of the environmental policy, which is then carried out by implementing each of the subsequent steps.  This approach applies a type of Plan-Do-Check-Act cycle that is common to quality management approaches, such as TQM and TQEM.[14]

An organization's EMS may formally follow this classic ISO 14001–TQEM structure, as does P&G Mehoopany's EMS, or may be more informal, as is WDWR's EMS.  Ben and Jerry's Homemade, Inc., is another example of a company that has a less traditional TQM-TQEM style (Wever, 1996, p. 40).  Whether the EMS is relatively formal or informal, effective implementation of an integrated facility management approach requires a system that includes the basic EMS functions listed above.

## Overview of P&G Mehoopany's EMS

P&G's global EMS is of the ISO 14001–TQEM type; it goes beyond ISO 14001 by being more proactive in a number of areas, including environmental policy, training, and an emphasis on P2.  An overview of P&G's EMS follows:

1. Policy and commitment.  The earlier discussion of P&G's environmental management goals captures P&G's environmental policy well.  The policy is articulated through a set of clear

---

[14]For more details on how to implement an EMS and relationships with TQM approaches, see the numerous materials on this topic, such as Jackson (1997) and Wever (1996).

principles and goals at the companywide and P&G Mehoopany levels.

2. Planning process.  The planning process incorporates specific environmental goals, objectives, and legal requirements and includes P&G's audit and rating process (which will be discussed in more detail in Chapter Five).  Key environmental aspects are identified, and system capability is verified.

3. Implementation.  The organizational structure of P&G's EMS clearly defines resources, roles, and responsibilities.  Critical elements are well documented and well communicated to all site personnel.  The EMS also includes appropriate skills training and awareness programs (which will be discussed in Chapter Seven).

4. Measurement and evaluation.  Monitoring performance and making necessary corrections are important parts of P&G's EMS. For instance, compliance issues must all be remedied within 12 months.  P&G also has extensive environmental record keeping and annual EMS audits to verify performance.

5. Management review.  Global, regional, and local site managers review the EMS annually to help drive future risk reduction and overall environmental performance improvement.  P&G's EMS emphasizes continuous improvement.

### Overview of WDWR's EMS

At WDWR, the EMS is not of a formal, standard ISO 14001–TQEM or traditional industry type.  The system tends to be less structured and more informal because the organization and culture are very decentralized, relaxed, and not highly structured.  For example, Disney traditionally has been very relaxed about documentation; it has not even printed organizational charts.  Even though WDWR's EMS is less formal, many of its policies and its implementation philosophy tend to fit into the ISO 1400–TQM framework because they are proactive and focus on customers and continuous improvement. The implementation process includes effective training and awareness programs, incentives, communication procedures, monitoring and measurement activities, and continuous improvement efforts (see Appendix B for the details).  Therefore, despite its unique approach, WDWR has the policy and commitment, planning process, implementation, measurement and evaluation, and review elements of an effective, proactive EMS.

## SUMMARY

This chapter has reviewed the central questions of defining goals for a proactive environmental management program and then preparing for and executing an implementation program to realize these goals.  It has reviewed the role a formal EMS can play in such activities.  The remaining chapters address in more detail three important activities that support implementation:  the development of effective metrics and assessment tools to link environmental activities to strategic organizational goals (Chapter Five); the development and sustainment of effective relationships with important stakeholders (Chapter Six); and the use of training, incentives, and other programs to enable and motivate all employees to promote the organization's environmental goals (Chapter Seven).  Experience in the best commercial firms tells us that, without effective support activities in each of these areas, the activities discussed in this chapter will most likely fail.

# Chapter Five

# ENVIRONMENTAL ASSESSMENT, METRICS, AND PRIORITY SETTING

A critical component of industry's environmental management activities is how companies develop, analyze, prioritize, and choose environmental projects for implementation. The process and metrics that are used to determine and choose projects, such as P2 activities, are important issues for DoD installations. Commercial facilities and defense installations face the same difficulties when choosing and justifying environmental projects. In many companies, environmental projects must meet the same rate-of-return requirements as other business projects. Given the inherent difficulty and uncertainty of assessing the costs and the benefits of many environmental activities, understanding the methods that proactive companies use is especially important.

## USING ENVIRONMENTAL ASSESSMENT, METRICS, AND ACCOUNTING

Proactive company sites facilitate and conduct environmental assessments and use accounting practices that integrate environmental concerns into core business processes. In such companies, management encourages and supports comprehensive and innovative environmental accounting practices. The support often includes accepting some nontraditional approaches, since there is as yet little tradition for environmental accounting and economic analyses. Proactive companies also provide effective analytic environmental assessment tools, both formal and informal, and maintain a supportive organizational environment for their use. These companies also effectively use environmental metrics to help measure progress toward corporate goals, assist environmental assessments, and help motivate behavior.

## Environmental Accounting

Historically, many environmental costs, such as costs associated with raw materials, manufacturing processes, and product design, were hidden in conventional accounting categories, such as labor, maintenance, research and development, overhead, and marketing. Such traditional financial accounting practices meant that innovative environmental cost-saving activities, such as P2, were not being implemented within companies and that proactive managers were not credited when they achieved innovative environmental savings. However, new environmental and full-cost accounting tools and techniques are changing such practices.

The definitions of *environmental accounting* and such related terms as *full-cost accounting* and *environmental cost accounting* depend on the user. In general, *environmental accounting* refers to the incorporation of environmental costs and information into a variety of corporate decisionmaking and accounting processes.[1] Environmental accounting techniques try to capture the full range of costs associated with environmental activities, including conventional, hidden, contingent, and image costs. *Conventional costs* refers to costs from chemical purchases and storage, maintenance, labor, and utilities. *Hidden costs* are costs associated with such items as ancillary chemical and material inputs; waste management, treatment, and disposal; regulatory compliance; fees and taxes; insurance; and production costs. *Contingent costs* are associated with unexpected future occurrences, such as liabilities for spills, cleanup, and worker injuries. *Image costs* are the costs associated with facility image and relationships outside the company, such as "good neighbor" activities, bad publicity, affects on clients or consumers, and the affects of a good or bad relationship with regulators.[2]

---

[1] For discussions of different environmental accounting terms and the application of such techniques, see Ditz et al. (1995), Bailey and Soyka (1996), and Graff et al. (1998).

[2] For examples of where to find convention and hidden costs and more complete discussion of all these costs, see Kennedy (1998).

Collecting these data and assessing the environmental costs, especially the hidden, contingent, and image costs, can be very difficult. In addition, companies that are proactively taking an integrated facility approach are focused on addressing the hidden, contingent, and image costs. Such approaches have expanded the traditional definition of *costs*, taking both a short- and a long-term view. For example, cost assessments focus not just on immediate regulatory compliance but also on such long-term issues as potential future liabilities, financial savings from implementing new environmental technologies, and the effects on corporate reputation.

Proactive firms recognize that environmental accounting offers a wide range of benefits. In an effort to educate businesses about environmental accounting, U.S. EPA (undated) has argued that environmental accounting can help companies

- gain competitive advantages
- increase profits
- guide new product and process development
- increase revenues through improved EMSs
- guide improvements in product and material use
- reduce costs through energy and resource efficiency
- identify opportunities to minimize compliance costs
- support the capital budgeting process
- improve investor return
- improve community satisfaction and confidence.

The decreasing costs of complying with current and potential future regulations and assessing costs of operational flexibility are two very important benefits, as the Intel P2 permit and the WDWR 20-year development permit illustrate. In both cases, an understanding of the costs of current and future regulations and increasing operational flexibility helped convince upper management that the permitting efforts were worthwhile business investments.

Businesses have traditionally considered environmental costs when selecting a product mix, evaluating manufacturing inputs, costing processes, pricing products, and comparing costs across facilities. More-proactive companies and facilities also use environmental cost information in evaluating waste-management options, prioritizing environmental initiatives, assessing opportunities for P2, making capital investment decisions, and doing strategic planning. For example, Witco Corporation's Newark, New Jersey, plant conducted a facility P2 planning process that developed facilitywide and process-level material inventories with associated costs. The plant's staff used this analysis to identify a potential cost savings of $30,000 that could be achieved by improving process efficiency and other P2 projects (Graff et al., 1998, pp. 92–93). As another example, the staff of the Amoco refinery in Yorktown, Virginia, analyzed environmental costs throughout the facility to understand how much was being spent and why, then used this information to aid capital budgeting and other decisions related to the environment.[3]

Financial accounting tends to focus on the past, while environmental accounting focuses on the future. But while the latter often focuses on identifying and supporting business planning and decisions about the future, it also uses historical data as appropriate.

P&G Mehoopany has effectively used environmental accounting data and approaches to identify environmental costs, link them to business units, and act to reduce them by, for example, converting some wastes into salable commodities. P&G Mehoopany currently spends $23 million a year on environment-related expenditures but also generates revenues and implicit benefits equal to about half this through, for example, actual sales of waste and displacement of expensive fuel oil. By cutting environmental expenditures in half, some actions have an explicit beneficial effect on the bottom line. Figure 5.1 shows how this contribution to the bottom line has grown, year by year, over the last decade or so for waste revenues.

## Supportive Organizational Context for Environmental Accounting and Assessments

Proactive companies promote routine use of databases, assessments, and analytic tools that help decisionmakers see how environmental

---

[3]One of the most interesting things about this plant's effort is that it provides a detailed illustration of the complexity of calculating environmental costs. For example, Amoco found that assigning these costs to process units could be misleading and suboptimal compared with a full understanding of facility-level costs (Ditz et al., 1995, pp. 47–81).

decisions affect all parts of the organization. These companies recognize that improved tools can enhance environmental management. The range of desirable tools includes environmental audits; resource, energy, and/or material tracking systems; accounting systems that link environmental effects to various decisions; and engineering models of core production and remediation activities that help firms compare the effects of alternative environmental actions. For example, some companies, such as AT&T and Chrysler Corporation, have promoted the use of activity-based costing for environmental accounting. This costing methodology traces environmental costs back to the activities that are directly responsible for them and then uses the information to improve environmental and business decisionmaking, such as decisions related to current processes and future designs (McLaughlin and Elwood, 1996, p. 18).

Corporate and facility management also gives flexibility in the choice and implementation of such tools, given their limitations. Such

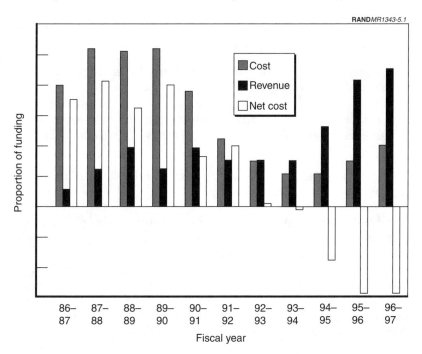

Figure 5.1—P&G Mehoopany Waste Disposal Costs Versus Waste Revenue

accounting systems as life-cycle assessment, total cost assessment tools, and activity-based costing remain primitive. Firms typically rely on existing cost accounts and draw the information needed to support specific decisions from these accounts as needed. Such analyses typically require considerable discretion and judgment. Using such tools is complicated because they cannot always account for all environmental costs, such as image costs, and because the appropriate data are often lacking and too expensive to acquire. Thus, innovative environmental and management professionals often use approaches that are more informal. Management accepts such judgments in setting priorities for such environmental activities as P2.

For instance, P&G Mehoopany made a strategic decision to favor incineration over land disposal, even though incineration appears to cost more. The staff decided to pursue the use of a waste-to-energy facility because land disposal is too uncertain, especially given the potential liabilities. This decision, which eliminated high-end risk, was made without formal cost analysis because the uncertainties associated with land disposal could not be formally laid out.

Ultimately, organizational concerns tend to dominate tool development; until a firm organizes itself in a way that allows it to use a tool effectively, the political support for tool development will be limited. That said, objective tools can provide a strong basis for shifting corporate attention toward environmental concerns in a company.

## Quantitative and Qualitative Metrics Used to Stimulate Innovation

Successful firms manage what can be measured. This cliché can be overstated, but proactive firms rely on metrics as the foundation for managing improvement. Accounting is often called the language of business. Metrics extend this notion more broadly to reflect the importance of nonmonetary, as well as monetary, measures of performance. Proactive environmental facilities effectively use environmental metrics to help measure progress toward their goals, aid their environmental assessment processes, and help motivate behavior.

Motivational metrics measure a team's or a manager's success and provide a basis for allocating the net value added that the firm generates among its units. Proactive facilities use environmental metrics to measure progress and help motivate behavior. For example, BRT (1993, p. 10) found that all six facilities it studied used P2 metrics to measure progress, communicated the progress, and used the metrics to assign responsibility and accountability for the P2 results.

Such metrics apply throughout the company, from top to bottom. Metrics designed to motivate behavior must be carefully crafted to each decisionmaking setting throughout the firm to ensure that the metrics

- induce the decisionmaker to pursue firmwide goals

- are compatible with the constraints that the decisionmaker faces in each setting

- are easy to collect and verify

- are mutually understood and accepted by the decisionmaker and oversight authority (Kaplan, 1990; Kaplan and Norton, 1996).

In practice, successful firms find that metrics that meet these criteria more nearly approximate firmwide goals because the decisionmaker has more discretion. Hence, metrics vary at different levels and locations in the firm.

Dow Corning's Carrollton, Kentucky, facility is a good example of using a metric both to measure progress toward an environmental goal and to motivate the environmental behavior of all employees. The facility uses an innovative metric and compensation system based on corporate and unique facility goals to reduce emissions cited in the Superfund Amendments and Reauthorization Act of 1986 (SARA). This facility developed and implemented a P2 plan that reduced SARA emissions by 92 percent over about ten years, beginning in 1988. The plan used a tracking system that included annual reduction goals and that targeted specific waste streams. The facility created a variable compensation package based on level of achievement of corporate and facility goals to reduce the SARA emissions. In 1998, every facility employee received a 3-percent bonus based on his or her annual salary for meeting or exceeding this goal (Kentucky Pollution Prevention Center, 1998).

It is, however, important to note that quantitative metrics alone can rarely capture everything important about a decisionmaking position. Proactive firms typically supplement these data qualitative metrics on the overall operation of important processes. The managers may also have the discretion to adjust the quantitative metrics associated with particular options under consideration to reflect subjective judgments about how cost-effective these options would be for the organization as a whole.

These considerations present a special challenge for environmental management. As noted earlier, integrating environmental management with other management concerns is about innovation. Metrics provide the basis not just for inducing everyone to execute the existing production process as well as possible but also to improve that process continually to reduce the associated environmental damage. Innovative circumstances typically call for metrics that reflect an unconstrained work environment and hence, as broadly as possible, the firm's goals. But environmental management must ultimately be implemented in constrained circumstances, with metrics that reflect this. The tension between unconstrained metrics aimed at innovation and constrained metrics that implement an innovation is not easy to resolve, especially when change is continuing.

In individual firms, engineering groups affiliated with production often drive innovation but are able to take a broader perspective. In these circumstances, the engineers can work with metrics closer to the corporate environmental goals than would be appropriate for the workers on the production line. For example, the engineers might use metrics that reflect the companywide costs associated with using a chemical, while the workers on the line would use metrics that track their implementation of the tighter housekeeping and pharmacy practices the engineers had developed. Making this distinction is more problematic in firms that rely more heavily on the production teams than on others for innovation.

**P&G's Use of Metrics.** P&G uses different environmental metrics at many different levels within its organization, including the corporate and facility levels and within the business units. P&G effectively uses environmental metrics to help measure progress toward environmental goals, help assess environmental processes, and motivate behavior.

An important metric is the plantwide environmental Key Element Assessment (KEA) number, which P&G calculates each year for each facility. This number, which takes three days to calculate,[4] is derived from an environmental auditing and assessment process that P&G uses to evaluate systems and how well they are addressing environmental issues. The company has a facility standard of 8 for the environmental KEA (10 being the highest rating). Some plants are at a disadvantage in this calculation because of the complexity of the environmental issues they face. The Mehoopany plant is a high-complexity site.

The calculations start with environmental audits of each facility, measuring against corporate performance standards in five areas:

1. government and public relations: compliance, inspections, and community relationships
2. people capacity: leadership, training, accountability, program support and expectations, etc.
3. direct environmental impact: includes monitoring emissions (air, water, solids), assessment of waste management, and management of process change.
4. incident prevention: includes a prevention plan, special risk programs for specific chemicals on site, emergency response plans and training, spill protection, etc.
5. continuous improvement: audit frequency and follow-up, waste and cost reduction, goals and measurement of progress, complexity reduction relevant to such environmental effects as disposal and recycling, etc.

The individual calculations for each of these five areas are blended together to arrive at the site-level KEA number.

The Mehoopany facility uses a range of monthly and periodic metrics for managing its environmental program, calculating progress for these standards, and calculating the yearly environmental KEA. The plant regularly tracks environmental measures in management, air

---

[4]P&G also does plant KEAs in the areas of safety and quality. It also takes three days to calculate the safety KEA.

quality, water quality, solid waste, and toxic and/or hazardous waste. Seventeen such measures are tracked on a monthly basis (see Table 5.1). The plant has good measures of pollution generation by medium, and the staff uses these measures effectively. However, the integrated facilitywide measures are not very good as yet; such measures are very hard to develop. KEA is as close as the staff gets. MEG also does not have any specific metrics for P2 but tracks P2 measures by looking at trends. MEG staff is working to develop better metrics, especially for P2 activities and at the site level.

**WDWR's Use of Metrics.** WDWR uses metrics less formally. WDWR uses energy usage metrics to continue improving environmental performance and to save money. Given WDWR's size and location,

### Table 5.1

### Environmental Performance Measures— P&G Mehoopany

|  | Measures | Units |
|---|---|---|
| Management | Assessment rating | 1–10 |
|  | Complexity rating | 1–10 |
|  | Compliance |  |
|  | —Actions | Number |
|  | —Chronic | Number |
|  | Incidents (P&G) | Number |
|  | Total waste to environment | MTPY |
|  | Public perception | 1–10 |
|  | Costs |  |
|  | —Net[a] | $ M |
|  | —Recovered | $ M |
| Air quality | Emissions (DER inv.) | Mtons |
|  | Incident releases | Lbs |
| Water quality | Discharges (NPDES) | Tons |
| Solid waste | Disposal | Mtons |
|  | Beneficial use | % |
| Toxic/Hazardous waste | Hazardous waste generation | Tons |
|  | SARA releases | Tons |
|  | Chlorine used (as $Cl_2$) | Tons |

SOURCE: P&G.

NOTE: Annual data on each category are tracked from 1983 to the present.

[a]Total recovery.

this is no small matter: One day in August costs millions of extra dollars because energy usage is at its peak. Therefore, the resort has developed an effective energy conservation program.

WDWR tracks energy usage and energy conservation savings at each property and functional area. Using these data, EI and RCES show properties how energy conservation saves money. For example, summary statistics about the current practices and potential revenue opportunities of different environmental practices, related to energy savings, by property area are used to help motivate properties to participate in the Green Lights program.

WDWR has also used such metrics to develop an effective energy conservation tracking and awards program for the different resorts. The award is based on percentage of improvement in energy savings for each of the 13 resorts. Each month, the improvement percentages for all the resorts are made public so that their staffs can compare the new data to their own performance the previous month and to how well the other resorts did. Keeping these data in a spreadsheet allows each resort to track how well it has been doing graphically. This tool is particularly useful for monitoring performance and motivating the staff to do better. These metrics are used to create a friendly energy conservation competition between the different hotels. WDWR uses metrics for tracking recycling rates at different business units in similar ways.

## ENVIRONMENTAL ASSESSMENT AND PRIORITIZATION TOOLS, TECHNIQUES, AND APPROACHES

Proactive facilities use a range of customized formal and informal analytical techniques in assessing and prioritizing environmental decisions. Whenever possible, information systems and analytical tools that identify the full, facilitywide effects of environmentally related activities are used to help integrate environmental concerns into the core interests of the facility. One example is the use of life-cycle assessment to identify the effects of a system's initial design during its operation and support. Another is activity-based costing, which fully attributes environmental compliance costs to decisions about the design and operation of a company's core production processes.

However, such tools are limited, and informal tools are also used, especially for P2.  P2 decisions are often a challenge that requires creative assessment approaches.  A key part of applying such tools, formal or informal, is that facility environmental managers use business goals to justify environmental activities.  Incorporating business goals in the justification and analysis process makes these activities acceptable to upper management and enables them to be integrated into the core business.

## Range of Tools and Techniques Customized for a Facility

Effective facility managers and environmental professionals use a range of environmental assessment techniques and tools that have been customized to meet the needs of their facilities, such as chemical and material tracking systems, life-cycle analysis tools, process evaluation tools, hazardous waste and other media analysis tools, regulatory assessments, environmental audits, and P2 assessments.

Some of these are formal, such as P&G Mehoopany's chemical safety management system (CHEMS), which the facility uses for detailed tracking and management of chemical use and for trying to minimize environmental impacts.  Other tools are more informal.  For example, the Celanese Engineering Resin, Inc., facility in Bishop, Texas, follows a waste-management hierarchy in environmental decision-making.  This facility's staff uses a waste-management hierarchy for environmental project priority setting.  The hierarchy emphasizes reuse or elimination of the waste at the source over waste treatment or emission (Graff et al., 1998, pp. 88–89).

Some of these tools, such as the chemical tracking and process analysis tools, focus on only part of the facility's environmental impact.  It is difficult to develop and apply tools that address all processes; all unit activities; complete use of chemicals, materials, water, and energy; and every media type (e.g., water, air, and waste).  Effective facility approaches try to integrate, analyze, and prioritize across many of these different facility systems, activities, and evaluation techniques.

Environmental audits have been one of the most powerful tools for making facility approaches more comprehensive.  An environmental audit or environmental assessment involves a comprehensive examination of all a facility's processes and activities and their environmental impacts for all media. An audit or assessment often focuses on identifying P2 activities. Such environmental audits have also helped senior leaders appreciate the pervasiveness of environmental concerns in their core activities.[5] Information from such audits has been instrumental in jolting the senior leaders of now-proactive firms into a proactive stance. Companies that are in highly regulated industries and those that are more proactive conduct regular environmental audits. For example, five of the six largest forest and paper companies have conducted regular environmental audits at their facilities since at least 1991.[6]

As briefly mentioned earlier, P&G conducts annual environmental audits at each of its facilities. The goal is to yield KEAs and other metrics that can be used to drive improvement over time. Strictly speaking, comparing the KEA and other measures across locations is difficult, but the human temptation to compete is irrepressible. Since P&G's facilities audit one another, objectivity could be an issue. However, the corporation has thoroughly trained a small group of people to avoid bias, with their own performance as auditors calibrated as part of a formal internal certification. The Mehoopany environmental staff has learned a lot about objectivity from these auditors over time while working with them on audits. Mehoopany environmental staff has found this process to be useful for helping to improve the environmental program over time.

But this process is costly. It takes three full days to generate the measures needed on Mehoopany itself. Also, more-complex operations are harder to audit and hence harder to benchmark across sites. Simplifying processes leads to better performance in part because it makes continuous improvement, driven by this auditing process, easier to achieve. P&G Mehoopany has been considered a highly complex site within P&G, especially because of the environmental impact of its pulping mill and high visibility in the community.

**P&G Mehoopany's Range of Tools.** To illustrate the range of tools available to a successful facility, consider the P&G Mehoopany plant.

---

[5]For an overview of auditing options, see Willig (1995).

[6]Champion International, Georgia-Pacific, International Paper, Kimberly-Clark, and Stone Container conduct periodic facility environmental audits (every three years or less) (Levinson, 1998).

Mehoopany staff uses a range of analytical, planning, and computerized tools to help assess the progress and identify priorities for its environmental activities. Most of these tools are unique to the facility, although some are corporatewide. We have already discussed some of these tools and will discuss others later in this chapter. However, it is worth briefly summarizing some of them here:

- the annual environmental KEA, the aggregate facilitywide assessment that P&G uses corporatewide to evaluate systems and how well they are doing on environmental issues (already described)

- monthly performance measures for air quality, water quality, solid waste, toxic and/or hazardous waste, and environmental management issues (already described)

- module environmental improvement plans, an environmental planning tool for business units at Mehoopany

- customized tools that the Process Services Module's EPT uses for efficiently tracking and managing environmental issues

- CHEMS, which provides a set of management tools that P&G can use to induce P&G employees and customers to use chemicals safely; includes tracking and educational components (described in detail in Appendix A)

- a P2 matrix to help prioritize P2 investment options (described later in this chapter).

EPT's efforts illustrate how P&G Mehoopany integrates and uses such tools to help with environmental and business decisions. Mehoopany uses module environmental improvement plans to help assess environmental priorities, tracking results and management of activities. EPT has been very successful at developing and using such a plan. This plan started by identifying the current state, the desired future state, and the known gaps between them. Analyzing the gap provided a basis for identifying specific action items to close the gap, which in turn became *strategies* that include

- specific action steps, sometimes broken into key subelements
- a responsible party for each step
- a standard to strive for, for each step
- actual status of each step

- classification of each step by priority:  breakthrough, control and improve, or backlog.

The team reviews each action step at least quarterly to track progress toward the desired state.

EPT's improvement plan also identifies a set of 14 specific measures that the team tracks monthly.  Four of these are compliance driven; ten are not.  The current list focuses on wastewater, but the team plans to add variables to reflect air and solid waste issues.  For each measure, the team identifies

- permit specifications
- average level for the month
- standard deviation for the month
- a "delta z" score (a measure of change from the previous month)
- a yes-no assessment of whether the variable is within bounds.

Each month, the team books the proportion of variables, all equally weighted, that are within bounds; this proportion becomes the measure of *environmental product reliability* for the module.  The team tracks this proportion and compares it in each period with a target level.  This target can and does vary by month to reflect an assessment of what the team thinks the module could reasonably expect to reach that month.  In effect, this approach to metrics normalizes the proportion so that a score of 100 percent is a "stretch" goal, and the target is a goal considered achievable within existing constraints.

The team reports its findings on each variable and the summary proportion score to the operational manager of the Process Services Module and to teams through the module every month.  When a variable fails to make its target level, the team also conducts a failure analysis, using a Pareto chart to locate the biggest problems.  The team then conducts a cause-and-effect analysis to trace failure to root causes and, for each root cause, identifies plan adjustments with a schedule and responsible person.  The team then tracks the status of action items that fall out of the gap analysis and evaluation of failures and changes made.  Each item has a named "owner" who can be held accountable for its status.

All the steps in this process are documented and tracked with a efficient computerized system, which is available to all relevant staff.

This system provides these tools in an organized set of simple charts and graphs and is a good tool for assessing current and potential future environmental issues and initiatives. In addition, the team manages a home page that allows anyone on the P&G Mehoopany in-house network to get information on a wide variety of environmentally relevant topics. Topics range from the agenda for team meetings to references on environmental topics. Included with this information are historical data on many variables that could potentially provide the basis for a CAAA Title V permit.

**WDWR's Range of Tools.** WDWR also uses a range of formal and informal assessment tools and techniques that are customized for the facility. To help properties participate in EPA's Green Lights program, EI staff helps them see the financial savings by using formal cost-accounting approaches to show the return on investment. For example, if the retrofitting cost at a hotel with Green Lights is $600,000, which is $500,000 more than with normal lighting choices, EI staff explains that, within three years, the hotel will begin to achieve savings because the return on investment is $200,000 per year. In the energy area, less-formal approaches are also used. For example, each guest room in the Contemporary Hotel has a Direct Digital Control device that allows occupants to control the heating, cooling, and humidity in their own rooms directly, including the actual temperature. This device cost about $25.00 extra per room. The guests like this control, and it enables WDWR to reduce temperature in unoccupied rooms to save energy. The operations manager did not have to compute an internal rate of return for this activity, since he acquired a large amount of functionality at a minimal cost.

At WDWR, EI also uses simple sample cost comparisons between traditional methods and more environmentally friendly alternatives to convince properties to invest in the latter. For example, EI staff has compared the total annual costs for purchasing and using traditional laser printer cartridges against purchasing and using recycled ones.

A good illustration of how corporate culture affects the assessment and choice of environmental activities is the system WDWR uses to reward employees. The company strongly supports activities to reward employees for doing a good job. EI has a yearly budget for its activities but often receives additional funding for special ideas. If EI staff asks for additional money, it normally must show Disney management a return on the investment. However, the staff has also justified such additional funds because they were for activities that reward employees for outstanding performance.

## Using Business Goals to Justify Environmental Actions

Facility environmental managers and champions that are environmental leaders are effective at using business goals to help justify their environmental actions. Such managers are creative in how they incorporate such justifications into traditional business practices. Environmental accounting tools are used whenever possible, but given the difficulties in quantifying some of the environmental costs, innovative justifications are also used. Such approaches are developed for the individual company and facility culture to integrate the environmental justification effectively into normal business practices. For example, Baxter International developed an innovative "environmental balance sheet" as a financial statement of the company's environmental costs and cost savings. This technique integrated environmental considerations into the bottom line by translating the environmental issues into terms upper management understood (Graff et al., 1998, pp. 82–83).

**P&G's Use of Business Goals to Justify Environmental Actions.** Such approaches often focus on strategic business issues, as P&G illustrates. An important part of the Mehoopany facility's environmental program is finding ways to contribute to traditional business goals. To do this, Mehoopany's perspective recognizes the need to focus more on strategy and broad thinking about environmental issues than on specific cost measurements, which can be hard to compute for their environmental concerns. Specific arguments used include the following:

- P2 and other proactive policies help P&G management stay focused on its own core issues by avoiding distracting and resource-consuming conflicts with regulators.

- Proactive policies help build relationships with external stakeholders by contributing to trust. This simplifies other problems by reducing regulation and oversight and making it less onerous when it occurs.

- Partnerships with regulators have led to an especially good relationship with Pennsylvania regulators, who have been able to target their work with the facility more effectively, confident that P&G will follow the regulations. Essentially, the plant is taking advantage of an operational two-tier regulatory system.

- Avoiding conflict with regulators allows P&G to work out solutions on its own schedule and without immediate constraints, which increases the likelihood that P&G will find the best solution to a problem. This is especially compelling when P&G anticipates expanded regulation in the future and wants to approach this prospect on its own terms.

- P&G recognizes managers who can reduce complexity because environmental results are part of the performance system. In general, anything that leads to emissions increases complexity because it introduces regulators and all the in-house overhead necessary to satisfy the requirements they impose. It is better never to get into this situation in the first place.

- Environmental policy and performance protect P&G's franchise to conduct business over the long term. Until environmental issues have been disposed of, the normal business is at risk.

These points are not independent; even when they seem at odds, they tend to support one another. Some of these business practices are P&G's, and some are unique to the Mehoopany facility.

In the end, the teams that organize policy issues for final decisions justify their recommendations using a variety of criteria, such as

- cost
- ease or complexity of operations (simpler is better)
- likely effects on external customers (ask how you would feel in their shoes in the face of different decisions)
- what is right to do, given P&G Mehoopany's basic principles, including doing prevention at the source as much as possible.

P&G Mehoopany recently reduced its use of chlorine and ammonium nitrogen when MEG staff applied this thinking about priorities to specific decisions. Chlorine reduction allowed Mehoopany to avoid paying for treatment, as well as to develop a response to a problem that would have had to be resolved eventually anyway. And evolving science had shown that ammonium nitrogen could be harmful to the ecosystem under certain conditions. So, to do the right thing, the plant reduced its use of ammonium nitrogen without any regulatory direction. This allowed the plant to maintain the initiative and hence control, even though doing so clearly increased near-term costs. Long-term effects were not specifically quantified, but P&G Mehoopany perceived the change as a source of business advantage, given potential long-term risks and costs. Similarly, as mentioned earlier, Mehoopany made a strategic decision to favor incineration over land disposal, despite the apparent higher cost of incineration, and invested $2.5 million in reducing odors, without any formal economic justification, simply because of community concerns.

P&G Mehoopany managers are more open to broad, strategic arguments when the implications for capital requirements or effects on operations are smaller. Whenever possible, the environmental manager looks for P2 candidates with low investment costs. In these cases, savings need not even be discussed, although the facility can also provide many examples of how much environmental actions cut total cost, such as the solid waste examples already discussed.

In justifying and choosing environmental initiatives, economic and strategic arguments for change and complexity come into play in different ways. On the one hand, specific solid waste issues are much easier to address because they all ultimately come down to how much you are going to pay to dispose of waste. Air and water issues are harder to address because the standards for performance are more complex. On the other hand, economic arguments themselves can get complex and confusing. In these circumstances, arguments that are more strategic, if presented effectively, can carry more weight with Mehoopany management.

**WDWR's Use of Business Goals to Justify Environmental Actions.** At WDWR, environmental projects often have to meet the same rate-of-return criteria as other business projects. However, other business reasons are frequently used to justify such projects, such as being compliant, avoiding potential future regulations, improving operational flexibility, and improving community and regulatory relations.

EAD has successfully justified its requests for hazardous waste investments because of the need to comply with regulations. For instance, improvements to the roof over the hazardous waste-management area were approved for compliance reasons, without having to meet the normal rate-of-return justification. Upper management knows it is more costly to receive a violation, not just because of fines and penalties, but also because of the potential to hurt the company's image: Avoiding bad publicity is an important project justification. Upper management realizes it has to act aggressively to avoid potential environmental compliance issues.

Public image concerns with respect to Florida's county recycling law helped justify the $4 million investment in the MRF. In fact, the MRF was primarily built because of this recycling law. The law itself is weak; there is no real penalty for not complying with it. However, Disney did not want to look bad to the public by not complying with the recycling law. And, because each county's recycling report goes to the state, WDWR did not want to be among Florida's worst-performing counties if the DEP compared them all.

WDWR managers often use a combination of such business reasons to help justify projects. As an illustration, RCES requested, and received, $1.3 million to extend the reclaimed water distribution system using the justification that the system could provide more reclaimed water. Further, this additional water reuse would look good in negotiations with South Florida Water Management District over the renewal of WDWR's water use permit. Finally, WDWR could do the extension concurrently with a road-widening project, and it would cost less to do it now rather than later.

## Facility P2 Assessments and Justifications

Facility environmental champions and managers are especially innovative when it comes to P2 decisions. Facilities that are effective at P2 have integrated P2 into business planning. For many of the more-proactive facilities, P2 is a core value. Management and workers throughout the facility recognize the importance of trying to reduce pollution at its source as much as possible. The philosophies and operations of many of these facilities integrate an explicit or implicit waste-management hierarchy. Such cultures help support creative efforts to develop and justify P2 projects. Effective environmental champions and managers also work within the facility's culture.

Since quantifying some P2 opportunities can be so difficult, informal methods are often used.  BRT (1993) found that, while none of the facilities it examined had a formal process for prioritizing P2 projects, they do prioritize informally.  The informal methods included tracking waste volumes, cost, and future compliance issues out to at least three years.  For example, the P2 prioritization process at Martin Marietta's facility in Waterton, Colorado, focused on understanding waste stream issues, including the volume of waste, toxicity, cost of disposal, related land-use issues, regulatory requirements, and impact to facility operations and liability.  The process at 3M's Columbia, Missouri, facility looked at quantity, toxicity, and potential hazard of waste streams, customer requirements, and the probability of success (BRT, 1993, pp. 11, 22).

Even though final P2 prioritization is often relatively informal, the underlying assessments often include the use of effective tools to analyze and understand a facility's manufacturing and other processes.  Such tools include process characterization and flow diagramming, material accounting, fishbone diagrams, Pareto charts, statistical methods to investigate processes, and material input-output analysis (BRT, 1998, pp. 26–28).

**P&G Mehoopany's P2 Justification and Assessment Processes.**  P2 is important to Mehoopany's environmental program.  The facility justifies P2 by looking at such factors as reduction of regulatory requirements, raw material values and savings, and community impact.  The long-term complexity of issues at the facility and the operational value of the effort also are factors.  The Mehoopany environmental staff receives broad operational support on P2 decisions from the plant manager.

Justifying P2 has been easier for solid waste at Mehoopany than for air and water, because staff can more easily show the benefits.  Air and water P2 investments are harder to justify.  To help with this problem, Mehoopany developed a simple matrix to rank alternatives in terms of their appropriateness for P2 actions.  A brief review of Mehoopany's actions over the past few years reveals that the facility has generally acted on the recommendations generated by this matrix.

The matrix has three columns of criteria:

• Cost: operating, capital, disposal

- Risk:  effects on environment, health, safety, business risk, and complexity
- Regulation:  current and future potential.

Then Mehoopany identifies eight potential target areas for action as rows in the matrix:

- For air:  $SO_2$, $NO_X$, particulates, chloroform, odor
- For water:  BOD per ton of pulp, ammonia, sulfite liquor carry-over to treatment.

For each target area, the analysis asks whether cost, risk, and regulatory concerns are high, medium, or low.  The answers fill out the matrix, supplying a simple summary judgment that locates the biggest problems and, hence, what management should emphasize in searching for P2 candidates.  The final product of the assessment is a "hit list" for potential P2 actions.  In using this tool, MEG works with the module operational staff and engineers to make P2 investment decisions.  For more-expensive P2 investments (as well as other environmental projects), the plant manager ultimately decides.  However, there is a good process to ensure alignment between the environmental group and the plant manager.

**WDWR's P2 Justification and Assessment Processes.**  As already mentioned, WDWR uses a range of approaches to justify environmental projects, and their P2 justifications are no different.  One prime justification is cost savings, as in the earlier printer cartridge example; others include concerns about potential future regulation, operational flexibility, and public image and relationships with regulators.  The zero-emission wastewater treatment facility, an investment of over $100 million, was justified using a variety of these reasons.  Similarly, in developing the 20-year development permit, Walt Disney Imagineering had to convince management that it would be worth the $40 million expense.  Operational flexibility, regulatory concerns, public image, and traditional cost savings were all part of the justification process.  WDI staff was able to show management the cost savings and net present value of this project because of all the property development WDWR would be able to do.  More importantly, the staff showed management the business advantage of this innovative permit—that WDWR could develop more of the site and do it more efficiently than with the traditional piecemeal approaches to development. This deal also provided WDWR numerous public-relations benefits—with the regulators, environmental groups, and community.

Even when informal approaches are used, proactive facilities integrate P2 into business planning. For example, Intel's Aloha, Oregon, facility P2 plans are business-based (BRT, 1993, p. 21).

# Chapter Six

# PROMOTING EFFECTIVE RELATIONSHIPS WITH RELEVANT STAKEHOLDERS

Effective relationships with all relevant stakeholders is important for successful environmental management. These stakeholders include regulators, stockholders, customers, community and environmental groups, journalists, and other interested parties. Some of the most successful innovative environmental approaches are especially effective in dealing with stakeholders who are active and have responsibilities in the surrounding community. Company employees are another important stakeholder group.

All proactive companies agree that continuous communication, in all directions, about the goals and status of the environmental management program is important to success. This includes not only internal communication, as discussed in Chapter Four, but communication with all stakeholders.

The EMS literature has numerous examples of the importance of stakeholder relationships to business success in many environmental areas, such as remediation management, EMS development, and P2. For example, BRT (1998, p. 25) found that the most frequently identified characteristic of high-quality P2 planning was that the facilities engaged stakeholders and understood and responded to government and community expectations. In fact, as discussed in Chapter Three, identifying customers and other key stakeholders and what they want now and in the future is an important element of TQM, TQEM, and ISO 14001–type approaches. For example, in applying TQEM, Xerox Corporation identified its customers and, to meet its EHS goals, is eliminating as much waste as possible. Xerox identified such external customers as local community and consumers of the company's products and services and such internal customers as product design teams, manufacturing, and corporate research and technology (Resetar et al., 1999, pp. 120–121).

## HONEST ENVIRONMENTAL REPORTING AND DIALOGUES WITH STAKEHOLDERS

Industry has found that facilities that are genuine and honest in their efforts to improve environmental management and performance and in communicating such activities accurately to the public, customers, regulators, and other stakeholders can have significant benefits both for the facility and for the company's bottom line. Intel provides an example:

> We are designing our future by building on the relationships with our communities, regulators, suppliers and customers. Proliferating our successes jointly with operational flexibility will improve the environment and maintain a safe work environment for our employees and communities while supporting Intel's continued growth. (Intel, 1999.)

The Project XL effort at the Chandler, Arizona, facility demonstrates this commitment. Intel has been working to ensure that those who have a stake in this facility are involved in the environmental design and impact assessment of the XL proposal, are informed, and have an opportunity to participate fully in project development. One example is the massive outreach effort to local citizens, which included hand delivery of 25,000 notices. Intel has also agreed to make all environmental data for the facility available on the Internet as part of a standard reporting mechanism.[1]

Proactive companies in the chemical industry provide another good example of the importance of honest dialogues with stakeholders. Responsible Care (the chemical industry's EHS performance-improvement initiative) has a code of management practices that

---

[1]See http://www.epa.gov/projectxl/intel/ for information on this project. This site also contains the detailed minutes from stakeholder meetings during the project's development. Also, significant stakeholder involvement is a requirement for Project XL experiments. See http://www.epa.gov/projectxl/ for more information about such requirements and other companies' experiences.

includes community awareness. Responsible Care emphasizes public outreach and communication about industry activities (Chemical Manufacturers Association, 1994, p. 19): "maintaining an honest dialogue with the public is crucial to the success of the chemical industry's efforts under Responsible Care."

Most proactive companies publish formal EHS or environmental reports every year or two to help educate stockholders, the general public, their customers, and other stakeholders about their environmental activities. In fact, by 1994, over 150 companies worldwide had issued such reports. Reports meeting the guidelines of the Public Environmental Reporting Initiative usually describe the organization, its environmental policy, and its environmental management program; what it releases; how it conserves resources, manages risks, and complies with regulations; and how it addresses product stewardship, employee recognition, and stakeholder involvement.[2] And some proactive companies also publish EHS reports for their individual facilities and business units. For example, IBM's Personal System Group published an environmental report in 1997. In addition to Disney's corporatewide environmental report, WDWR produces reports for EI and for WDWR itself. Similarly, P&G has a corporate environmental report, and P&G Mehoopany has published its own environmental reports (for example, P&G Mehoopany, 1997d).[3]

These reports inform key outside stakeholders about the goals and status of the company and the facility's environmental program. Communication with these groups also reflects the facility's views of each group. Depending on the corporate and facility visions, these communications can give special attention to customers, regulators, NGOs, or local communities, including employees who live there.

Both P&G Mehoopany and WDWR conduct honest environmental reporting and dialogues with stakeholders and have accrued benefits because of it. Trust and integrity are two of P&G Corporation's core values. These values focus on honest open dialogues based on trust:

---

[2]A business cooperative developed the Public Environmental Reporting Initiative to help provide consistency in public environmental reporting (Wever, 1996).

[3]For other example environmental reports, see IBM (1997a) and IBM (1997b). Also see the bibliography for additional examples, including the EHS reports of Intel, Georgia-Pacific Corporation, and DuPont.

> We respect our P&G colleagues, customers, consumers and treat
> them as we want to be treated. We have confidence in each other's
> capabilities and intentions. We believe that people work best when
> there is a foundation of trust. (P&G undated a.)

P&G Mehoopany carries out this value in its environmental activities.
MEG staff currently meets face to face with about five selected community "thought leaders" throughout the year to discuss the facility's
environmental activities. P&G recognizes the value of these ongoing
discussions. In these meetings, Mehoopany staff tries to be as open
and honest as possible; MEG once gave a sludge sample to a local
environmental group concerned about the contents of the plant's
sludge to analyze. The plant environmental manager has pointed
out that it is important for people to get to "know you as a person,
not as a company." Such honest meetings help company relations
and its environmental image.

Disney Corporation's experience also provides lessons about the
importance of honesty and true dialogues in dealing with stakeholders. WDWR has made open and honest dialogues with regulators,
the community, and other stakeholders a policy. This effort has
enabled them to implement innovative environmental activities,
such as the 20-year development permit. Some corporate Disney
staff tried unsuccessfully to develop a Disney theme park in Northern
Virginia near the District of Columbia. In this effort, Disney had not
actively and honestly engaged all relevant stakeholders, such as
members of the local community and environmental groups. Strong
local opposition and negative publicity defeated the Northern
Virginia park effort. To learn what might have gone wrong with its
community relations, Disney Corporate staff drew on the experience
of the person who had led the staff involved in WDWR's successful
20-year development project. This individual asked the corporate
staff whether they had talked to the local people in Virginia. They
had talked to the governor and the congressmen. He said that they
had talked with the wrong people and should have talked with local
community and environmental groups and engaged all community
members in an honest dialogue. Most important, in making development plans, the staff needed to listen, understand, and address all
the different community concerns.

## BUILDING TRUST AND PARTNERSHIPS WITH REGULATORS

Proactive facilities have developed good, open, and honest working relationships with their federal, state, and local regulators. Such facilities report any problems immediately, and this honesty has helped the facilities establish and maintain their credibility about environmental commitments with regulators. The resulting good working relationships help the facilities attain environmental and business objectives. For example, the companies that have been the most successful in remediation management have found that building and maintaining a strong, positive, and credible relationship with regulators that includes open communication is critical to success (Drezner and Camm, 1999, pp. X–XII, 43–45, and 74–76). Such a trusting relationship is especially important with local regulators. State and local regulators often have authority over the environmental issues at the local facility level.

Building trust and respect by nurturing relationships with regulators or other stakeholders is not the same as acquiescing to stakeholder demands. Managing stakeholders is always about balancing the interests of all stakeholders. A proactive firm seeks an open, frank exchange with each stakeholder that clearly articulates the basis for the firm's position with that stakeholder. Being open often facilitates discussion that leads to a mutually satisfactory outcome. But each stakeholder must understand that the firm respects all of its stakeholders' needs and reflects them, in good faith, in its discussions with each individual stakeholder.

P&G Mehoopany works hard to maintain good relationships with regulators, investing the time and effort necessary to build trust and respect. Mehoopany staff members meet with regulators regularly, explain what they are doing, help educate them about their industrial processes, and give tours of the facility. Mehoopany also participates in partnerships with regulatory entities in statewide environmental forums. For example, the plant environmental manager attends all meetings of the Air Quality Technical Advisory Committee. Mehoopany has, when requested, provided input on issues that have little direct effect on it. More broadly, two P&G employees participated in the Pennsylvania 21st Century Environmental Commission.[4] This commission of about 50 people developed recommendations about how environmental issues should evolve in Pennsylvania in the new century.

WDWR has been very effective at building trust and partnerships with regulators, as the negotiations with Florida DEP demonstrated. This allowed WDWR to avoid going through the state permitting process for each small water hookup. Because it trusts WDWR, Florida DEP gave WDWR the regulatory authority for an *intracompany* permitting system to handle these small hookups. WDWR staff thus acts as its own manager and watchdog.

This type of trust has not always existed. WDWR learned from experience how important it was to develop such trust. In 1988, WDWR was fined with a hazardous waste violation (a labeling violation). CNN even did a story on it. In response, WDWR hired a special staff to deal with hazardous waste compliance. There has not been a hazardous waste violation since then. WDWR also changed its relationship with the regulators by building trust and credibility. For example, Florida DEP used to automatically inspect if an employee called department with a complaint. Now, the DEP regulator calls EAD staff first and asks them about the issue. WDWR has a similar relationship with the state water regulators. Again, an important part of building this trust was being honest and open with the regulators. For instance, WDWR now calls the regulators if it has something wrong, instead of trying to hide it. WDWR has been very open about what it is doing, and its staff members talk with the regulators on a regular basis.

Another useful example of how WDWR has earned regulators' respect and trust has to do with wetlands and endangered species. Because WDWR has a staff expert knowledgeable in wetlands, native flora and fauna, and endangered species, it has not had to hire a contractor to handle these issues. On her own time, she also volunteers to work with local environmental groups; for example, she is on the board of the local chapter of The Nature Conservancy and is active in the National Audubon Society. She has won many environmental

---

[4]For more on the commission, see Pennsylvania 21st Century Environment Commission (1998).

awards for her efforts. The regulators trust her because of her dedication and her technical knowledge, and she can explain to them why WDWR does things the way it does. She has thus been quite an asset to WDWR in working with regulators on wetland and endangered species issues. For example, during the Animal Kingdom development, she identified some sand skinks (a small lizard with no legs), a state protected species, in the proposed development area. WDWR had found them in their site survey and immediately told the regulators about their existence. The local regulators had not even known the skinks were there. WDWR applied for and received a permit to relocate them to another site on the property, where the University of Florida is monitoring them. WDWR's staff honesty and expertise about relocating this species helped them earn the permit.

## Taking Advantage of Evolving Regulatory Flexibility

A trusting and open relationship with regulators, especially at the state and local levels, enables proactive facilities to take advantage of the evolving environmental policy context discussed in Chapter Two. Such facilities are reaping the benefits of two-track regulatory systems. Since these facilities have demonstrated superior environmental performance through their actions, regulators work with them as partners and essentially give them preferred treatment.

Preferred treatment, as discussed in Chapter Two, can include streamlining administrative requirements and the permitting process, easing inspection and enforcement policies, offering financial incentives, and waving some fines and penalties for companies that promptly report violations. It also includes allowing the facilities to implement creative projects that benefit the company and help the environment. For example, the P2 permitting experiment at Intel gave it operational flexibility. WDWR's 20-year development permit and small-hookup water permitting system also yielded important operational flexibility. Because state and local regulatory resources are limited, preferred treatment can also help government agencies. For example, knowing that certain facilities have demonstrated superior environmental performance allows regulators to concentrate their inspection and enforcement efforts on facilities other than those known to be proactive.

Our impression is that P&G Mehoopany's relationships are so good now that the facility already benefits from an effective two-tiered regulatory system. Pennsylvania state regulators have been moving toward giving less oversight on permits and other issues when past performance has been good. The facility has thus benefited from the mutually trusting relationship that the MEG staff has developed with Pennsylvania regulators.[5]

**WDWR 20-Year Development Permit.** In such regulatory flexibility project efforts, creative thinking and negotiating are often important to the relationships innovative companies have with regulators and with community members and other key stakeholders. The details of WDWR's effort to negotiate the 20-year permit for development of the entire Disney property regarding wetlands issues provides excellent lessons about this negotiation process. To develop such an innovative permit WDWR creatively engaged regulators, environmental groups, and the surrounding community. In fact, one of the most important parts of the process was dealing with the regulators and environmental groups, especially since so many different regulators were involved in the effort. This permit was approved by and incorporated permit requirements handled by at least seven regulatory agencies, including the U.S. EPA, the U.S. Army Corps of Engineers, Florida DEP state water resources regulators, the South Florida Water Management District, and the U.S. Fish and Wildlife Service. From the very beginning, a WDWR staff member met with different regulators and showed them the benefits of the plan both for the regulator and the environment. For example, the 20-year permit would save the regulators time and money and meet their comprehensive plans. In contacting regulators, the staff member started both at the highest level and the local level within each agency. For example, he started with both the EPA Regional Administrator and the local EPA regulator.

Similarly, from the start, this staff member met with all the local environmental and citizens groups to show them the benefit of the plan for the environment. He began with the most anti-Disney organizations, being open and honest with them and asking them what they wanted. The Nature Conservancy actually came up with

[5]P&G Mehoopany's EMS and environmental activities already come close to Pennsylvania's SEM efforts. P&G Mehoopany has even provided input to Pennsylvania DEP on the state's environmental business leadership piece of the evolving SEM approach. However, MEG differs with the DEP's SEM slightly in specific policies about sharing with the community.

the idea for Disney to purchase Walker Ranch.  All of the environmental groups accepted the permit deal, and there were no protests. At the time, the state had placed a high priority on purchasing Walker Ranch because of its interesting habitats and location.  Walker Ranch and the WDWR property are located at the headwaters of the Everglades system.

As noted earlier, but worth repeating, Disney's honesty and credibility were important to this process.  For instance, WDWR staff members honestly stated which wetlands were of low quality and which were of higher quality.  The staff then tried to see that their plans would have as little an impact as possible on the higher quality wetlands.  WDWR showed the regulators and the environmental groups the actual wetlands that the development would affect so that they could see for themselves that these wetlands were of low quality. WDWR proved that it was being honest and was trying to do as much as it could to minimize environmental impact.  WDWR won the trust of both groups.

At first, it was hard to get state regulators to agree.  However, Carol Browner, head of Florida DEP at the time, was open to the new idea. Also, WDWR showed the regulators that the small pieces of wetlands in past mitigation efforts were not doing very well.  Florida DEP regulators who had been anti-Disney before are best friends now because WDWR was honest and did not "play games."  WDWR did have a bit of a problem with some U.S. EPA regulators at the headquarters in Washington, D.C., who almost derailed the effort.

Another unique part of the process was convincing the regulators to deal with a global concept for the permit, i.e., general development areas rather than specific details for each building.  The plan did include specific details with respect to roads and utility lines because these had the main impact on the wetlands.  However, the plan mapped out general development areas rather than each individual building site.

## Educating and Training Regulators

The education and training of regulators is often important to developing a good relationship.  Defense installations are often large and unique facilities within a community.  Regulators often are not familiar with the types of activities, especially the industrial processes, that occur on the bases.  Both Mehoopany and WDWR have similar characteristics within their communities.

P&G Mehoopany is the only major industrial facility in a primarily rural area in northeastern Pennsylvania.  It also has a unique pulping facility.  Mehoopany has helped educate state and local regulators about its processes.  Such training is especially important, since state regulators often are junior and not very experienced.  Experience is especially lacking about industrial processes and the pulp and paper industry.  Mehoopany staff also gives facility tours to Pennsylvania DEP employees to demonstrate good environmental practices, for example, good industrial wastewater treatment.  P&G Mehoopany has also sponsored a course about the paper industry for state water permitters to help them better understand the industry's environmental issues.[6]

Similarly, WDWR has actively educated regulators about its operations, as the 20-year permit development process illustrated.  EAD staff members routinely invite the regulators to visit the facility to see what they are doing.  At WDWR, it is especially important to have the regulators visit and see what WDWR is doing, since its operations are not like the surrounding orange plants and are thus unique for the area.  WDWR has learned how important it is help the regulators understand the unique circumstances of the situation to provide a balanced view of the issues, rather than just black and white.

## ENGAGING THE SURROUNDING COMMUNITY, NGOs, GENERAL PUBLIC AND OTHER KEY STAKEHOLDERS

Continuing communication with regulators is only one part of a broader program for effective management of stakeholder relationships.  Proactive facilities recognize that the environmental views that the surrounding community, NGOs, stockholders, customers, and other key stakeholders have of facilities can affect their business goals.  These facilities are part of their communities, and their employees live in them, so it is desirable for the facilities themselves to be good community members.  Both P&G Mehoopany and WDWR

---

[6]Several MEG member used to be state regulators, which has also helped Mehoopany's relationships with regulators.  Environmental professionals in Pennsylvania often start by working in a regulatory agency and then later move into industry positions.

strongly emphasize public relations and communication with all stakeholders. Both facilities consider public image and community relations to be important to the success of their businesses. For instance, the Mehoopany staff does not want to see an article in the local paper that criticizes the plant. Part of Mehoopany's stakeholder philosophy is "think like your community" and "be a member of the community." The plant environmental manager states that his public vision is that the community does not "hear, smell, or see the facility in a negative way."

To engage these many different stakeholders, a facility develops different strategies and mechanisms. If the customer is another company, the facility may seek formal third-party ISO 14001 certification to verify that its environmental management practices meet the customer's needs.[7] If the customer is a household that prefers "green" products, a firm may maintain buyer loyalty by placing special emphasis building an "environmental profile" that differentiates its product from alternatives. This means building an objective case that it is sufficiently clean and communicating this case in language that the customer will understand and accept. Formal eco-labeling programs, when available, support this effort.[8] This also means communicating effectively with customers to understand what elements of environmental performance they value most.

If a local community or NGO is a key stakeholder, the facility gives a high priority to gaining and maintaining the stakeholder's trust, respect, and goodwill. As with regulators, trust is a basis for mutually attractive information exchange and negotiation. In such a situation, the facility and company may strongly emphasize community relations. Georgia-Pacific Corporation is one such company. One of its four main environmental principles is "Promote Community Awareness," which includes community involvement, responding to community concerns, and voluntary disclosure about its performance toward specific environmental goals (Georgia-Pacific, 1996).

As with regulators, an important part of such information exchanges is information the facility hopes will train the stakeholder about spe-

---

[7]As discussed earlier, many U.S. firms have not sought formal certification. However, for a useful discussion of available options, see Jackson (1994), pp. 61–69.

[8]See, for example, Kirchenstein and Jump (1994), p. 70.

cific elements of the facility's situation and goals.  Such training and risk communication can be critical when, as is often the case, the stakeholder is not as technically sophisticated as the facility itself.  Of course, stakeholders typically respond constructively to such training only if trust has already been established.  For community stakeholders, helping in community activities also helps to build trust.  Whoever the stakeholder is, these considerations encourage the facility to invest in its relationship with the stakeholder, seeking dialogue even when the company is not seeking to sell a specific product or win a debating point.

External environmental communication also can include actively exchanging information with the scientific community and national environmental groups.  The latest information from the external scientific and policy community supports a facility's pursuit of creative solutions.  Participation in the broader debate on environmental issues also helps shape the direction of ongoing scientific research and regulatory reform.

### Employ Diverse Range of Communication Mechanisms Based on Facility and Stakeholder Needs

Proactive facilities regularly engage stakeholders in a diverse range of mechanisms customized to meet their needs.  Effective facility strategies for engaging stakeholders include regular meetings with community leaders, public meetings, and formal community advisory panels (CAPs)[9] that participate in community environmental activities; meetings with the press; surveys of attitudes toward the facility; and meetings with the facility's main environmental opponents, such as local environmental NGOs. Creating and distributing facility environmental literature and information through open houses, plant tours, Earth Day fairs, newspaper articles, company environmental newsletters, and informational environmental brochures are also effective ways to educate and engage other stakeholders.

For example, Olin Corporation, a leader in remediation management, develops site-specific community outreach plans to maintain communication, avoid surprises, and assure community support

---

[9]Also called *community advisory boards* and *stakeholder boards*.

when needed.  An Olin facility develops an outreach strategy and an implementation plan for remediation issues that include specific goals, roles of key players, processes for conveying and obtaining information, key audiences, key messages, and notional questions and answers (Drezner and Camm, 1999, p. 75).

P&G Mehoopany employees use a diverse range of activities to engage the community and other stakeholders about environmental activities.  Employees meet with stakeholders face to face, conduct public surveys, have open houses, and sponsor and participate in community environmental activities.  Mehoopany helps build off-site environmental awareness, both for both members of the community and for its own employees.  For instance, the plant held a large fair to celebrate the 25th anniversary of Earth Day in 1995.  This fair was open to the public, and such outsider environmental groups as The Nature Conservancy also participated.  Staff members have also built a nature trail across the street from the plant.  P&G Mehoopany has partnered with Pennsylvania Department of Conservation and Resources to provide 30 volunteers to work at local parks.  For 17 years, the Mehoopany staff has participated in an Environmental Day for 5th and 6th graders at the local school.  For some of these activities, such as the nature trail, Mehoopany has even paid employees for part of their time.

Mehoopany has also actively worked in partnership with another key local stakeholder group on environmental issues:  the wood suppliers.  Mehoopany has promoted sustainable forestry to protect local forest health and to increase the safety of logging in these forests, even though P&G owns none of these forests and has no financial liability in them.  For instance, Mehoopany's forestry group has given technical training to its suppliers to improve practices that affect environmental and safety performance.  In 1996, the group trained 300 loggers in such environmental practices as controlling erosion, creating buffer strips around streams, and using harvesting strategies.  Such practices are compatible with the hardwood forests that dominate around Mehoopany and that P&G Mehoopany relies upon to ensure the quality of its pulp.  Mehoopany has also reached agreements with some suppliers to avoid logging during the muddy spring and fall "breakup" periods, when logging operations can especially damage the forests.  Participating suppliers continue to pay workers during this period, and P&G helps the suppliers avoid cash-flow problems that might accompany such a break in production (cash flow is important because suppliers tend to work very close to the edge, hand to mouth, without much financial slack). P&G Mehoopany also participates in a Pennsylvania state sustainable forestry program.  These examples illustrate how seriously Mehoopany takes its stewardship role and the importance of working with suppliers.  Suppliers are also an important stakeholder group for DoD facilities.

WDWR also uses a range of mechanisms to engage community stakeholders, including community and school presentations, open houses, printed materials, employee participation in community environmental efforts, and special environmental events.  EI has a slide show on Environmentality for community and environmental groups.  When giving this presentation, staff members discuss both what has and what has not worked, which has enhanced WDWR's credibility—its staff is not perfect but learns from its mistakes.  EI also gives talks about Environmentality at local schools and has put up displays at local parks and other community special events.  EI developed a brochure on Environmentality in response to the many requests from the general public for information about WDWR's environmental efforts.

Employee involvement in local and national environmental group activities helps foster good relationships with the groups.  For example, a Disney vice president sits on the board of The Nature Conservancy.  One of the best examples of how Disney uses its own creative entertainment style to engage and educate the public about environmental efforts is the release of ladybugs at the Contemporary Hotel.  Although discussed earlier, this deserves repeating here because of its value in stakeholder relations with WDWR's customers. A costumed cast member, Dr. L. Bug, helps the children guests release ladybugs to help control aphids, while their parents take pictures.  The cast member also explains to the guests how this helps the environment and about WDWR's other IPM activities.  This IPM activity has become a fun and educational experience for guests and an effective public outreach mechanism for WDWR's environmental program.  Other properties also include environmental educational experiences for guests, such as at Discovery Island and the Land Pavilion.

## Effectively Using Opinion Surveys

Surveys are effective for measuring the stakeholders' satisfaction with the facility's environmental program and to help target and prioritize EHS activities. Facilities ask the following kinds of questions:

- Does the EHS program effectively meet your need for regulatory information?

- What are your environmental concerns regarding the facility?

- Do you consider the facility to be a good neighbor?

- Are you satisfied with your interaction with the facility—for example, the response time to questions and concerns?

- What are the public's views on the facility's environmental record and stewardship activities?

- For employees: How do you rate the EHS leadership and performance?[10]

Many proactive facilities have started using community opinion surveys to help improve their environmental programs and community relations. For instance, several Intel facilities have used community perception surveys (Intel, 1998, p. 20).

P&G Mehoopany has effectively used such surveys to improve stakeholder relationships and to help in the development and implementation of its environmental activities. Mehoopany has twice conducted a facility public perception survey of community stakeholders, once in 1992 and again in 1996. The most recent attempt yielded information that Mehoopany was still processing in 1997.

The first round conducted detailed discussions with employees from the community and used a random telephone survey to reach others in the community. It also selected community "thought leaders"—people who shape local opinion for detailed discussions: elected officials, environmental leaders, regulators, teachers, newspapers editors, neighbors, health professionals, business people, and others. In-depth interviews ran for one-half to a full hour and were designed

---

[10]For more details and examples about stakeholder surveys, see Wever (1996), pp. 173–175.

to elicit views about P&G Mehoopany.  The interviews were highly structured to draw information objectively without allowing the interviewer to inject his or her own views.  Time was left open at the end of each interview to allow the respondent to ask questions and for the interviewer to become freer and more proactive.  The goal was to get an objective picture of where P&G Mehoopany stands in the community; one question asked people what they would do if they were the plant manager.  The survey was conceived of as being much like a marketing survey in that the goal was to collect data as objectively as possible to support future decisionmaking.  And the effort grew out of wanting to find ways of understanding "how one would feel if you were standing in the other guy's shoes"—in this case, the community's shoes.

The second round refined these methods.  For example, a random telephone survey identified individuals willing to participate in an in-depth, face-to-face interview in exchange for gifts of P&G products. P&G Mehoopany went out of its way to schedule interviews with "thought leaders" to get an inclusive sample.

The public perception survey had two important main results.  First, Mehoopany got a good picture of its image, including particular indications of concern about

- odor
- negative effects of the plant on a local river, if any (nothing specific; the Mehoopany plant is just so big, some people feared it must be threatening the river)
- traffic
- basic lack of trust in large industry without any specific foundation.

Mehoopany responded to these concerns by developing structured responses for each.  For example, the plant responded to the concern about odor by putting together a community advisory team that met every six months for several years.  After the team broke up, Mehoopany continued to share information with former members. To address the river's health, the plant sponsored and invited the public to attend a workshop, which the Academy of Natural Sciences of Philadelphia actually put together and ran.

Second, Mehoopany staff met face to face with many important external players and used these opportunities to promote the sort of continuing dialogue that could proceed without being prompted by an immediate concern or need on P&G's part. The resulting discussions would lack an agenda or the pressure that accompanies a need to make a decision. Since this promoted better long-term relationships, it was at least as important as the first product. The plant environmental manager found that personal relationships support a continuing bond of trust between organizations even when the organizations take different positions on specific issues. The differences do not become personal and hence remain open to rational discussion and management.

This exercise was valuable, but expensive. The second time around, Mehoopany offered P&G products in exchange for the random interviews and worked hard to accommodate the needs of the more-targeted influential individuals. On average, each interview basically took two hours, including all the preparation, give and take, etc. Interviewing notables cost about 400 hours of MEG staff time—and public affairs staff members also attended this particular group of interviews, which increased the cost. Mehoopany is now seeking ways to continue this dialogue, with better targeting to allow greater frequency but without such a heavy cost. MEG staff members currently continue to meet with about five thought leaders a year.

## Use of Community Advisory Panels

Proactive facilities also may create formal CAPs to create ongoing dialogues with their communities. CAPs have been used effectively in industry for remediation sites, and many defense installations also have effectively used remediation advisory boards. Project XL, for example, features stakeholder boards to help in the development of these innovative programs. Such stakeholder boards can be an effective means of actively engaging surrounding communities in education and discussions about facility EHS programs.

For example, the chemical industry's Responsible Care members use CAPs to promote ongoing dialogue with the general public. These CAPs provide ongoing links between the facilities and their surrounding communities. At CAP meetings, the public can ask questions, make comments, raise concerns, and receive direct responses from the facility. More than 300 Responsible Care facilities have formal CAPs. The structure and focus of CAPs are based on unique facility needs. CAP members meet monthly and set most agendas. Facilities often hire professionals to lead the panel meetings and formally write up the meeting minutes. Community members volunteer their time to serve on a CAP.

CAPs help with community relations, project implementation, and even company management improvement, as three diverse examples illustrate. First, the Huntsman Corporation was building a new facility in Port Neches, Texas, and used a CAP to present the facility plans and discuss EHS plans. Second, an Intel facility in New Mexico used a CAP in 1997 to develop an environmental education program for elementary students and to provide community input to the facility's risk assessment efforts. Third, it benefits company management at a Velsicol Chemical Corporation facility; as the corporation's president, Art Sigel, explains:

> The panel broadens the perspective and vision of the company participants and the result is better, more-progressive managers who have built a strong relationship with their neighbors.[11]

It should be noted that such formal CAPs can be time consuming, as some Project XL facilities have discovered.

---

[11]Except for the Intel example, all this information about Responsible Care and CAP examples came from Chemical Manufacturers Association (1994), pp. 20–25. The Intel example is from Intel (1998).

# Chapter Seven

# TRAINING AND MOTIVATING ALL EMPLOYEES

An effective environmental management program depends on having a well-trained and motivated workforce throughout the organization. Even employees who are not directly responsible for environmental functions should be aware of environmental goals and policies. Training and motivating all employees about environmental issues can be difficult, especially when environmental concerns are not the primary focus of the business. Defense installations face similar challenges, given that environmental concerns are not their primary mission. Facilities that have been effective at integrated facilitywide environmental management approaches have also been effective at training and motivating all their employees about environmental issues.

## ENVIRONMENTAL TRAINING FOR ALL EMPLOYEES

For an EMS to be effective, all staff members need to know their roles and responsibilities and the proper procedures. The educational process includes introductory training for new employees, refresher courses, specialized courses for management, and courses on such special issues as hazardous materials. The training also needs to incorporate appropriate motivational approaches.

### Employees Are Empowered with Formal Training

Perhaps the most common error companies have made when trying to make a large cultural change, such as implementing an EMS, is to adjust formal responsibilities and metrics without explaining the expectations to employees. Proactive environmental facilities recognize the importance of formal training. Five types of formal training are important to improving environmental management:

1. A firm trying to raise the perceived relative importance of internal environmental concerns will provide training about the general social importance of environmental issues and the role the firm can play in this broader setting. Such training often integrates factual presentations, emotional appeals, and open discussion groups to try to change the attitudes or even the values of the firm's employees.

2. A firm using new management methods (such as cross-functional teams) to promote integration will train its employees to use these teams and to use more-general consensus-building and problem-solving techniques relevant to the success of the teams. Similar training is important to any manager being asked to be more creative and persistent about environmental issues, although general management experience is often the best teacher of these skills.

3. A firm seeking to develop environmental specialists who can operate confidently in many aspects of environmental decision-making—for example, specialists who can function effectively as decisionmakers on cross-functional teams—will develop databases these employees can use for self-paced instruction. Such databases offer current information on technologies or case studies of past decisions that young employees can access when facing specific day-to-day problems.

4. A firm facing new regulations, introducing new P2 programs, or adopting new databases or analytic tools will offer targeted training to employees that these changes will affect most directly.

5. A firm seeking to establish a critical mass of expertise on environmental issues that can sustain experts over time and help them work together to keep their skills up to date form centers of excellence or competence centers. Such centers can support the training options listed above and provide points of focus for longer term career development.

Training takes time. Formal training will be more time intensive the more interaction the firm seeks between trainer and trainee. Over the longer term, informal on-the-job training related to the execution of new programs and procedures will continue indefinitely.

## General and Specialized Environmental Training Classes Customized for the Facility

Proactive environmental facilities use a range of customized environmental education and training mechanisms effectively, including both general and specialized environmental courses. For instance, Georgia-Pacific Corporation has developed a general video and course materials about its environmental policies and positions for all employees. This company also has developed individual special environmental training modules for Title V CAA requirements, P2, and Georgia-Pacific's forestry practices (Georgia-Pacific, 1996).

All proactive environmental facilities provide some sort of general and introductory classes to help educate and train employees about environmental issues. General classes include overviews for new employees and management, as well as periodic updates, covering general environmental policies, procedures, issues, and concerns.

Introductory overview courses often motivate as well as educate. They explain facility policy and procedures but also explain the importance of the broader environmental issues in general and how they relate to the facility's bottom line. Motorola's Protecting Our Environment course, which they began giving to all employees in 1993, illustrates this point. This companywide course explains why environmental issues are important to Motorola and its employees. The course was designed to help increase employees' environmental awareness, review Motorola's environmental game plan, and help each employee take action. The course includes a section about several global environmental problems, such as stratospheric and ground-level ozone, and explains the impacts of these problems and how participants could help prevent them. The course also covers the corporate environmental expectations for the business units and how regulations affect their business. Finally, the course describes the advantages of going beyond compliance and suggests ways employees can participate in P2 activities at home as well as at work (Eagan, Koning, and Hoffman, undated).

Such general introductory courses are often given to all employees. However, proactive facilities also offer such general courses by individual business unit and management functions. Both P&G Mehoopany and WDWR empower their employees with a range of courses. For instance, P&G Mehoopany has a New Employee Environmental Orientation Training course that everyone attends.  Each new employee receives a one-and-one-half hour presentation on his or her environmental role and ownership, according to the position's responsibilities.  Part of this presentation shows how environmental excellence gives the business a competitive advantage.  Because every employee owns company stock, this business linkage can help motivate employees to pay more attention to environmental issues. All module safety functional leaders receive periodic environmental overview training.  Individual modules also provide general environmental courses that are customized for their own business units. For instance, the Process Services Module gives a three-hour course on environmental issues to each of its new employees, including 30 minutes on why good environmental performance is important. This course is structured to raise a series of specific questions and promote open discussion among the participants.  The questions help new hires understand why environmental issues are important, what P&G Mehoopany expects of them, and what they can do to promote the environmental goals of the firm.

All new WDWR cast members must attend the Disney University orientation, which includes a quick two-minute talk about Environmentality and the circles.  Many of the properties also have their own orientations for newcomers, which often include some information about environmental issues, such as recycling.  The Magic Kingdom actually has a paid full-time environmental person, a custodian, who explains environmental issues to other cast members, such as recycling and waste minimization.  The Magic Kingdom justifies his salary because of the money it makes on recycling and the money it saves on landfill fees.

Proactive environmental facilities, such as P&G Mehoopany and WDWR, also give specialized training on selected environmental topics, such as compliance and hazardous waste.  P&G Mehoopany conducts classes and on-the-job environmental training on specific topics, such as its annual hazardous waste training and emergency response training and drills.  Training in other areas is less frequent. For example, P&G gives "new role" environmental training to individuals moving into roles with direct environmental responsibility, such as engineering.  The company also targets special environmental areas, such as waste reduction, for training, if it appears to be needed.  Mehoopany also has on-the-job training for selected areas, such as prework and involvement in regulatory visits. At WDWR, EAD has formal training on compliance issues, especially in the hazardous waste area, and on biohazardous waste.

## Less-Formal Environmental Education Activities

Proactive facilities also provide less-formal environmental education: articles in facility newspapers, company brochures, environmental open houses, informal meetings, Earth Day fairs, etc. Such mechanisms often serve other purposes, including sharing information internally and with the community and other external stakeholders, as well as helping to motivate employees. Both P&G Mehoopany and WDWR have a range of informal education activities.

**P&G Mehoopany.** P&G Mehoopany provides special environmental information meetings periodically for selected staff, on such topics as the results from the public perception survey. A large display inside the facility's entrance explains the importance of environmental issues in plant operations. Other environmental educational activities include articles in the company paper; special environmental brochures that help educate employees, their families, and the general public; and other forms of community outreach (as discussed earlier). For instance, P&G Mehoopany's environmental brochures include *The Solid Waste Utilization Handbook* (undated b), *25 Years Treating Nature as a Customer* (undated a), and *Environmental Update 1997* (1997d). *The Solid Waste Utilization Handbook* describes the solid waste responsibilities of Mehoopany employees, performance expectations, definitions, and successes. In addition, MEG staff participates in national, regional, and local environmental conferences, such as the Air and Waste Management Association meetings.

**WDWR.** Because WDWR has over 50,000 employees, a high turnover rate, and many low-paying service jobs, training and retraining are often challenging. For instance, it is hard to train resort housecleaning staff, especially because many of them speak only Spanish. Therefore, WDWR does a large amount of informal environmental training and education along with its formal activities. These informal techniques are often integrated with motivational techniques, many of which will be discussed later in this chapter.

About once a year, EI helps organize an environmental fair at each property. The purpose of these Environmental Awareness Days is to educate cast members about environmental activities, and employees receive a gift for participating.[1] But to receive their gifts, the cast members had to fill out a survey asking how they learned about Environmentality, what they think WDWR should do, etc. This survey was then used for updating the training program and for developing new environmental activities.

Each year, many of the properties have an Earth Day fair that helps educate both employees and guests. Other awareness activities include a computer bulletin board, the Environmentality brochure, and environmental displays. WDWR developed an Environmentality display for the Magic Kingdom to educate the guests as well as employees. Once a month, EI publishes a full page on Environmentality in *Eyes and Ears*. This page mainly highlights program successes and new activities and mentions how employees can become more involved. In 1996, the newspaper also included a "Conservation Corner" column to help educate cast members about native species in Florida, such as manatees. The idea was to motivate and educate cast members about local issues so that they would be more environmentally responsible both on and off site. EI staff members also track other companies' activities and read environmental literature to find new ideas and educate themselves.

## MOTIVATING ALL EMPLOYEES

Training is a fairly standard process of providing knowledge and information to employees. One of the most difficult parts of an effective EMS is motivating employees, from the highest level of management to the lowest-skilled and lowest-paid worker, to implement what they have learned in their everyday operations. This implementation is especially difficult for environmental issues because they are often not the primary focus of the organization.

The industry facilities that have been the most effective at motivating employees combine certain key elements in their operations: The strategic vision and business thinking of the parent organization

---

[1] The gift was a clock in 1996, a radio in 1997, and a watch in 1998; EI has since stopped widespread distribution of such gifts.

have shown that it values environmental issues.  Appropriate cost mechanisms and other procedures have been developed and implemented that demonstrate real belief in the importance of environmental issues.  Incentives deserve special attention and should be chosen in keeping with the prevailing corporate culture.  Depending on the culture, incentives may target individuals, teams, or organizations; can be direct or indirect; and can be monetary or nonmonetary (Hoffman, 1992–93, pp. 1–11).  Finally, explaining the business rationale for environmental activities, such as cost savings, helps to educate employees and motivate environmental behavior.  All these elements reflect the integration of environmental issues into the core business operations of the facility.

Monetary incentives, such as tying management salaries to environmental performance, are important.  However, they are often not enough or may not be feasible for all parts of the organization.  For example, linking employees' environmental performance directly to their salaries is not usually very feasible, except for selected management personnel.  Additional innovative incentives and techniques are required to motivate all workers to address environmental issues throughout the facility's operations:  appealing to individual workers' values, ethics, and common sense; empowering the workers to develop their own incentives; showing the business justifications for environmental actions; and special recognition programs that employees value.

The environmental staff plays an important role in this motivational process.  The staff must be able to help employees throughout the facility see the benefits of working with the environmental staff and of paying attention to environmental issues on the job.[2]

## Placing Appropriate Corporate Values on Environmental Issues

Aside from the benefits previously discussed, demonstrating environmental stewardship and stressing the importance of environmental issues at all levels in a company can strongly motivate employees.

---

[2]For a good discussion of how an EHS manager can go about showing the benefits to other staff, see Brown and Larson (1998).

Such values are reflected through company policy, philosophy, strategic thinking, and implementation. It is extremely important for a facility to show that it considers environmental issues to be central to doing business. Making this an integral part of the facility's own business will encourage employees to take environmental concerns just as seriously and to see them as important to the mission of both the facility and the company mission.

As discussed earlier, many corporations and their individual facilities are making environmental issues central to the company vision, philosophy, and strategic-thinking process. For instance, WBCSD companies have recognized that environmental stewardship is an important part of a strategic business vision. Proactive companies have found that such values help motivate employees to do the right thing with respect to the environment.

As has already shown, both P&G and Disney companies and the P&G Mehoopany and WDWR facilities clearly value environmental issues and foster a strong environmental ethic and stewardship throughout their organizations. For instance, P&G Mehoopany has shown this stewardship by engaging in many proactive activities, including the environment in its vision and policy, and even creating a facility environmental motto—"treating nature as a customer." WDWR has shown this commitment through its environmental vision and its investment and support in EI and Environmentality. Such values helped to motivate the facility's employees.

## Monetary Incentives and Environmental Accountability

Having successful EMS requires appropriate procedures to integrate environmental performance directly into the different parts of a facility's business operations. This often involves formal methods of directly linking environmental performance with monetary rewards. Many companies point to the importance of placing key environmental management positions on a promotion path that attracts highly qualified managers and rewards them for good performance with promotions.

At Eastman Kodak, the pay of senior managers is based in part on their environmental performance (U.S.–Asia Environmental Partnership, 1997, p. 52). Similarly, P&G Mehoopany employees who deliver results are rewarded accordingly, and the results in question, especially for management personnel, include environmental performance.

Team-oriented firms use formulas to allocate profit-sharing bonuses to team members; proactive companies write these formulas to reflect environmental management activities. Some companies argue that cost-effective environmental management improves overall corporate profits and that all employees should benefit through profit-sharing arrangements. For instance, as discussed earlier, Dow Corning's Carrollton, Kentucky, facility has a variable compensation package for all employees based on the status of achieving corporate and facility goals to reduce SARA emissions. In 1998, every facility employee received a 3-percent bonus on his or her annual salary for meeting or exceeding this goal (Kentucky Pollution Prevention Center, 1998).

Formal procedures also include consequences for lack of appropriate environmental performance, such as salary penalties, disciplinary actions, and even firing for more-extreme violations of environmental procedures. In areas with significant environmental and health risks and with potential regulatory penalties, such as handling hazardous materials, a plant's environmental policy often includes punishment for not meeting minimum performance criteria.

P&G Mehoopany has minimum expectations for all employees' environmental performance. If an employee does not meet this standard, there is a formal plan with explicit consequences to make sure that, at least, the employee gets back to the standard. For example, a person may not advance because of his or her environmental performance.

But punitive approaches are not sufficient, especially because many environmental actions, such as P2, may be voluntary and may not be required for the job. Reward systems are often more effective for motivating some workers.

Mehoopany prefers to motivate people with positive, rather than negative, incentives, such as special rewards. WDWR motivates most of its employees through incentives, except for selected management personnel and EI staff. Unlike many companies, monetary incentives are not part of the Disney culture. However, as a management incentive, WDWR does have a financial award. If an employee saves the company a large amount of money through an environmental activity or other special projects, he or she can receive a financial award.

## Special Incentives and Techniques for Average Employees

Although monetary incentives can be extremely important, especially for management, they are often not enough, especially for lower-paid and lower-skilled workers, such as WDWR's hotel and restaurant workers. For such individuals, a range of key techniques is available: appealing to workers' own values, ethics, and common sense; empowering workers to develop the incentives; and developing special recognition programs that employees value. Recognition programs can include useful and fun environmental competitions for workers.

The most common form of special incentive appears to be a direct, nonmonetary award to individuals who have tangibly improved environmental management. Companies emphasize the importance of giving such awards often, even for small improvements, to emphasize the importance of environmental management throughout the organization. BRT (1993) found that all six P2 teams had facility and/or corporate recognition programs that helped to sustain employee motivation for P2 activities. For example, Intel's Aloha, Oregon, facility had a formal division-level recognition and reward process for major P2 accomplishments and some informal peer-to-peer recognitions for smaller achievements (BRT, 1993, pp. 11, 29). Another example is 3M, which has a companywide award for individuals or teams of employees "who are environmental, health and safety pioneers at work and in the community" (3M, 1998).

## Incentives at Mehoopany

P&G Mehoopany also uses special incentives to motivate employees. Its ECOS award is a noncash environmental recognition program. The award winners appear in the company newspaper, *Mehoopany News*, receive a plaque, and dinner. However, some employees are still not very aware of this program. Outside recognition for the facility's overall environmental record is another incentive. In 1996, the plant received the Pennsylvania Governor's Environmental Excellence Award. The operational employees met the governor to accept this award. Such recognition makes employees feel good about their environmental accomplishments and helps motivate them to continue the good work.

## WDWR's Creative Motivational Incentives

WDWR has been especially successful and creative at motivating average employees through special incentives. The facility has a range of motivational techniques that appeal to individual workers' values, ethics, and common sense and that empower the employees to decide what environmental activities to do and how to motivate other employees. WDWR has also created fun and friendly competitions and provided individual awards and recognition. Some of these techniques are described in thorough detail here because they are especially relevant to defense facilities.

**Circles.** WDRR's ECEs, discussed briefly earlier, are effective at empowering cast members. Although not every property has these voluntary grass-roots environmental groups, over 20 did in 1996. EI helps set up the circles, whose purpose is help implement Environmentality at the local level. Circles help to increase environmental awareness, reinforce training, generate new ideas, and implement day-to-day operational environmental projects. Circle members also motivate other cast members to do Environmentality. Members run the circles themselves. The activities of the circles and how often they meet vary from property to property; they generally meet every two weeks or once a month.

Employees participate in the circles because they care. The majority of participants attend the circle meetings on company time, although some meet during the lunch hour. Meetings are limited to one hour. There are about 6 to 25 people per circle. Some properties, such as the Magic Kingdom, have minicircles because so many cast members wanted to participate in the program. Because meeting size is limited, the employees who attend the circle represent other cast members who are active but do not attend the circle meetings. The representatives may hold separate meetings for the other cast volunteers.

Many ECE groups watch to see that fellow employees are doing the right thing with respect to the environment and help motivate them to do environmental activities. For example, one cast member noticed that another was washing food containers out in the storm drain rather than in the sanitary drain, which violates WDWR procedure. The circle member told EI staff, which in turn educated the other individual about the proper procedure. In another instance, a cast member noticed that an area needed more recycling cans. The circle passed this along to EI staff, which worked to get more cans at the site.

In 1996, the Contemporary Hotel's SEES was one of the best examples of the success of ECEs. The SEES committee had a whole series of different recognition activities that the cast members developed. This employee recognition program has been very successful. The recycling rate increased from 11 to 58 percent within 9 months thanks to a complete turnaround in employees' attitudes about recycling.

**EE Pins.**  At WDWR, it can be difficult to get cast support for an activity, yet getting cast involvement is very important. The operations manager stressed over and over again how important it is to give local recognition to employees to make them accountable for their actions. Pins have been a useful motivating incentive in the Disney culture. The lowest-level incentive is receiving a unique, specially designed Jiminy Cricket pin for attending the SEES meetings. Because these pins cannot be bought anywhere, they were very popular for a while.

In addition, the Contemporary Hotel's operations manager challenged the hotel's ECE to create an award for verified accomplishments that would be unique to WDWR or to the Disney Company.[3] Volunteers from SEES designed the "EE" pin. They decided to have silver and gold pins and specified the criteria for receiving each. A silver pin indicates that the cast member has demonstrated a commitment to the environment. The recipient must routinely come to SEES meetings and participate in such activities as recycling. Silver pins can be awarded at any time, and about 30 were given in 1996 and 1997.

---

[3]Note that this award system has changed since 1996.

A gold pin represents a specific environmental accomplishment. These pins are awarded once a year at the Earth Day ceremonies at Epcot Center. At this event, the Disney Corporate Vice President for Environmental Policy announces the accomplishments and names, then presents the pins. This formal presentation enhances the significance and desirability of the award. Gold pin winners are also mentioned in *Eyes and Ears*. At the Earth Day celebration in April 1996, about 10 gold pins were awarded.

**Friendly Competition.** The SEES group also has created a fun competition for the cast members at the Contemporary Hotel. Every month, the SEES groups give out a department award to the leading (the best) department and a "nonaward" to the laggard (one that did not do very well), for each SEES issue. Safety and security have been combined in this award system, yielding a total of six awards. The actual awards are statues to be displayed for the month in the winning departments. The general manager ensures that the awards are promptly displayed in the department managers' offices. The next month, each award moves to a new award winner. For the nonaward, the department "winner" has 5 days to do better. If it succeeds, then the nonaward is taken away, so the department does not have to display it for the entire month.

For energy, the positive award is a 9-inch statue of Sorcerer Mickey, and the nonaward is a statue of a burnt-out lightbulb. For safety and security, the positive award is a statue of Ludwig von Drake, and the nonaward is a miniature statue of a broken crutch. For the environment, the positive award is a statue of Jiminy Cricket, and the nonaward is a clear plastic case containing a hangman's rope with a dead rubber chicken on it. Clearly, no one wants to have the rubber chicken nonaward in his or her office: Everyone performed so well during the closing months of 1996 that the chicken had not been awarded for four months in a row. The award system had been in operation for about a year and a half at that point. The operations manager found that this game was a fun way to keep people motivated and that it kept the program from becoming monotonous.

Other incentives at WDWR include Jiminy Cricket certificates for recycling activities and free gifts for attending the environmental awareness days.

**Appealing to Personal Values.**   WDWR also motivates the staff to become interested and get involved in environmental issues by appealing to individual cast member's values, ethics, and common sense.

For instance, the Contemporary Hotel's operations manager motivates cast members by helping them see that they are doing the environmental activities for themselves, their children, and their grandchildren. He shows how things are linked, presents simple facts that make the issues important, and makes the impact seem real. For example, he explains that it takes 352 years for a Styrofoam cup to degrade completely.

This manager also uses the "shock factor" to educate and motivate, presenting large, scary statistics to help cast members understand the full significance of an environmental impact. The shock factor captures the individual's attention and interest; then, direct involvement in the group (SEES) can transform the interest into creative and positive environmental actions.

These actions begin at the cast member level, not from management. The staff generates the ideas, and the operations manager provides the resources to carry them out. The operations manager has said that the fact that the casts members generate the ideas themselves and make things happen is an important part of successful motivation. Having ongoing consistent support is also important. The manager has found educational resources from the local elementary school to be useful because they explain things simply and quickly and include interesting game ideas.

**For DoD.**   Given DoD's culture, such employee-run ECEs and friendly environmental competitions could be useful motivational techniques for defense installations to help motivate military and civilian personnel.

## Showing Business Cost Savings from Environmental Activities

Demonstrating the cost savings to management and other workers can also help motivate employees. For example, Volvo environmental personnel found that it was easier to get personnel to carry out environmental activities, such as recycling, when environmental effects were put in monetary terms (Resetar et al., 1998). Showing the cost justification for environmental actions is especially important for management. One very effective way of doing this is to tie costs directly back to business units. Some companies do this by allocating compliance costs to the overhead costs of business units before assessing unit profits; others tax business units for using external sources for disposal or recycling services not included on a preapproved list. Such techniques help to motivate all business units to take environmental issues seriously.

Both P&G Mehoopany and WDWR use business reasons to motivate environmental behavior.

**Cost Savings at Mehoopany.** P&G Mehoopany is especially effective at using business cost methods to motivate employees' environmental performance. Ownership and accountability stand at the heart of P&G's idea of management, including environmental management. This is most directly reflected in the strong support within P&G for allocating environmental costs to the business units responsible for generating the costs. The basic idea is simple:

- Place all environmentally related costs in well-defined cost pools.
- Develop simple rules and supporting practices to allocate each pool to a product module.
- Use the financial system to enforce this accounting system.

The plant has a very good system for allocating cost to business units. For example,

- The cost of MEG itself is allocated to product units according to simple rules that are subject to revision each year.
- The plant tracks all waste streams and either charges business modules for waste disposal costs or credits the modules for revenues from selling wastes or for the cost displaced by finding uses for the waste in-house. Displaced fuel is valued at its full associated cost savings.
- Allocating the costs of disposing of solid waste can be a problem because all solid wastes pass through a single transport point on the way to disposal. To allocate the cost of all material passing through, Mehoopany simply weighs each container coming from

a product module to the transport point and allocates the cost proportionally.  While this method is not absolutely precise, it is close enough to allocate costs.

**Cost Savings at WDWR.**  Showing cost savings is an important part of the Environmentality program.  EI's presentation to properties on the cost savings of Environmentality is entitled "Compelling Business Reasons for Environmentality."  The presentation includes 20 money-saving examples to show the properties:  using recycled laser printer cartridges, using hardwood mulch (better for the environment and cheaper than cypress), making double-sided copies, composting food waste (instead of landfill), using energy saving lights, etc.  EI presents sample cost comparisons between traditional methods and more environmentally friendly alternatives, such as the total costs in a year of using traditional laser printer cartridges versus using recycled ones.  EI also shows summary statistics about the current practices and potential revenue opportunities of different environmental activities.

In all of these areas, many companies use competition among business units to heighten the incentive effects of these options and to gather internal benchmarks that can be used to allocate incentives among units.  Friendly competition, such as the fun and competitive games at WDWR's Contemporary Hotel, helps motivate employees.  Extending the friendly competition to business units can address specific issues.  For example, WDWR's monthly comparisons of the energy savings of all 13 of its hotels allow their staffs to compare their own success against that of the previous month as well as against the improvements of the other hotels.  The resulting peer pressure and friendly competition create the desire to do even better the next month.

In sum, all proactive facilities recognize the importance of incentives in the successful implementation of environmental management, and each facility uses the specific incentives it is most comfortable within its cultural setting.

## Manage Failures to Limit Disincentives for Risk Taking

A special incentive issue that proactive firms recognize is the challenge of dealing with failed experiments with P2.  Because integrated facility environmental management approaches are new, experimental, and difficult, allowing failures is especially important.  Trial and error offer great potential to any learning organization and are especially important when refining changes to an ongoing production process.  Systematic learning depends on flexibility and tolerance of the right kinds of mistakes (Ochsner, Chess, and Greenberg, 1995–96, p. 71).  The most important aspect of successful experimentation is to recognize that failure is part of the learning process.  The term *failing forward*—that is, as Leonard-Barton (1996) puts it, "creating forward momentum with the learning derived from failures"—usefully describes this process.  Operationalizing this belief involves distinguishing between intelligent failure and unnecessary failure and setting up systems to learn from both (Leonard-Barton, 1996, p. 119).

Both P&G Mehoopany and WDWR expected failures as part of the experimentation process required in trying out innovative approaches.  In fact, WDWR even uses its failures to help build credibility with stakeholders.  EI's community slide show presentation on Environmentality discusses both WDWR's successes and its failures. EI has found that it helps WDWR's credibility to show that WDWR is not perfect and learns from its mistakes.

Most proactive firms seem to understand this, but we found few insights about specific ways of implementing such an understanding. How big a failure is acceptable?  How many failures are acceptable? Who should be held accountable for failure when so many things can contribute?  What kinds of decision screens can reduce the probability of failure without unduly discouraging experimentation?  What kind of safety net can limit the effects of failure?  Corporate cultures typically encourage conservative decisionmaking, supported by standard information sources and appeals to standard operating procedures that make failure far less likely than any attempt to change standard operating procedures.

Implementation of the kind of change discussed here will raises question about all these points until a new culture, more tolerant of an increased emphasis on environmental considerations, takes the place of the old. Until firms develop good answers to such questions, an important disincentive to serious change will persist.

# Chapter Eight

# CONCLUSIONS

What does all this information about how commercial facilities have approached proactive environmental management mean for DoD? Our research suggests that, as DoD pursues more-integrated, holistic approaches to environmental management of its installations, it should

- track and participate in the evolving policy development on facility environmental management

- fully participate in integrated environmental management approaches and experiments

- implement environmental management systems that align all DoD environmental activities with core DoD values

- promote and creatively use environmental assessment and metrics

- promote effective relationships with all relevant stakeholders

- train and motivate all employees about environmental issues.

As previously noted, DoD organizations, from the Office of the Secretary of Defense to individual defense installations, are already trying to do many of them. These are not easy tasks, either for companies or DoD. Successfully completing them relies on how they are implemented. Below, we discuss the key implementation lessons for DoD for each of the six areas.

## TRACK AND PARTICIPATE IN THE EVOLVING POLICY DEVELOPMENT IN FACILITY ENVIRONMENTAL MANAGEMENT

The U.S. environmental policy context has been changing over the last decade or more. The emphasis has been shifting away from traditional centralized command-and-control approaches to environmental protection. There is a new emphasis on all stakeholders collaborating to address environmental issues in more-proactive ways, such as P2. There is also a new emphasis on regulatory flexibility and on incentives for improving environmental protection, such as states encouraging facilitywide permitting experiments. There is increasing emphasis on state and local governments having more authority and control to customize regulatory programs and environmental approaches to unique local place-based needs. Such evolving policies and activities have yielded many regulatory and financial benefits for industry and other regulated entities, such as reduced inspections and reporting requirements. Given these changes, three main policy trends are of special concern for DoD facilities, as discussed in the following subsections.

### The Expanding Roles of State and Local Governments

The expanding roles that state and local governments have begun playing present unusual challenges and opportunities for DoD facilities. At the highest level, OSD and the services should continue to engage in the policy dialogue regarding states' authority and expanding policy efforts. As state and local governments have been customizing their regulatory programs to meet their own individual needs, it has become more difficult for defense installations and industry facilities alike to keep on top of environmental issues in different states.

National environmental policies, regulations, and standards help provide a consistent playing field for complying with environmental regulations and implementing EMSs. OSD and the services can help determine how flexibility develops by actively participating in national environmental policy debates and forums about the devolution process. They should actively engage organizations helping to evolve such policies. Several organizations are helping to develop such policies; for example, the Environmental Council of the States helped create NEPPS, and NPPR is instrumental to the development of state P2 planning laws and incentives. OSD and the services have already actively engaged some of these organizations and should continue to do so. They should also consider expanding these efforts as the environmental policy context evolves. For example, it is very difficult for federal agencies, especially DoD, to engage local governments in policy dialogues because there are so many. However, DoD may want to engage some national-level local organizations, such as NALGEP, more actively if trends continue and evolving environmental policies focus even more at the local level.

At the regional, state, and local levels, defense installations and regional defense organizations should actively participate in state and local activities, including development of new environmental laws and new incentive programs. For instance, state environmental leadership experiments and P2 incentive program development are areas that defense installations should be tracking and becoming engaged in. P&G Mehoopany's engagement in the Pennsylvania SEM development process and participation on the Pennsylvania Governor's Twenty-First Century Environmental Commission are good examples of a proactive facility keeping involved with the state's evolving environmental policy context.

## Proactive Environmental Performance Based on Collaboration

In their involvement in such policy efforts and their activities to implement more-innovative environmental management approaches, all parts of DoD should look for opportunities to take advantage of the new emphasis on partnerships and collaboration. Many of the industry examples of proactive facility environmental management approaches took advantage of collaboration. WDWR's 20-year development permit effort is an excellent example. DoD policies and practices, from the highest levels in OSD to the installation level, should focus more on developing collaborations between defense installations and regulators and other stakeholders. DoD itself has already participated in many collaborative processes, but given the innovative collaborative experiences of proactive business facilities, defense facilities may find more opportunities in this area. However, it is important to note that the collaborative efforts of DoD facilities must be consistent, open, and honest and must include all appropriate stakeholders to earn the trust and respect of regulators and other stakeholders. The Disney experience in Northern Virginia, compared with its experience at WDWR, provides specific evidence to support this point.

## Evolving Two-Track Regulatory System

Lastly, DoD should capitalize on the evolving two-track regulatory system as much as possible. If defense installations can demonstrate their superior environmental performance and earn regulator trust, they can reap the benefits of this evolution, as such proactive industry facilities as P&G Mehoopany and WDWR have. DoD also has the opportunity to transfer lessons one facility learns to others because its more-proactive facilities have already participated in such activities.

There is also the opportunity to participate in the broader environmental policy debate and evolution in this area. This point refers to the fact that the ways this evolving two-track regulatory system plays out at specific facilities can have important implications for evolving national policies about regulatory reinvention. Therefore, DoD should track and analyze its own facility experiments and how they can engage in this regulatory reinvention policy process more effectively.

## FULLY PARTICIPATE IN INTEGRATED ENVIRONMENTAL MANAGEMENT APPROACHES AND EXPERIMENTS

Industry and federal, state, and local governments are participating in many new and innovative approaches to improving environmental performance more efficiently and effectively. Many companies are trying to be more-integrated and holistic in how they address environmental issues and are starting to implement integrated facilitywide environmental management approaches.

Integrated facility approaches address environmental issues by examining an entire system as comprehensively and proactively as possible. These approaches analyze, compare, prioritize, and address environmental concerns across traditional boundaries, including environmental media and issues (air, water, land, hazardous waste, species, etc.) and the different functions and activities of the organization and facility. The functions include different processes, products, and business units, and the activities include industrial, commercial, residential, natural resource, facility support, and any other activities that occur at the facility. Such approaches integrate environmental issues into other business and operational concerns as much as possible. These approaches not only examine environmental issues across an entire facility but also examine the potential interrelationships among them. All of this his leads to the implementation of actions designed to minimize the facility's environmental impact. Governments and industry often provide incentives to help motivate and promote implementation of such approaches.

Such integrated approaches include proactive EMS–ISO 14001 approaches; environmental leadership experiments, such as Project XL; facilitywide P2 planning and implementation activities; facility-wide permitting approaches; sustainability activities; and ecosystem management. These categories are not mutually exclusive. In fact, facilities often combine these approaches, and there is often synergy among them. Many of the more–environmentally proactive companies are trying to implement a variety of these activities and approaches within their organizations.

Industry has gained numerous benefits from such efforts, including cost savings, operational flexibility, improved facility image, and improved environmental performance. DoD facilities have also been participating in some of these efforts; Vandenberg AFB's Project XL effort is just one example. However, opportunities to increase participation in such efforts exist. DoD should continue to support and encourage this, especially by trying multiple experiments and finding synergies. DoD also has been transferring the lessons it has learned from such experiments through such means as the national Air Force P2 conferences. These efforts should also continue and be increased to include transferring lessons across facilities, especially across the services. For instance, a more-assertive activity in this area would be to organize a DoD-wide conference focusing specifically on integrated environmental management approaches at facilities. At such a conference, innovative defense facilities and industry facilities could provide lessons learned.

## IMPLEMENT ENVIRONMENTAL MANAGEMENT SYSTEMS THAT ALIGN ALL DoD ENVIRONMENTAL ACTIVITIES WITH CORE DoD GOALS

DoD facilities need to ensure that they have implemented effective EMSs for promoting and facilitating innovative integrated facility approaches. To implement such proactive environmental policies, DoD needs to clarify its environmental goals, then help every part of the organization align its activities with them.

DoD must understand how its own environmental goals help it pursue its core goals: the goal of increasing military capability, which justifies DoD's existence, and the goals of managing resources efficiently and complying with federal socioeconomic policy and public administrative law, which pertain to any federal agency. Each of these core goals plays an important role in installation management. From here, DoD can clarify specific environmental goals in terms of the core goals.

Next, a mechanism will be needed for helping all parts of DoD align their activities—environmental activities at individual installations and others—with these clearly stated organizationwide goals. DoD should start by sharpening its environmental vision, principles, goals, targets, and priorities, making sure that these clearly link to the core priorities. These should support an approach to environmental stewardship that gives DoD greater control, flexibility, and agility in dealing with major environmental challenges it may face. The goals that drove Intel's pursuit of agile permitting methods provide a useful template.

Such an approach to environmental management sets the stage for individual installations to take more-specific actions. The formal implementation paradigm described in Chapter Four is ideally suited to driving high-level environmental goals into individual installations and their associated activities:

- Secure the support of the senior leadership.
- Build coalitions of those who must change to support implementation.
- Give a champion responsibility for day-to-day oversight.
- Use cross-functional teams to integrate relevant points of view.

- Assign clear roles and responsibilities for implementation.
- Decentralize execution to ensure proper integration at the local level.
- Use ongoing information gathering and sharing for continuous improvement.
- Facilitate creative and persistent change agents.
- Develop an effective EMS.

Next, we will briefly describe how this paradigm applies in the DoD context.

The paradigm starts with leadership from the top, in this case, the Secretary of Defense, the Chairman of the Joint Chiefs of Staff, and the civilian and military leaders of each service and defense agency. Environmental managers at each level should develop coalitions with each function that must adjust its policies and practices to implement a proactive approach. For the sake of proactive installation environmental management, the coalition should include operational combat activities, relevant combat support and combat service support activities, groups that keep and audit relevant accounts (such as financial management and the inspector general), those who oversee contractors operating on defense installations, and so on. The resulting coalition will be quite broad because defense activities on installations affect the environment in many ways and in ways that are integral to ongoing core defense activities. And the goals described above must help the whole coalition understand its relationship with the effects that activities at DoD installations have on the environment.

The coalition should work with its leadership to choose a champion who will have day-to-day responsibility for coordinating and overseeing activities designed to promote DoD's environmental goals. Each line manager on a DoD installation will retain responsibility for the environmental effects of his or her line activity; the champion will help each manager pursue DoD's goals and keep DoD's leadership informed about ongoing efforts to achieve these goals. To be most effective, this champion should be a widely respected leader with broad and long experience in the kinds of core activities found at the installations for which she or he is responsible. There should be some environmental experience, but experience with core activities should dominate. P&G's MEG director and WDWR's Contemporary Hotel operations manager are good examples of such champions at different organizational levels. DoD needs to help facilitate such champions as creative and persistent change agents.

At each level, the functions that must adjust their policies and practices will work together on a day-to-day basis in cross-functional teams. DoD now has extensive experience with integrated process teams and process action teams. Environmental management teams will work best if

1. Each member has authority to speak for his or her function without consultation.

2. Each member's performance review explicitly compares the team's performance against DoD's environmental goals.

3. The teams are formally trained to develop options and decisions in such a team setting.

Some teams will be permanent. Others will form and disband as needed. Some will integrate activities on a single installation; others will bring together representatives of several locations with common interests. P&G's corporatewide sector and facilitywide teams are models of the use of such teams for environmental purposes.

In this approach, DoD should clarify its goals for each installation and give each the flexibility and capability to develop creative solutions for its own specific environmental effects and regulatory setting. For the most part, the regulatory and forward-looking aspects of environmental policy at an installation are local; DoD should use the policies suggested above to empower installations to make the most of their circumstances and then hold each installation accountable for doing so. Promoting and encouraging ongoing information gathering and sharing for continuous improvement is an important part of this process. Gathering information is especially important because integrated facility environmental management approaches are new, experimental, and dynamic. DoD facilities should practice extensive benchmarking; partner with other facilities and institutions; and participate in ongoing communications about facility environmental practices with other DoD installations, between facilities and across different services.

DoD cannot plan and execute such an approach in one fell sloop. It will take time. It will also take commitment, persistence, and the willingness and ability to learn from the experience of taking a more-proactive approach. This will be particularly difficult for DoD because of the short tenure of its leadership at all levels. Choosing an incremental approach will allow each set of leaders to see tangible progress toward the long-term goal of flexibility and agility that will give DoD greater control over decisions about its environmentally responsibilities. The inability to move as fast as some commercial firms have should not discourage DoD from maintaining the pressure required to improve its environmental policy; practice; and ultimately, performance over time.

Proactive organizations pursuing such change benefit from effective EMSs. DoD should adjust its installation EMSs at every level to track not only compliance but also opportunities to increase military capability, reduce costs, or improve compliance with socioeconomic goals and administrative law. ISO 14001 and more-aggressive versions of TQEM offer DoD tools for doing this, either by benchmarking its EMS to these tools or, even better, by seeking third-party certification to a standard form of EMS.

DoD will benefit from an EMS that supports a more-proactive stance, but it is important to remember that proactive facility environmental management and EMS implementation also require a much broader set of supporting activities, such as the development of effective metrics and assessment tools, good working relationships with key stakeholders, and effective training and motivation for all employees.

## PROMOTE AND CREATIVELY USE ENVIRONMENTAL ASSESSMENT AND METRICS

Measuring environmental performance and tracking execution against environmental performance goals will be critical for successful implementation of facilitywide environmental management at DoD installations. Doing so will require effective metrics and, typically, an assessment framework in which to apply them. Effective metrics and assessment tools will improve DoD's ability to

1. specify its environmental goals clearly
2. translate these goals into specific targets

3. hold teams accountable for pursuing these targets by measuring team performance against the targets

4. help teams compare costs and benefits to DoD as a whole when prioritizing and pursuing different environmental projects.

DoD needs to promote and use environmental assessment, metrics, and priority setting creatively in analyzing and choosing environmental projects. To affect actual behavior in the workplace, these metrics and assessment tools must be compatible with—and easy to square with—the goals that DoD teams pursue as part of their normal, day-to-day planning and operations.

Given the apparent differences between DoD's core goals and the nation's environmental priorities and the difficulties and uncertainties associated with measuring the costs and benefits relevant to environmental performance, it may not be easy to develop an effective set of metrics and supporting assessment tools. To move in this direction, DoD should

- provide a supportive organizational context for environmental accounting and assessments
- promote environmental accounting
- use quantitative and qualitative metrics to stimulate innovation
- use a range of tools and techniques customized for the installation
- use DoD's core goals to justify environmental actions.

OSD and the services should continue to provide a supportive organizational context, facilitating and conducting environmental accounting and assessments. This will help integrate environmental concerns into core processes effectively throughout DoD. For instance, all defense installations should conduct annual holistic facility environmental assessments focused on P2, as many already do.

Managers throughout the different defense organizations need to encourage and support comprehensive and innovative environmental accounting practices. Providing this support may include accepting some nontraditional methods because traditional accounting and economic analyses cannot adequately handle many environmental issues. DoD needs to allow for the forward thinking and flexible reasoning that proactive and innovative companies use. An example is P&G Mehoopany's investment in odor control for the sake of environmental strategy and community relations, not because of current regulations or cost justifications.

Also important to the process is providing and developing effective analytic environmental assessment tools, both formal and informal, and maintaining a supportive organizational environment for their use. The tools need to be flexible enough to be customized for individual facility needs.

Effective environmental metrics that help measure progress toward specific facility goals at different levels are also needed, both to aid the environmental assessment and to help motivate behavior. A useful industry model here is WDWR's tracking recycling and energy rates by property and then using the data to track progress toward goals and motivate behavior through friendly competition.

Finally, and most importantly, DoD needs to use its core goals—to sustain military capability and to control costs—to help justify environmental actions. It is very important for DoD, the services, and individual defense installations to try to understand the implications of current and future environmental policy and the regulations that may affect current or future military missions. Looking at long-term costs and adopting an environmental stewardship role should be part of this process. Again, such reasoning may not fit into traditional accounting terms. A sample military mission would be ensuring military operational flexibility, which is the type of justification WDWR used in developing innovative permitting activities. WDWR also looked at the very long-term implications of such activities, including the long-term impacts on wetlands and the ecosystem.

## PROMOTE EFFECTIVE RELATIONSHIPS WITH ALL RELEVANT STAKEHOLDERS

Good stakeholder relations are important in implementing integrated facility environmental management approaches. Proactive facilities identify and manage relationships with all relevant stakeholders: regulators, the general public, suppliers, community and environmental groups, employees, etc. To manage and take advantage of stakeholder relationships effectively, DoD should

- promote and conduct honest environmental reporting and dialogues with all relevant stakeholders
- engage the surrounding community, NGOs, general public, and other key stakeholders
- build trust and partnerships with regulators
- take advantage of evolving regulatory flexibility
- employ a diverse range of communication mechanisms, according to the needs of both the facility and the individual stakeholders.

OSD and the services should actively promote honest dialogues with and environmental reporting to all relevant stakeholders. For DoD, the stakeholders include everyone: employees; communities; contractors and suppliers; environmental and other NGOs; the press; federal, state, and local regulators; other federal agencies; Congress; industry; and the general public. This honest reporting should include formal EHS and specialized environmental reports every year or two, to help educate the general public and other stakeholders about installation environmental activities. DoD facilities should also actively engage the surrounding community, NGOs, general public, and other key stakeholders in ongoing, honest dialogues about installation environmental issues. For the sake of effective stakeholder relations, it is critical to report and discuss environmental activities honestly, especially those that might be perceived negatively.

OSD and the services should also work at all levels to develop and maintain good working relationships with federal, state, and local regulators by building trust and partnerships. Installations should report any problems immediately to regulators. Such honesty will enable the facilities to establish and maintain their credibility with regulators about environmental commitments and activities. A trusting relationship is especially important with local regulators. Having a good working relationship will help DoD to achieve environmental and core mission objectives more effectively and to take advantage of evolving regulatory flexibility.

To build such trust and partnerships more effectively, DoD installations should work to educate and train regulators. Like WDWR and P&G Mehoopany, many DoD installations are unique within their communities. Giving tours and courses about installation operations, as the WDWR and P&G Mehoopany did, will help educate regulators about installation-unique environmental concerns and military mission needs. The result will be regulators who are more understanding and willing to work in collaboration with DoD installations in meeting their goals. Moreover, DoD should participate in and take advantage as much as possible of evolving regulatory flexibility, especially at the state and local levels. Such programs often provide more flexibility and have the greatest direct impact on DoD installations.

The needs of installations and community stakeholders are diverse and unique. Therefore, DoD facilities should use a diverse range of communication mechanisms based on these needs. Effective facility strategies include regular meetings with community leaders; meetings with the public and the press; formal CAPs that participate in community environmental activities; surveys of attitudes toward the facility; and meetings with the facility's main environmental opponents, such as local environmental NGOs. Creating and distributing facility environmental literature and information through open houses, plant tours, Earth Day fairs, newspaper articles, company environmental newsletters, and informational environmental brochures are also effective ways to educate and engage other stakeholders. Obviously, DoD already does many of these things. However, all parts of DoD, especially defense installations, should have systematic, consistent, and regular activities for different stakeholder groups.

Two mechanisms that are especially useful for DoD relations with the community and the general public are CAPs and opinion surveys. Many DoD installations have already successfully used CAPs, in the form of community Remediation Advisory Boards. These should be extended, or new ones could be created, to address all environmental issues and to address selected controversial topics. Opinion surveys are effective ways to measure stakeholder satisfaction with an installation's environmental program, to help target and prioritize environmental activities, and to help avoid unexpected future stakeholder problems. P&G Mehoopany's survey of community stakeholders (the public perception survey) is a good model for DoD to follow.

It should be noted that such stakeholder efforts can take time and cost money, but they are well worth the ongoing investment to enable OSD and the services to implement innovative integrated facility approaches.

## TRAIN AND MOTIVATE ALL EMPLOYEES ABOUT ENVIRONMENTAL ISSUES

Effective training and motivation of all employees is also important for successful implementation of facility environmental management approaches.  To train, educate, and motivate all its employees effectively, DoD should

- set appropriate values for environmental issues
- supply regular formal training to empower employees
- provide general and specialized environmental training customized for facility needs
- provide less-formal environmental education
- offer some monetary incentives and introduce environmental accountability for employees
- provide special incentives and techniques that appeal to average employees
- demonstrate the business cost savings that accrue from environmental activities.

For effective employee motivation and training, DoD must make clear at all levels that it values environmental issues, that they are important both to individual jobs and to the DoD mission.  To take these issues seriously, military personnel and civilian employees have to understand that these issues are important to DoD.  If part of the organization, such as a base operations manager, does not truly value environmental issues, attempts to train and motivate employees will be undermined.  Environmental stewardship needs to be valued in both policy and actions.

DoD should use ongoing periodic training and retraining to empower its employees, to make sure that they (1) are aware of the importance of the environmental issues, (2) know what their responsibilities are, and (3) know what DoD expects of them.  DoD should provide training customized for individual facility needs and should include general (e.g., introductory environment) and specialized (e.g., hazardous materials) courses.

Defense facilities should encourage and provide less-formal environmental education activities, such as Earth Day fairs, because these are an important ways to educate, train, and motivate employees.

DoD should make sure that appropriate incentives and environmental accountability mechanisms are in place for military personnel and civilian employees. Performance appraisals for managers and selected employees should include their environmental records, which will allow providing appropriate monetary incentives for management and will show that the organization does value environmental issues. However, direct monetary incentives for environmental performance are not necessarily appropriate or realistic for DoD. Instead, DoD should integrate environmental accountability with its customary incentives, which are primarily nonmonetary.

In addition, DoD should use special incentives and techniques that appeal to average employees and should empower employees to develop such incentives. WDWR's employee-run ECEs are an excellent model of an empowerment process. An important part of the ECE effort was the fact that the employees themselves decided what the best incentives were to motivate fellow employees and created friendly peer pressure to encourage participation. Defense facilities should develop friendly competitions around environmental performance, as WDWR did with recycling and energy, to motivate employees to do better. Given military culture, such incentives would be especially effective for motivating enlisted personnel and blue-collar civilians.

DoD should demonstrate to managers and other employees the cost savings that environmental activities can provide. This is especially important for management. While this does include actual money saved, the potential beneficial effects for DoD's core missions are more important to many DoD employees. Proactive environmental approaches could, for example, increase an installation's operational flexibility. Such demonstrations can help motivate military personnel and civilian employees to take environmental issues seriously because they show how these approaches affect the military mission.

## CONCLUDING REMARKS

Implementing integrated facility approaches to environmental management is not easy. Commercial facilities are experimenting and making some progress with such new and innovative approaches. Given DoD's size, organizational structure, culture, and other unique aspects, it is even more difficult for DoD to implement such approaches throughout its organization. Promising steps are being taken throughout DoD, but this process will take time. By implementing some of these ideas and the lessons of best commercial practices, DoD can improve its effectiveness and timeliness in implementing such approaches, which will ultimately help DoD achieve both its military and its environmental goals.

# PROCTOR & GAMBLE MEHOOPANY
# ENVIRONMENTAL MANAGEMENT CASE STUDY

This case study is based primarily on interviews of Procter & Gamble
(P&G) Mehoopany staff members that took place in October 1997.
P&G company brochures and written information were also used
when applicable. Please note that case studies are snapshots of a
particular organization at a particular time and that Mehoopany's
program has continued to evolve since the interviews. Subsequent
communications with P&G Mehoopany have indicated that, while
some of the details may have changed, the message is largely the
same.

This appendix describes P&G Mehoopany's environmental program,
emphasizing its successful implementation. Brief overviews of the
facility, its general organizational structures, and some of the environmental accomplishments are followed by discussion of the policy, goals, visions, and structural elements of the environmental
management system (EMS). Next, the appendix describes the facility's processes for environmental assessment and priority-setting, its
effectiveness at stakeholder relationships, and how it trains and
motivates its employees. A brief conclusion follows.

## CASE STUDY OVERVIEW

The largest P&G plant in the world, with about 2,700 employees
drawn from six counties, is set in a rural valley along the
Susquehanna River in Mehoopany, Pennsylvania. P&G Mehoopany
has two basic product lines: tissues and towels, and diapers. The
facility houses a diverse set of functional activities, including pulp

production at a sulfite pulp mill,[1] water purification, drinking water treatment, and wastewater treatment.  Given its diverse activities, which have a high potential environmental impact, and high visibility in the community, the facility is highly complex compared to other P&G facilities.

P&G Mehoopany has a strong, well-run, and efficient environmental program that has implemented innovative facilitywide approaches. The plant has achieved substantial reductions in air, water, and waste emissions.  It has also addressed natural resource issues, such as working with wood suppliers in sustainable forestry.  The facility has won numerous environmental awards and been recognized as a best-in-class P2 facility.  The environmental program is built on a strong corporate EMS philosophy and ethic with a total-quality environmental management (TQEM) approach.  Management is effective at integrating environmental issues into the business units, including allocating environmental costs back to them and emphasizing P2 initiatives.  The managers base their environmental decisions on strategic thinking about the long-term impacts and the economics. They have been effective at reducing the plant's environmental impact and finding cost savings from environmental initiatives, especially in the solid waste area.  The plant's very good relationships with the regulators and community feed back into increasing internal management support for additional proactive, innovative environmental approaches.  The managers effectively train and motivate the employees to support the environmental program.

## THE COMPANY

P&G produces and sells a wide range of paper, laundry, cleaning, beauty care, health care, and food and beverage products to more than five billion consumers in more than 140 countries.  The company markets approximately 300 consumer product brands, including Tide, Pampers, Ariel, Crest, Always, Whisper, Vicks, Pantene Pro-V, Oil of Olay, and Pringles.  P&G employs 110,000 people worldwide, with headquarters in Cincinnati, Ohio, and operations in 58 countries.  For the fiscal year ending June 30, 1998, P&G's worldwide net

---

[1]One of the changes since the original interview is that P&G Mehoopany no longer produces its own pulp.  Environmental practices and programs have remained in place during the transition to a nonpulp facility.

sales were over $37 billion and net earnings were $3.78 billion (P&G, 1998). P&G's primary motivation is to serve its customers.

Paper products are one of P&G's main product lines. P&G's paper products plants are located throughout North America, including facilities at Mehoopany, Pennsylvania; Albany, Georgia; Green Bay, Wisconsin; Modesto, California; Cape Girardeau, Missouri; Greenville, North Carolina; Belleville, Ontario (outside Toronto); Auburn, Maine; and Oxnard, California.

P&G's company culture and philosophy are very much focused on leadership, integrity, customers, and company reputation. The core values focus on high-quality employees, leadership, ownership,[2] integrity, being the best, and trust. Similarly, company principles include respect for all individuals, keeping company and individual interests inseparable, focusing strategically, innovation as a cornerstone of success, and being externally focused; Tables A.1 and A.2 present the full list of core values and principles. These corporate values are reflected throughout the organization and its environmental program.

In environment activities, P&G also strives to be a leader; to emphasize innovation; to focus on customer, community, and regulator relations; to value the company image and reputation; to be strategic, proactive, and forward thinking; and to promote integrity. To help facilitate these activities, the corporate organizational structure includes a fair amount of decentralized environmental authority that allows individual facilities to innovate and customize their environmental activities for local needs.

## THE FACILITY

In 1997, the P&G plant in Mehoopany, Pennsylvania, covered about 1,200 acres and had about 85 acres of roof space. The plant opened as a Charmin Paper Products Company facility in 1966. The workers living in the region at the time were employed in declining industries, especially coal mining. Charmin moved into this location to

---

[2]*Ownership* is a term of art at Mehoopany and conveys a sense of accountability and responsibility.

## Table A.1

## P&G's Core Values

| P&G is its people and the core values by which they live. |
|---|
| P&G PEOPLE. We attract and recruit the finest people in the world. We build our organization from within, promoting and rewarding people without regard to any difference unrelated to performance. We act on the conviction that the men and women of Procter & Gamble will always be our most important asset. |
| LEADERSHIP. We are all leaders in our area of responsibility, with a deep commitment to deliver leadership results. We have a clear vision of where we are going. We focus our resources to achieve leadership objectives and strategies. We develop a capability to deliver our strategies and eliminate organizational barriers. |
| OWNERSHIP. We accept personal accountability to meet the business needs, improve our systems and help others improve their effectiveness. We all act like owners, treating the Company's assets as our own and behaving with the Company's long-term success in mind. |
| INTEGRITY. We always try to do the right thing. We are honest and straightforward with each other. We operate within the letter and spirit of the law. We uphold the values and principles of P&G in every action and decision. We are data-based and intellectually honest in advocating proposals, including recognizing risks. |
| PASSION FOR WINNING. We are determined to be the best at doing what matters most. We have a healthy dissatisfaction with the status quo. We have a compelling desire to improve and to win in the marketplace. |
| TRUST. We respect our P&G colleagues, customers, and consumers and treat them as we want to be treated. We have confidence in each other's capabilities and intentions. We believe that people work best when there is a foundation of trust. |

SOURCE: P&G (undated a).

take advantage of this labor; the surrounding forestry assets, especially the mature forests; and the water in the Susquehanna River. In 1976 Charmin Paper Products Company's name was changed to The Procter & Gamble Paper Products Company.[3]

The P&G Mehoopany site has two plants, producing two basic product lines: the tissue/towel plant and the diaper plant. For management purposes, these two plants are run in a thoroughly integrated

---

[3]This report simply refers to the facility as P&G Mehoopany.

## Table A.2

## P&G's Core Principles

| These are the principles and supporting behaviors that flow from our Purpose and Core Values. |
| --- |
| WE SHOW RESPECT FOR ALL INDIVIDUALS. We believe that all individuals can and want to contribute to their fullest potential. We value differences. We inspire and enable people to achieve high expectations, standards, and challenging goals. We are honest with people about their performance. |
| THE INTERESTS OF THE COMPANY AND THE INDIVIDUAL ARE INSEPARABLE. We believe that doing what's right for the business with integrity will lead to mutual success for both the Company and the individual. Our quest for mutual success ties us together. We encourage stock ownership and ownership behavior. |
| WE ARE STRATEGICALLY FOCUSED IN OUR WORK. We operate against clearly articulated and aligned objectives and strategies. We only do work and only ask for work that adds value to the business. We simplify, standardize, and stream-line our current work whenever possible. |
| INNOVATION IS THE CORNERSTONE OF OUR SUCCESS. We place great value on big, new consumer innovations. We challenge convention and reinvent the way we do business to better win in the marketplace. |
| WE ARE EXTERNALLY FOCUSED. We develop superior understanding of con-sumers and their needs. We create and deliver products, packaging and concepts that build winning brand equities. We develop close, mutually productive rela-tionships with our customers and our suppliers. We are good corporate citizens. |
| WE VALUE PERSONAL MASTERY. We believe it is the responsibility of all individ-uals to continually develop themselves and others. We encourage and expect outstanding technical mastery and executional excellence. |
| WE SEEK TO BE THE BEST. We strive to be the best in all areas of strategic impor-tance to the Company. We benchmark our performance rigorously versus the very best internally and externally. We learn from both our successes and our failures. |
| MUTUAL INTERDEPENDENCY IS A WAY OF LIFE. We work together with confi-dence and trust across functions, sectors, categories, and geographies. We take pride in results from reapplying others' ideas. We build superior relationships with all the parties who contribute to fulfilling our Corporate purpose, including our customer, suppliers, universities, and governments. |

SOURCE: P&G (undated a).

way.[4] The Tissue/Towel Plant makes Bounty kitchen roll towels and Charmin bathroom tissues. Plant processes begin with chipping and pulping and continue through final distribution of the products. The Diaper Plant makes Pamper and Luvs disposable diapers. The diaper operation is strictly an assembly plant, drawing all inputs from other plants. Workers think of the diapers in process as carcasses, just like car assemblies.

The Mehoopany facility also maintains a major distribution space for all P&G products in the northeast part of the country; actual boundaries vary continually with market demand. P&G makes direct dock-to-dock shipments—P&G to final retailer—from this facility.

The Mehoopany facility is unusual for P&G because it has retained key support structure elements in house, including pulp production, water purification, drinking-water treatment, and wastewater treatment. The Mehoopany pulp mill was the last pulp mill owned by P&G and is now closed. Mehoopany also maintains a gas-powered 65-megawatt cogeneration plant on site to generate waste heat for drying paper in production before it goes to the converter. The facility operates this way because

- The plant is so large relative to the surrounding community that it cannot contract with anyone else close by to take on these workloads.

- Mehoopany has performed these functions well enough so that it is not worth seeking new sources, even as P&G increases its strategic focus by divestiture and outsourcing.

This facility was even more unusual in that it was a sulfite pulp mill, whose basic technology was 150 years old. This mill was rare, since only about 14 sulfite plants remain in the United States. Most U.S. pulp mills have moved toward a Kraft or sulfate approach, which is more attuned to higher-quality (e.g., writing bond) papers. However, sulfite papermaking yields a lower strength, chemically cleaner product, which is well suited for paper towels and tissues.

In 1997, Mehoopany produced about 50 percent of the pulp it needed. The remainder came from recycled pulp or other external

---

[4]All references to Mehoopany, the facility, or the plant throughout this appendix refer to this integrated site.

sources that provide the specific input attributes the facility needs to achieve the product attributes it seeks.  The wood input has to be monitored closely and the mix has to be adjusted continually because the specific attributes of inputs change continually.

As it has from the beginning, Mehoopany operates 7 days a week, 24 hours a day.  All employees own some stock.  Flexible work rules are the norm.  Pay is based on performance, not seniority or job classification.  Mehoopany was one of the first P&G plants to introduce each of these practices, which are now standard throughout P&G.  The plant is nonunion.

## Mehoopany Modules

The basic unit of business organization at Mehoopany is the *module*. In 1997, Mehoopany had about 23 modules; the exact number changes over time.  Modules are operationally focused and correspond roughly to what might normally be called a business unit. Some examples are

- environmental[5]
- process services[6]
- Bounty conversion[7]
- papermaking
- engineering
- technology
- wood supply.

A module's operations manager is responsible for its environmental results.  The modules are the focus of specific environmental plans on site.  These issues will be discussed more below.

---

[5]This module is discussed in more detail later.

[6]This module provides pulp mill, utility, and wastewater services for the whole site (note the status of pulp as a basic ancillary to the main business of the plant, which is producing retail consumer products).

[7]This module cuts Bounty paper from gigantic rolls and assembles it into individual rolls suitable for home use.

## Teams

The plant uses a flat ownership model with cross-functional teams, and these lie at the heart of much decisionmaking. In the environmental area, teams within Mehoopany bring together environmental people and engineers; integrate the environmental and line modules; and integrate input from different paper product sites within P&G, including P&G headquarters in Cincinnati. Teams tend to be small (six or so) and senior. The members represent their own organizations and can also act on their behalf. Some teams go on for years; others address a simple issue and disband. Their longevity depends on their demonstrated utility.

The teams do not actually make decisions, but feed information and recommendations to a single decisionmaker, who retains ultimate responsibility. The idea is to encourage bottom-up initiative through the teams by encouraging them to formulate concepts for senior review, although the senior official makes the final decision. This approach promotes employee empowerment and helps Mehoopany develop more-junior talent that will grow into the leadership in the future. While this occurs, the current leadership retains ultimate responsibility. For example, teams developed the basic approaches that led to recent reductions in use of $NO_x$ and chlorine at Mehoopany; the general plant manager ultimately made the specific decision in each case. This manager is responsible for controlling resources on the site and, as part of this responsibility, makes the decisions that ultimately affect resource allocation.

Sector teams across different P&G facilities provide the strongest links between Mehoopany and the rest of P&G on environmental policy. The North American paper team is one of the strongest and most effective, followed by North American soap. Outside North America, sector teams form by region, not product. All the teams look across P&G to find common issues and to promote efficiency by diffusing ideas. Plant members are supported by legal, regulatory, and environmental health and safety input from P&G headquarters in Cincinnati. Key corporate environmental policies and activities have come from these sector teams, such as the "Designing Waste Out" initiative, which started within a couple of the sector teams and spread to the whole company because it succeeded in these sectors.

## Forestry Group

In 1997, Mehoopany maintained a forestry group of ten professionals as part of its procurement module (wood supply). This module acquired wood and prepared it for pulp production. The forestry group assured a continuing, reliable supply, giving cost and quality close attention. It also assisted suppliers in practicing forestry in a way that is compatible with P&G's values and needs. The group has addressed safety issues for ten years.

## GENERAL ENVIRONMENTAL INFORMATION AND ACHIEVEMENTS

The Mehoopany plant has a very active and aggressive environmental performance record and program in terms of environmental and financial achievements and effort. In 1996, P&G spent $23.5 million on environmental improvement operating costs (including salaries) at the facility. With offsets from the waste reduction and recovery programs, such as in solid waste and energy, the plant recouped about half the investment, so the total environmental facility spending was about $11 to 12 million in 1996.

The plant has received several environmental achievement awards, including the Pennsylvania Department of Environmental Protection (DEP) 1996 Pollution Prevention (P2) Recognition, two different Pennsylvania Governor's awards, the U.S. Environmental Protection Agency 33/50 Success Story in 1996, and Renew America's *Environmental Success Index* from 1990–1997 for P2 results.

Mehoopany has substantially reduced its air, water, and waste emissions (see Table A.3). For example, overall site air emissions have been reduced 80 percent since the plant started up. The plant's solid waste reduction and recovery program is very aggressive. Mehoopany has traditionally recovered and sold or reused 90 to 92 percent of its waste streams. Although much of the reuse is in the form of broke, the waste paper that is traditionally put back into the pulping process in papermaking, the actual proportion of reuse of other materials is high. The absolute value of the waste sold or reused has grown substantially, yielding a net cost earnings of over $2.5 million in 1996 and 1997 (see Figure A.1).

## Table A.3

## P&G Mehoopany Environmental Summary Information

**OVERALL SITE**

We have a strong history of environmental performance.  Our people are proud of our accomplishments in "Treating Nature as a Customer."

Each year we spend over $13 million for environmental protection.

Since start up, we have invested more than $60 million in capital for environmental equipment.

Some 50 people work full time for environmental protection.

We don't use recycled paper from off-site in our paper products.  We have explored this, but haven't found a high quality, cost effective source for recycled fiber that fits our consumers' desire for our high quality products.  Between 5–10% of our product is made from internally recycled paper (broke).

Our pulp is made without chlorine.  We are one of the few pulp producers in the US to have completely eliminated chlorine from the bleaching process.  We use a substitute material that breaks down into air and water.

The Mehoopany site has been recognized by external groups and agencies.  Recent recognition includes:

* PA Governor's Waste Minimization Awards (1989 and 1994)

* PA Department of Environmental Protection 1996 "Pollution Prevention Recognition"

* Renew America's Environmental Success Index (1990–1996)

* US EPA "33/50" Success Stories—for chlorine elimination (1996)

**AIR QUALITY**

Overall site air emissions have been reduced by 80% since initial start-up.

We have recently (1997) completed a $4 million project to further reduce sulfur dioxide emissions from our pulping process.

The odor you can sometimes smell comes from our pulping process.  We've taken steps to reduce the odor and have made lots of progress in the past few years.  In 1995, we installed an odor control system that has helped, not eliminated, the odors.  Reducing the odor further is one of our top site environment priorities.  A team is working on this now.

Most of the emission you can see at the site is steam from the drying of paper.

**Table A.3—Continued**

| WATER QUALITY |
|---|
| A multi-million dollar wastewater treatment plant protects the Susquehanna River. Each year we employ scientists from the Academy of Natural Sciences of Philadelphia to study the fish and insects living above and below the plant. Their studies over the past 30 years tells us we are having no negative effects on the health of the River. |
| We typically operate at less than 1/2 of permitted discharge levels. |
| Nutrients are an important issue to the Chesapeake Bay, which gets much of its fresh water from the Susquehanna River. We've reduced our nutrient (nitrogen) discharge to the river by 40% in the past few years. |
| We withdraw roughly 12 million gallons per day from the Susquehanna River, and return over 90% of this back to the river after treatment. (The remaining 10% is vented as steam or water vapor in the drying of paper) |
| Our water withdrawal represents less than half of one percent of the river flow during normal conditions. |

SOURCE: P&G Mehoopany (undated c).

In 1997, P&G used little chlorine and no elemental chlorine in its Mehoopany operations because of a decision made in the early 1990s to shift to chlorine-free bleaching processes. Mehoopany was one of the few U.S. pulp producers to eliminate chlorine from the bleaching process, first shifting the broke and then the entire paper process. No regulations governed this chlorine reduction, so the decision was made based more on strategy than on pure cost. A range of issues helped management decide that this elimination was good for long-term business health, including public affairs difficulties, the state and cost of treatment technologies, and the uncertainty about health issues and future regulatory impact. This remains the largest change in environmental policy undertaken at the plant.

## OVERVIEW OF P&G'S EMS

P&G has a proactive corporate environmental policy and management system, which the Mehoopany facility has built on to develop and implement its own site program. The corporate philosophy and support of environmental issues have helped facilitate a strong environmental program at Mehoopany.

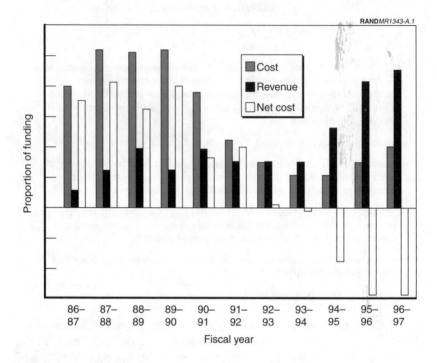

SOURCE: P&G.

**Figure A.1—Waste Disposal Costs versus Waste Revenue**

To manage the environmental impact of its operation, P&G has a global EMS for all its facilities. The EMS program is built on a framework that includes a corporate environmental quality policy, standards of performance, standard operating procedures, continuous improvement, current best approaches, and annual audits.

The overall environmental quality policy is designed to facilitate the improvement of the environmental quality of its products, packaging, and operations around the world (see Table A.4). This policy is the foundation of the EMS. Elements of the policy are translated into system requirements that are implemented as standards for all facilities. These standards are further developed into standard operating procedures for actual site implementation. Current best

## Table A.4

## P&G's Environmental Quality Policy

Procter & Gamble is committed to providing products of superior quality and value that best fill the needs of the world's consumers.  As a part of this, Procter & Gamble continually strives to improve the environmental quality of its products, packaging, and operations around the world.  To carry out this commitment, it is Procter & Gamble's policy to:

**Ensure our products, packaging, and operations are safe for our employees, consumers, and the environment.**

**Reduce, or prevent, the environmental impact of our products and packaging in their design, manufacture, distribution, use, and disposal whenever possible.** We take a leading role in developing innovative, practical solutions to environmental issues related to our products, packaging, and process. We support the sustainable use of resources and actively encourage reuse, recycling, and composting. We share experiences and expertise and offer assistance to others who may contribute to progress in achieving environmental goals.

**Meet or exceed the requirements of all environmental laws and regulations.** We use environmentally sound practices, even in the absence of governmental standards. We cooperate with governments in analyzing environmental issues and developing cost-effective, scientifically based solutions and standards.

**Continually assess our environmental technology and programs, and monitor progress toward environmental goals.** We develop and use state-of-the-art science and product life cycle assessment, from raw materials through disposal, to assess environmental quality.

**Provide our consumers, customer, employees, communities, public interest groups, and others with relevant and appropriate factual information about the environmental quality of Procter & Gamble products, packaging, and operations.** We seek to establish and nurture open, honest, and timely communications and strive to be responsive to concerns.

**Ensure every employee understands and is responsible and accountable for incorporating environmental quality considerations in daily business activities.** We encourage, recognize, and reward individual and team leadership effort to improve environmental quality. We also encourage employees to reflect their commitment to environmental quality outside of work.

**Have operating policies, programs, and resources in place to implement our environmental quality policy.**

SOURCE:  P&G (undated b).

approaches in documentation, training programs, and other techniques support the standards implementation.

Continuous improvement involves ongoing feedback on performance, measurements of accomplishment, and evolving changes in the overall system. Annual environmental audits fuel this process, and customers and other stakeholders are central to it. This EMS, relying on continuous improvement, is basically a total quality management (TQM) process.

With the assistance of a third-party auditor, Environmental Resources Management, Inc. (ERM), P&G conducted a detailed assessment of its EMS between June 1996 and February 1997, comparing the EMS with ISO 14001 requirements (see P&G, no date). ERM reviewed and evaluated the relevant documentation and records; formally interviewed corporate and regional personnel; and visited typical P&G manufacturing facilities in the United States, Mexico, Japan, and Italy to verify EMS implementation and documentation. Table A.5 summarizes ERM's findings, comparing the building blocks of the EMS to the five major categories of performance outlined in the ISO 14001 standard. ERM also identified some areas needing improvement, which P&G then addressed. The resulting changes allowed the audited P&G facilities to meet or exceed the intent of ISO 14001 in all subcategories of the standard (see Table A.6).

Thus, the comparison concluded that P&G's existing EMS met the intent of ISO 14001 in all but one or two details, and the company adjusted its process to make the correspondence complete. After going through this process in 1997, P&G saw no reason to seek ISO 14001 certification. The company considered self-certification but could not find any economic justification for that, either.

But internal environmental audits continue on a regular basis. A team with members from the plant being audited, corporate headquarters, and other plants makes the actual environmental audits. At any given site, the auditing team is led locally one year, and by corporate headquarters the next, and so on. Team reviewers have one year on, then one off. Mehoopany's environmental manager has been involved in audits at plants in Toronto and California. He has learned a great deal from these that he could use at Mehoopany.

**Table A.5**

**Comparison of P&G's Global EMS with ISO 14001**

| ISO 14001 | Compared to | Procter & Gamble's Global EMS |
|---|---|---|
| ISO requires a written policy, which guides company decisionmaking. It must exist, and it must be widely communicated. | Environmental policy | Procter & Gamble's policy includes necessary commitments and drives continuous improvement. It is widely communicated. |
| A systematic, broad-based process must exist to identify, evaluate, and prioritize environmental aspects/impacts that need improvement. | Planning | This is part of Procter & Gamble's Audit/Rating Process. Key aspects are identified, and system capability is verified. |
| ISO requires that resources, roles, and responsibilities be clearly defined. Documents and operational controls must be in place to drive results. Processes to prevent or mitigate accidents must exist. | Implementation & operations | Procter & Gamble's EMS clearly defines roles and responsibilities. Critical elements of the EMS are documented and well communicated to site personnel. Emergency response systems are in place. |
| Performance is verified against compliance requirements and stated objectives. Outstanding issues are worked and appropriate records are maintained. | Checking & corrective action | Annual EMS audits are conducted to verify performance. Clear improvement plans are expected. Compliance issues are remedied within 12 months. |
| Top management must conduct documented EMS reviews to address the possible need for modifications due to changing situations. | Management review | Global, regional, and local site managers review the EMS annually to help drive future risk reduction and overall environmental performance improvement. |

SOURCE: P&G.

Table A.6

Areas in Which P&G EMS Meets or Exceeds ISO 14001

| P&G Fully Meets the Intent of ISO 14001 | | P&G Goes Beyond the Intent of ISO 14001 | |
| --- | --- | --- | --- |
| Communication | Monitor & Measure | Environmental Policy | Structure, Responsibility |
| EMS Documentation | Corrective Action | Environmental Aspects | Training & Competence |
| Document Control | Management Review | Legal, Other Requirements | Emergency Response |
| Operational Control | | Objectives & Targets | Record Keeping |
| | | Management Programs | EMS Audits |

SOURCE: P&G.

The goal of this audit process is to yield measures that can be used to drive improvement over time. Strictly speaking, scores are difficult to compare across locations, but the human temptation to compete is irrepressible. Since P&G's facilities audit one another, objectivity could be an issue. However, the corporation has thoroughly trained a small group of people to avoid bias, with their own performance as auditors calibrated as part of a formal internal certification. The Mehoopany environmental staff has learned a lot about objectivity from these auditors over time while working with them on audits. Mehoopany environmental staff has found this process to be useful for helping to improve the environmental program over time. Again, the key is ultimately to improve at home.

This process is costly. It takes three full days to generate the measures needed on Mehoopany itself. Complexity takes on a special meaning in this context; more-complex operations are harder to audit and hence harder to benchmark across sites. Simplifying processes leads to better performance in part because it makes continuous improvement, driven by this auditing process, easier to achieve. In 1997, Mehoopany was considered a highly complex site within P&G because of its pulping mill's environmental impact and its high visibility in the community.

## MEHOOPANY'S ENVIRONMENTAL POLICY, PHILOSOPHY, AND PRINCIPLES

Speaking broadly, the Mehoopany facility is organized around six values:

- safety and the environment
- quality
- cost
- production (quantity)
- organizational capacity and development, and productivity (development of skills and leadership; production per unit of input)
- appearance.

Management monitors these aspects quite closely and has metrics for each. These values also factor strongly in the development of the environmental program.

In developing its facility EMS, Mehoopany also created an overarching vision to help guide its actions (see Table A.7), as well as using the general P&G Environmental Quality Policy (see Table A.4). The plant's policy, principles and implementation program also follow a basic TQM-TQEM framework.[8] As a result, four main themes drive Mehoopany's environmental program:

1. **Good principles and values as a company.** These principles include ownership, integrity, and trust. *Ownership* focuses on total business ownership of environmental aspects and the personal responsibility and accountability of individuals. *Integrity* means doing what is right and obeying the letter and spirit of the law. *Trust* refers to respecting the customers and treating them as you would want to be treated—the culture focuses on the customer.

2. **Environmental success and business success are absolutely linked.** Environmental performance is viewed as a business strategy. Business and environmental staff are partners linked in setting the direction for the site. The business units internalize environmental costs as much as possible. The consistent strategy is to take a "zero loss/total quality approach."[9]

3. **Broad ownership of all employees key to success.** Employees are networked across the site with respect to environmental issues. The operation owns environmental issues. Training, awareness building, and recognition are important parts of this process. Environmental teams also are important part of this approach.

4. **Environmental systems approach.** The fundamental environmental structure, both for the company as a whole and for Mehoopany, is to have a good broad EMS framework with a site "system ownership" focus. The focus is on maintaining owner-

---

[8]For more details on the relationships of TQM and TQEM frameworks, see the numerous materials on this topic, such as Jackson (1997), Wever (1996), and Wever and Vorhauer (1993).

[9]This quote and these aspects are from P&G Mehoopany (1997b).

ship and using a systems approach to develop and implement solutions for environmental issues.

Mehoopany management has made these values and guidance visible and checks against them daily in decisionmaking. Employees at

### Table A.7

### Mehoopany Environmental Vision

We are visionaries and broad in our approach to environmental protection. Today's actions move us toward greater knowledge, better technologies, and more reliable systems, all ingredients to our products—a safe and clean environment for our employees, community, and future generations, and full public acceptance of our operations.

Elimination of waste is a principal thrust. Air emissions, solid wastes, and wastewaters have declined to a minimum level in volume, strength, and hazard. We beneficially use all unavoidable solid wastes. We are moving well toward our goal of no landfill use.

Treatment and disposal systems for those wastes we can't avoid are reliable. Our performance is well within all environmental needs and regulatory expectations. Unplanned releases, spills, and permit deviations are extremely rare, and repeat incidents are non-existent. Our plant operations virtually cannot be seen, smelled or heard from offsite. Our total wood resource is managed in partnership with others for environmental protection, sustainability, ecosystem health, and long-term availability.

Chemicals are fully understood by users, and our risk management system prevents harmful impacts on our employees, products, the environment, and the community. Our use of hazardous chemicals is minimal. Our neighbors are comfortable with their knowledge of our chemicals and safety related systems. Together we are prepared to deal effectively with any unexpected situations.

Our environmental customers express satisfaction and pride in our performance. Relationships with these customers reflect trust, confidence, and openness. Our customers seek us out for environmental expertise and help, and contacts are continuing rather than incident-related. Environmental customers can obtain information, their feedback counts, and improvements follow identified opportunities.

Ownership for our environmental results is with those positioned to produce them—all site personnel operating from the principle—do what's right—and finding reward in doing so.

The Mehoopany Environmental Group

November 1995

SOURCE: Mehoopany Environmental Group (1995).

all levels check to see if their own actions are consistent with this guidance.

P&G seeks to associate its name with cleanliness, health, and nutrition in the products that it designs, manufactures, and sells to retail customers. The company sees environmental performance as having a natural fit with these values, flowing from them and reinforcing them. Given the general P&G culture, corporate interest in pursuing environmental performance feels natural.

Mehoopany had an employee contest to develop an environmental motto for the facility; the winner was "treating nature as a customer." This is a restatement of P&G's view of itself as a consumer products company, for which the customer is always at center stage. The motto effectively turns the spotlight to a new customer—the environment itself. This motto came from an employee with a broad and deep appreciation of P&G's culture.

In implementing its environmental policy, Mehoopany has four basic principles to help guide many of its decisions:

1. **Comply with all environmental laws and regulations.**

2. **Protect the environment as much as possible**, which means "doing the right thing," going beyond laws and regulations, and considering risk reduction to be an important customer.

3. **Work in partnership with internal and external customers,** including regulators, neighbors, the community, and the environment itself (the river, forests, etc.).

4. **Aggressively pursue P2**, including trying to minimize waste, management costs, and lost material value.

Given its values, culture, and approach, Mehoopany seeks ways to turn environmental excellence into a competitive advantage. Some of these ways include

- Enabling a focus on the core business, which includes providing a way to reinforce the core P&G values and principles.

- Providing a vehicle for promoting a better understanding of how production processes work, opening the door for improving them. Essentially, this is a TQM approach that reduces waste and rework.

- Integrating environmental aspects into the TQM approach.

- Creating a proactive environment policy that removes regulators from the decision space and helps focus high-level decisionmaking attention on core corporate issues.

- Promoting a better relationship with employees in terms of the quality of the working conditions and with the community in terms of the quality of its environment.

- Promoting long-term business health by thinking and acting strategically with a long-term vision and by removing problems that could threaten the business over the longer term.  This strategic approach includes considering external stakeholders.[10]

## STRUCTURE OF ENVIRONMENTAL ORGANIZATIONS

Mehoopany has about 50 people working on environmental issues. Eight are part of the environmental group; the rest work directly in the other business modules at Mehoopany.

### Mehoopany Environmental Group

The Mehoopany Environmental Group (MEG) is the staff support group with overall responsibility for environmental issues, reporting directly to the plant manager.  MEG's leader is the site facility environmental manager.  Group members oversee all environmental policy, management, operations, and training on site.  The facility environmental manager is responsible for understanding the applicable company and government requirements, evaluating the site's ability to meet those requirements, and developing improvement plans.  The group's personnel tend to align themselves by medium and by business unit.

The MEG staff works with the business modules, which retain line responsibility and control of resources on the line.  Almost all of

---

[10]Odor control is an example.  P&G has worked to reduce the sulfurous odor traditionally associated with papermaking, despite the fact that no regulations govern such odor.  Cutting it now could reduce the probability of future regulation.  Odor reduction has been justified on these grounds all along without reference to cost.  Chlorine use was also reduced more to preserve future options than in response to a formal economic analysis.

MEG's budget (80 to 90 percent) covers its staff. The business modules actually provide the money for this budget; each unit's share is calculated annually using a rough formula. The business modules do the day-to-day environmental work, providing MEG the operational information and budget to support it.

As the cheerleader for environmental issues at Mehoopany, MEG is working to build environmental ownership within each module. The operations manager for each is responsible for its environmental results, just as he is responsible for such other core areas as safety and quality. An operations manager delegates environmental responsibilities within the module.

MEG is trying to get each module to write an environmental improvement plan (described later in detail) as a way of defining and sustaining a clear sense of module ownership of environmental policy. At Mehoopany, owning a policy means being accountable for its implementation and success.

## Process Services Module Environmental Product Team

The Process Services Module (PSM) makes pulp, provides the site's steam and water, and treats wastewater. This module thus faces the largest environmental issues of any of the service modules. Indeed, these issues are integral to its day-to-day operations. The module employs about 250 people.

To deal with its environmental issues, this module has formed the Environmental Product Team (EPT), which has helped make PSM the most successful module at developing an environmental improvement plan and at taking ownership for environmental issues. The EPT mission is to be

> a champion and maintain a focus for the Process Services Module on those environmental areas that have a direct impact on our environmental customers as measured through our environmental reliability. This work is done through our current leadership structure. (P&G Mehoopany, 1997c.)

## Solid Waste Utilization Task Force

Mehoopany's Solid Waste Utilization Task Force has been instrumental in the facility's high success rate in reducing the amount of solid waste disposed of and in achieving the related cost savings. Task force members represent key business units, energy, MEG, and finance, with half coming from the plant floor. The task force develops strategy and priorities for waste minimization. The members have made sure that waste revenues and costs are directly costed back to the appropriate business units. An important part of the effort has been helping to implement the "three Rs" (Reduce, Reuse, and Recycle) throughout the plant and assisting development and implementation of P2 ideas for solid waste.

The task force also helped develop the Designing Waste Out team and initiatives. The team focuses on redesigning products and processes to minimize waste. This idea has been transferred to the corporation as a whole, with strong participation from P&G's European facilities. Designing Waste Out is a high priority at Mehoopany and throughout P&G.

## ASSESSMENT AND PRIORITY SETTING

An important part of the implementation process of the Mehoopany EMS is figuring out which activities to initiate and when. Mehoopany uses a standard TQM approach to set general priorities for all activities, including environmental activities. This general system routinely identifies areas for "breakthrough" investment. Although these have included environmental investments in the past, none did so in 1997.

Compliance is the bedrock of corporate environmental policy. Nothing else happens until this is assured. P&G works hard to verify this in truth and in appearance and has reaped a good relationship with regulators as a result. Mehoopany errs on the conservative side to eliminate any doubt about its compliance.

As part of its implementation process, plant management also makes its principles visible to everyone and exercises them in daily decisions. When tough situations arise, decisionmakers appeal to the principles to find an outcome compatible with as many as possible. For example, to manage toxic chemicals, Mehoopany has checked individual chemicals against a list of regulated chemicals and stopped emissions of any chemicals that could yield toxic levels of emissions over the long term. The principles applied are to do the right thing and to avoid any significant environmental effect.

Mehoopany has also justified P2 initiatives in implementing this approach without formal economic analysis. On one occasion, about 10 years ago, Mehoopany curtailed production during a period of particularly low water to avoid emissions at toxic levels. Again, this decision flowed from strict application of principles. The approach succeeded because Mehoopany had defined its boundaries clearly in advance so that no one could object effectively when a serious problem arose.

Members of the operational, engineering, and environmental staffs work together to make decisions about environmental issues, such as P2 activities. Although the plant manager ultimately decides when more-expensive environmental investments are proposed, there is a good process to ensure alignment between the environmental group and the plant manager.

## USING BUSINESS GOALS TO JUSTIFY ENVIRONMENTAL ACTIONS

Another important part of implementing the environmental policy is finding ways to contribute to traditional business goals. To do this, Mehoopany has focused more on strategy and broad thinking than on specific cost measurements, which can be hard to compute for environmental concerns. The specific arguments included the following:

- P2 and other proactive policies help P&G management stay focused on the company's core issues by avoiding distracting and resource-consuming conflicts with regulators.

- Proactive policies help build relationships with external stakeholders by contributing to trust. This simplifies other problems by reducing regulation and oversight and making them less onerous when they do occur.

- Partnerships with regulators have led to an especially good relationship with Pennsylvania regulators, who have been able to target their work with the facility more effectively, confident that P&G will follow the regulations. Essentially, the plant is taking advantage of an operational two-tier regulatory system.

- Avoiding conflict with regulators allows P&G to work out solutions on its own schedule and without immediate constraints, which increases the likelihood that P&G will find the best solution to a problem. This is especially compelling when P&G anticipates expanded regulation in the future and wants to approach this prospect on its own terms.

- P&G explicitly recognizes managers who can reduce complexity, because environmental results are part of the performance system. In general, anything that leads to emissions increases complexity because it introduces regulators and all the in-house overhead required to serve them. It is better never to get into this situation in the first place.

- Environmental policy and performance protect P&G's franchise to conduct business over the long term. Until environmental issues have been disposed of, the normal business is at risk.

These points are not independent; even when they appear to be at odds, they tend to support one another. Some of these business practices are P&G's and some are unique to the Mehoopany plant.

In the end, the teams that organize policy issues for final decisions justify their recommendations around a variety of criteria, such as

- cost

- ease and/or complexity of operations (simpler is better)

- likely effects on external customers (stand in their shoes and ask how you would feel in the face of different decisions)

- what is the right thing to do, given Mehoopany's basic principles, including doing prevention at the source as much as possible.

A recent example of how MEG staff applies this thinking in making specific decision is the reduction in the plant's use of chlorine and ammonium nitrogen. Reducing chlorine use avoided treatment expenses and allowed Mehoopany to address a problem that would have to be resolved eventually anyway. Since evolving science showed that ammonium nitrogen could be harmful to the ecosystem under certain conditions, the plant chose to reduce its use of this chemical. Even though regulations did not require this, Mehoopany chose to do the right thing. This also allowed the plant to maintain the initiative, and hence control, even though near-term costs clearly increased. The long-term effects were not specifically quantified, but

Mehoopany perceived the change as a source of business advantage, given the potential long-term risks and costs.

Similarly, Mehoopany has made a strategic decision to favor incineration over land disposal, even though incineration appears to cost more. Management decided to pursue the use of a waste-to-energy facility because land disposal poses too many uncertainties, especially with respect to liabilities. This eliminated high-end risk. This decision was made without formal cost analysis because the uncertainties associated with land disposal could not be formally laid out.

Community concerns have led Mehoopany to invest $2.5 million in reducing odor, without any formal economic justification. And because the community still complains about odor at times, even though it has improved significantly over time, the plant is considering additional actions. No regulations even play here, although they could in the future. Decisions on odor are being made strictly on the basis of subjective judgments about the value of community support and the potential for future restrictions.

On the other hand, changes in the process of producing diapers were motivated by cost considerations. What Mehoopany can do after the product is designed is limited, but changing cutting patterns and the width of paper rolls used to manufacture diapers cut the amount of waste paper, thereby justifying the additional cost.

Mehoopany managers are more open to broad, strategic arguments when the implications for capital requirements or effects on operations are smaller. Whenever possible, the environmental manager looks for P2 candidates that have low investment costs. In these cases, savings need not even be discussed.

That said, Mehoopany provides many examples of ways in which environmental activities have cut total costs. For example, the plant currently invests $23 million a year in environmental activities but recoups about half of that investment through their revenues and implicit benefits, such as actual sales of waste and displacement of expensive fuel oil. By cutting net environmental expenditures in half, some actions have explicitly benefited the bottom line. Figure A.1 shows how the contribution of waste revenues to the bottom line has grown, year by year, over the last decade or so.

Economic and strategic arguments for change and complexity play different roles in justifying and choosing environmental initiatives.

On the one hand, specific solid waste issues are much easier to address because they all boil down to how much disposal costs, and air and water issues are more difficult because the performance standards are more complex. But on the other hand, economic arguments can themselves be complex and confusing, so more-strategic arguments can carry more weight with Mehoopany management, if presented effectively.

## POLLUTION PREVENTION

P2 is an important part of Mehoopany's environmental program. The plant justifies P2 through such factors as reduced regulatory requirements, reduced use of valuable raw materials, and reduced community impact. The long-term complexity of issues at the facility and the operational value of the effort also are factors in P2 activities. MEG receives broad operational support on P2 decisions from the plant manager.

Solid waste P2 has been easier because the benefits are easier for MEG to demonstrate, while the benefits of air and water P2 are less easy to show. To help with this problem, Mehoopany developed a simple matrix several years ago to rank alternatives according to their appropriateness for P2 actions. A brief review of Mehoopany's actions since then reveals that Mehoopany has generally acted on the recommendations generated by this matrix.

The matrix has three columns of criteria:

- Cost: operating, capital, disposal
- Risk: effects on environment, health, safety, business risk, complexity
- Regulation: current and future potential

Then Mehoopany identifies eight potential target areas for action as rows in the matrix:

- For air: $SO_2$, $NO_X$, Particulates, Chloroform, Odor
- For water: BOD/ton of pulp, ammonia, sulfite liquor carryover to treatment

For each target area, the analysis asked whether cost, risk, and regulatory concerns were high, medium, or low. Filling in the answers filled out the matrix provided a simple summary judgment of which were the biggest problems and hence deserved the most management emphasis in the search for P2 candidates. The final product of the assessment is a "hit list" for potential P2 actions.

## ASSESSMENT TOOLS

Mehoopany's staff uses a range of analytical, planning, and computerized tools to help assess progress and identify priorities for environmental activities. Most of these tools are unique to Mehoopany, although some are used companywide. This section explains four main tools:

- the environmental key element assessment (KEA), an aggregate facilitywide assessment that P&G uses corporatewide
- the module environmental improvement plan, an planning tool for business units
- EPT's efficient tracking and management of environmental issues
- the Chemical Safety Management System (CHEMS).

### P&G's Environmental KEA

P&G uses KEAs to evaluate systems and how well they are doing on environmental issues, as well as safety and quality issues. Each assessment yields a plantwide environmental "KEA number." This number is calculated once a year at every P&G paper plant, using the same formula. Facilities help audit each other. The process takes three days (as does calculation of the safety KEA). The company's facility standard for the environmental KEA is 8 (10 being highest).

The various facilities have a friendly competition over their annual KEA numbers, although the main goal of the competition is for each facility to better its own KEA each year. Some plants are at a disadvantage in this competition because of the complexity of their environmental issues. Mehoopany is a high-complexity site.

The environmental KEA is calculated based on performance standards in five areas:

1. **Government and public relations**: compliance, inspections, community relationships, etc.

2. **People capacity**: leadership, training, accountability, program support and expectations, etc.

3. **Direct environmental impact**: monitoring emissions (air, water, solids), assessment of waste management, management of process change, etc.

4. **Incident prevention**: a prevention plan, special risk programs for specific chemicals on site, emergency response plans and training, spill protection, etc.

5. **Continuous improvement**: audit frequency and follow-up, waste and cost reduction, goals and measurement progress, reduction of the complexity related to such environmental effects as disposal and recycling, etc.

Measurements are calculated for the activities and performance in each of the five areas. These results are combined to determine the site-level KEA number.

Mehoopany uses a range of monthly and periodic metrics to help manage its environmental program, to calculate progress for these standards, and to calculate the yearly environmental KEA. The plant regularly tracks environmental measures in such areas as management, air quality, water quality, solid waste, and toxic and/or hazardous waste. These 17 monthly measures are shown in Table A.8. The plant has good measures of pollution generation by medium, and the staff uses these measures effectively. However, in 1997, the plant's integrated facilitywide measures were not yet very good, since these are very hard to develop. KEA is the closest the plant came. MEG also lacked specific metrics for P2 but tracked it by looking at trends. Members of the MEG staff have been working to develop better metrics, especially for P2 activities and at the site level.

## Module Environmental Improvement Plans

Mehoopany uses module environmental improvement plans as a tool for assessing environmental priorities, tracking results, and managing activities. Each plan should include the following items:

- objectives and a basic sense of direction—what makes a change "good"
- specific goals and plans
- specific responsibilities for organizations and individuals
- identification of people knowledgeable about the relevant policies
- measurement and communication of results
- plans for internal assessment and feedback, independent of any external oversight
- standards systematically attained.

**Table A.8**

**Environmental Performance Measures—P&G Mehoopany**

|  | Measures | Units |
|---|---|---|
| Management | Assessment rating | 1–10 |
|  | Complexity rating | 1–10 |
|  | Compliance |  |
|  | —Actions | Number |
|  | —Chronic | Number |
|  | Incidents (P&G) | Number |
|  | Total waste to environment | MTPY |
|  | Public perception | 1–10 |
|  | Costs |  |
|  | —Net[a] | $ M |
|  | —Recovered | $ M |
| Air quality | Emissions (DER inv.) | Mtons |
|  | Incident releases | Lbs |
| Water quality | Discharges (NPDES) | Tons |
| Solid waste | Disposal | Mtons |
|  | Beneficial use | % |
| Toxic/hazardous waste | Hazardous waste generation | Tons |
|  | SARA releases | Tons |
|  | Chlorine used (as $Cl_2$) | Tons |

SOURCE: P&G

NOTE: Annual data on each category are tracked from 1983 to the present.

[a]Total recovery.

The environmental manager would like each module to have such a plan. PSM has been the most successful at developing such a plan and taking ownership, that is, responsibility, for environmental issues. The operations manager "owns" environmental policy for his or her module but does not prepare its improvement plan. This is done instead by a member of the module staff. MEG acts as a cheerleader, supporting this effort from a distance and offering technical assistance as needed. PSM's reliability leader, who developed its improvement plan, serves as a single point of contact and acts as both a leader and a cheerleader for the environmental perspective.

Developing these plans is integral to the environmental manager's efforts to maintain a network of contacts between the MEG and the business units. The network tends to include environmentally oriented personnel in each module, not necessarily the operating managers. But ownership can become somewhat ambiguous. Operating managers, by definition, are responsible for all performance, including environmental performance, in their modules. One of the six basic attributes considered in manager's performance reviews is environmental issues. But environmental specialists tend to design improvement plans for these modules and to participate in the broader Mehoopany environmental network.

## PSM EPT Activities

EPT links the key players in PSM and creates, "owns," and manages the module's environmental improvement plan, among many other things. This team has existed since the late 1980s and currently meets monthly or as needed. Regular members are

- a representative from each operating department (pulp, boiler house, and environmental services)
- a representative from the module's Process Technology Group, to help weigh priorities
- a representative from the MEG, who provides information on external regulatory and community issues and links this team to teams at other sites
- the reliability leader for the module.

The team pulls in others as needed.  For example, the business unit responsible for the wastewater treatment plant sits in when water is at issue.  People may substitute for the principals but must come prepared to speak for their departments, with full authority to make decisions.  Subgroups may meet separately to discuss specific issues. At each team meeting, the team reviews results from the previous month's meetings, works on an action plan for the next 12 to 18 months, and allocates resources to execute plans.

The improvement plan has a simple TQM structure.  It starts by identifying the current state, the desired future state, and the known gaps between these states.  The gap analysis provides a basis for identifying specific action items to close the gap.  These become strategies that include

- specific action steps, sometime broken into key subelements
- a responsible party for each step
- a standard to strive for each step
- the actual status of each step
- classification of each step by priority (breakthrough, control and improve, or backlog).

The team reviews each step at least quarterly to track progress toward the desired state.

The EPT plan also identifies a set of 14 specific measures that the team tracks monthly.  Four of these are compliance driven; 10 are not.  The current list focuses on wastewater, but the team plans to add variables for air and solid waste issues.  For each measure, the team identifies

- the permit specifications
- the average level for the month
- the standard deviation for the month
- a delta z score (a measure of change from the previous month)
- a yes-no assessment of whether the variable is within bounds.

Each month, the team records the proportion of variables, all equally weighted, that are within bounds; this proportion becomes the measure of "environmental product reliability" for the module.  The team tracks this proportion over time and compares the value for each period with a "target" level. The target can and does vary by month to reflect an assessment of what the team thinks the module could reasonably expect to reach in that month. In effect, this approach to metrics normalizes the proportion so that a score of 100 percent is a "stretch" goal and the target is a goal considered achievable within existing constraints. The team reports its findings on each variable and the summary proportion score to the PSM operations manager and to teams through the module every month.

When a variable fails to make its target level, the team also analyzes the failure, using a Pareto chart to locate the biggest problems. A cause-and-effect analysis then traces the failure to its root causes. For each root cause, the team identifies plan adjustments, a schedule for making them, and a responsible person.

The team then tracks the status of action items that fall out of the gap analysis, the evaluation of failures, and the changes made. Each item has a named owner who can be held accountable for its status. All the steps in this process are documented and tracked with a efficient computerized system, available to all relevant staff, that organizes these tools through simple charts and graphs. The system is a good tool for assessing current and potential future environmental issues and initiatives.

EPT also manages a home page that allows anyone on the Mehoopany in-house network to get information on a wide variety of environmentally relevant topics. Topics range from the agenda for team meetings to references on environmental topics and include historical data on many variables that could potentially provide the basis for a CAAA Title V permit.

## Managing Chemical Safety

CHEMS provides a set of management tools that P&G can use to induce P&G employees and customers to use chemicals safely. The system

- tracks what chemicals P&G buys and in what quantities (among other chemicals, covers all relevant to specific regulatory requirements, such as SARA, OSHA, and others).

- does not capture by-products generated during manufacturing or other chemical use in house.

- educates people on how to use these chemicals

- identifies implications of use for waste streams, by chemical

- seeks to reduce the number of chemicals used and to reduce the toxicity of the chemicals used[11]

- provides a vehicle for the MEG to raise questions about potential substitutes for specific chemicals.

In practice, CHEMS focuses attention on chemicals with the largest volume and that are the most hazardous. Anhydrous ammonia and chlorine would come near the top of a list of these.

CHEMS has also supported Designing Waste Out initiatives and provided the vehicle for eliminating isopropyl alcohol from one manufacturing process, during a full-scale pilot test at Mehoopany. CHEMS also appears to have supported a review of a decision to cut waste streams that postponed the opening of an additional disposal site. Mehoopany assembled a broad team to address this question; CHEMS supported the team. The team ultimately found ways to extend the life of the existing disposal site by cutting specific waste streams.

## PROMOTING EFFECTIVE RELATIONSHIPS WITH RELEVANT STAKEHOLDERS

Stakeholder relationships are very important to the Mehoopany plant. The plant's environmental staff members work in partnership with both internal and external customers, who are considered to include regulators, neighbors, the community, and the environment itself (river, forest, etc.). Maintaining the stakeholder franchise is an important way for the plant to retain control of its own business.

---

[11]However, the reduction of the number of chemicals used at the plant has been somewhat limited. In fact, the diversity of paints used is rising, even though CHEMS has pointed out the negative environmental effects. The environmental manager is more confident that he can use CHEMS to cut the number of oils used because only minor effects on broader corporate performance would result.

## Relationships with Regulators

Mehoopany's staff invests time in its relationships with regulators, especially since state regulators are often junior and not very experienced, particularly with industrial processes and the pulp and paper industry.[12] So, the staff has helped train state regulators on such environmental issues as the different types of technologies used in the industry. Tours of the facility for Pennsylvania DEP personnel highlight good environmental practices, such as good industrial wastewater treatment. Mehoopany has also sponsored a course about the paper industry for state water permitters to help them better understand the industry's environmental issues.

Plant staff members also participate in statewide forums on environmental issues; the environmental manager, for example, attends all meetings of the Air Quality Technical Advisory Committee. Mehoopany has also, when asked, provided input on issues that have little direct effect on itself.

Even more broadly, a representative of MEG participated in the Pennsylvania Governor's Twenty-First Century Environmental Commission. This commission of about 25 people thought about how environmental issues should evolve in Pennsylvania in the 21st century. Over the course of a year, the commission addressed land use, environmental governance, natural resource protection and restoration, and environmental education issues. The membership included moderate environmental groups, firms, educators, and consulting firms.[13]

Pennsylvania state regulators have been moving toward reducing oversight of permits and other issues when past performance has been good. This heightens the importance of tending relationships. MEG staff members have a mutually trusting relationship with Pennsylvania regulators. It is our impression that the relationships are so good now that P&G Mehoopany already benefits from an effective

---

[12]In fact, several members of MEG used to be state regulators. Environmental professionals in Pennsylvania often start by working in a regulatory agency and then later move into industry positions.

[13]This report has come out since this case study was conducted; see Pennsylvania 21st Century Environment Commission (1998).

two-tiered system. It appears that ISO 14001 implementation would add nothing, either from a business or from a regulatory standpoint. The plant's program already comes close to Pennsylvania's Strategic Environmental Management (SEM) efforts. Mehoopany environmental staff even provided input to Pennsylvania DEP on the environmental business leadership piece of this evolving SEM approach. However, MEG's views on SEM differs slightly from those of Pennsylvania DEP with respect to total community sharing policies.

The MEG staff would like to see Pennsylvania DEP create a much-enhanced two-tier system in which facilities are rewarded for good performance and for having a SEM system, such as ISO 14001, in place. Elements of such a system that would interest P&G include

- permits with 10-year validity

- sitewide permits

- reduced inspections—for example, every other year rather than annually

- greater discretion to comply, especially with regard to administrative failures, paperwork, etc.

## Community Relations

Community relations and company image are especially important. MEG works with the plant public affairs office on community outreach. Members of the Mehoopany staff do not want to see an article in the local paper that criticizes the plant. Part of their stakeholder philosophy is "think like your community" and "be a member of the community." The plant environmental manager describes his public vision as follows: The community does not "hear, smell, or see the facility in a negative way." This community philosophy, as well as concerns about potential future regulations, motivated the plant's voluntary reduction of plant odors.

Mehoopany also helps build off-site environmental awareness, both for employees and for members of the community. In 1995, the plant held a large public fair to celebrate the 25th anniversary of Earth Day which included such environmental groups as The Nature Conservancy and the Audubon Society. Mehoopany staff members have built a nature trail across the street from the site and, in partnership with the Pennsylvania Department of Conservation and Resources, have provided 30 volunteers to work at local parks. For 17 years, Mehoopany staff have participated in the local school's environmental day for 5th and 6th graders. Mehoopany has even paid employees for part of the time they spend in such activities, such as building the nature trail. The plant also has a can recycling program, primarily to help create environmental awareness.

## Public Perception Survey

In the 1990s, Mehoopany tried a new approach for engaging its external stakeholders—a public perception survey of community stakeholders. The PPS has been completed twice, once in 1992 and once in 1996. The most recent survey yielded information that Mehoopany was still processing in 1997.

The first round involved detailed discussions with employees who live in the local community and used a random telephone survey to reach other community members. It also selected community "thought leaders" in the local community—people who shape local opinion for detailed discussions: elected officials, environmental leaders, regulators, teachers, newspaper editors, neighbors, health professionals, business people, and others. In-depth interviews ran for one-half to a full hour and were designed to elicit views about Mehoopany. The interview was highly structured to draw information objectively without allowing the interviewer to inject his or her own views. Time was left open at the end of each interview to allow the respondent to ask questions and for the interviewer to become freer and more proactive. The goal was to get an objective picture of where Mehoopany stands in the community; one question asked people what they would do if they were the plant manager. The survey was conceived of as being much like a marketing survey in that the goal was to collect data as objectively as possible to support future decisionmaking. And the effort grew out of the perceived need to find ways of understanding "how one would feel if you were standing in the other guy's shoes"—in this case, the community's shoes.

The second round refined these methods. For example, a random telephone survey identified individuals willing to participate in an in-depth, face-to-face interview in exchange for gifts of P&G products.

Mehoopany went out of its way to schedule interviews with thought leaders to get an inclusive sample.

The PPS has had two main important results. First, Mehoopany got a good picture of its image, including particular indications of concern about

- odor
- negative effects of the plant on the river, if any (nothing specific; the Mehoopany plant is just so big, some people feared it must be threatening the river)
- traffic
- basic lack of trust in large industry, without any specific foundation

Mehoopany responded to these concerns by developing structured responses for each. For example, the plant responded to the concern about odor by putting together a community advisory team that met every six months for several years. After the team broke up, Mehoopany continued to share information with former members. To address the river's health, the plant sponsored and invited the public to attend a workshop, which the Academy of Natural Sciences of Philadelphia actually put together and ran.

Second, Mehoopany staff met face to face with many important external players and used these opportunities to promote the sort of continuing dialogue that could proceed without being prompted by an immediate concern or need on P&G's part. The resulting discussions would lack an agenda or the pressure that accompanies a need to make a decision. Since this promoted better long-term relationships, it was at least as important as the first product. The plant environmental manager found that personal relationships support a continuing bond of trust between organizations even when the organizations take different positions on specific issues. The differences do not become personal and hence remain open to rational discussion and management.

This exercise was valuable, but expensive. The second time around, Mehoopany offered P&G products in exchange for the random interviews and worked hard to accommodate the needs of the more-targeted influential individuals. On average, each interview basically took two hours, including all the preparation, give and take, etc. Interviewing notables cost about 400 hours of MEG staff time—partly because public affairs staff members also attended this particular group of interviews. Mehoopany is now seeking ways to continue this dialogue, with better targeting to allow greater frequency but without such a heavy cost. The MEG staff currently continues to meet with about five thought leaders a year. The staff members recognize the value of this ongoing face-to-face discussion with selected community leaders. MEG tries to be open and honest as possible in these meetings, for example, giving a sludge sample to a local environmental group to analyze when the group was concerned about its contents. The plant environmental manager said that it is important for people to get to "know you as a person, not as a company."

## Working with Suppliers in Sustainable Forestry

The plant has aggressively reached out to its wood suppliers on environmental issues. Mehoopany has promoted sustainable forestry to protect the health of and to increase the safety of logging in local forests, even though P&G neither owns them nor has potential financial liability in them.

In this vein, Mehoopany's forestry group has given technical training to its suppliers to improve practices that affect environmental and safety performance. In 1996, the group trained 300 loggers in such environmental practices as controlling erosion, creating buffer strips around streams, and using harvesting strategies. Such practices are compatible with the hardwood forests that dominate around Mehoopany and that P&G Mehoopany relies upon to ensure the quality of its pulp. Mehoopany has also reached agreements with some suppliers to avoid logging during the muddy spring and fall "breakup" periods, when logging operations can especially damage the forests. Participating suppliers continue to pay workers during this period, and P&G helps the suppliers avoid cash-flow problems that might accompany such a break in production (cash flow is important because suppliers tend to work very close to the edge, hand to mouth, without much financial slack).

Mehoopany is on the verge of formalizing these initiatives by requiring certain green and safe practices of its suppliers. If this occurs, the formal certification process will be coordinated with a broader effort to impose quality, safety, and environmental requirements as part of a qualification process. Mehoopany may already have stopped purchasing from some suppliers who have avoided making the "long-term investments" in better practices that P&G wants as part of its long-term relationships. In 1997, such a decision would have been made on strictly subjective grounds. Mehoopany's commitment to sustainable forestry is reflected in its continuing participation in a Pennsylvania program on sustainable forestry.

## TRAINING AND MOTIVATING PEOPLE

Mehoopany tries to build employee support and ownership of environmental issues through education and training programs and other motivational activities.

### Education and Training

Mehoopany conducts a range of environmental education and training activities for its employees, from general to more-specific activities. Most of these activities are summarized in Table A.9.

In Mehoopany's New Employee Environmental Orientation Training, everyone receives a one-and-one-half hour presentation on his or her environmental role and ownership. Part of this presentation shows how environmental excellence gives the business a competitive advantage. Because every employee owns company stock, this business linkage can help motivate employees to pay more attention to environmental issues.

Mehoopany also conducts area-specific environmental training. For example, annual hazardous waste training and emergency response training are annual, while other areas are less frequent. The plant also targets special environmental areas for training if management feels there is a need. All module safety functional leaders receive periodic environmental overview training. Mehoopany also periodically provides special environmental information meetings for selected staff.

The PSM also gives a three-hour class on environmental issues to every new employee, which includes a 30-minute presentation explaining why good environmental performance is important. This class is structured to raise a series of specific questions and to promote open discussion among participants.  The questions help new hires understand the importance of environmental issues, what Mehoopany expects of employees, and what they can do to promote the environmental goals of the firm.

Other environmental educational activities include articles in the company paper; special environmental brochures that help educate employees, their families, and the general public; and other forms of community outreach (as discussed earlier).  For instance, P&G Mehoopany's environmental brochures include *The Solid Waste Utilization Handbook* (undated b), *25 Years Treating Nature as a Customer* (undated a), and *Environmental Update 1997* (1997d).  *The Solid Waste Utilization Handbook* describes the solid waste responsibilities of employees, performance expectations, definitions, and successes.  A large display at the facility's entrance explains the importance of environmental issues in plant operations.  In addition, MEG staff members participate in local, regional, and national environmental conferences to learn from other organization's environmental activities, such as Air and Waste Management Association meetings, and to share their own experiences, such as giving a presentation at NPPR.

## Motivation

Mehoopany rewards its employees according to their performance, i.e., delivering results, and this includes environmental performance. For each employee, there are minimum expectations for environmental performance.  If an employee does not meet them, there is a formal plan with explicit consequences to make sure the employee gets back at least to the standard.  For example, a person's environmental performance may prevent his or her advancement.

Mehoopany managers prefer to motivate people using incentives rather than punishment.  One incentive they use to motivate employees is the Environmental Council of the States (ECOS) award, a noncash environmental recognition program.  ECOS award winners appear in the company newspaper, *Mehoopany News*, receive a plaque, and dinner.  However, some employees are still not very aware of this program.

Table A.9

Mehoopany Environmental Education—Building Site Environmental Support and Ownership

| | Audience | Content | Frequency |
|---|---|---|---|
| Environmental orientation for new employees | All new employees | Corporate environmental policy, individual expectations, site environmental overview including environmental systems, chemical management and right-to-know, solid waste reduction and recycling, Toxic Substance Control Act (TOSCA) information, wastewater issues, community tour and perspective, air emissions control systems, environmental resources, and roles | Not applicable |
| Annual Right-to-Know refresher | All employees | Chemical safety refresher, material safety data sheet and right-to-know information | Annual |
| Department of Transportation Training | General: services, stock preparation, storeroom | Overview of the Department of Transportation's hazardous materials shipping management system and expectations | Every 2 years |
| | Detail: approved shippers | Function-specific training in shipping hazardous materials | |
| Hazardous Waste Operations Training | Emergency responders (Process Services), hazardous waste technicians | Training and certification of hazardous materials technician and of hazardous materials operations-level personnel | Annual |

**Table A.9—Continued**

| | Audience | Content | Frequency |
|---|---|---|---|
| Module safety functional leader environmental overview | Site incident command leaders | Incident command training, plus initial 24 hour, refresher 8 hour HM operations training | |
| | Module safety functional leaders | Broad environmental "refresher" training (objectives, expectations, systems, roles) | Periodic |
| "New role" environmental training | Individuals moving into roles with direct environmental responsibility (e.g., Process Services, Papermaking, Engineering, Diaper Delivery, Diaper Facilities organizations) | Specific training and expectations for the area and role involved, general environmental refresher training | Periodic |
| Process Services Module environmental training | All process services personnel | Environmental performance, issues, opportunity review, teamwork plan review | ~Annual |
| | New Environmental Services Department employees | Specific environmental education and corporate policy discussions | As new employees enter area |
| *Mehoopany News* articles | All site personnel | Specific to topic. Recent articles include chlorine reduction, governor's waste minimization award, river survey results, emergency response drill results, etc. | ~3/year |

SOURCE: P&G Mahoopany.

Another incentive has been outside recognition of the facility's overall environmental record. In 1996, the Mehoopany plant received the Pennsylvania Governor's Environmental Excellence Award, which the governor presented to the operations employees. Such recognition makes employees feel good about their environmental accomplishments and helps motivate them to continue such good work.

Whatever the incentive, ownership and accountability are the heart of P&G's idea of management. For environmental issues, this is most directly shown by the strong support within P&G for allocating environmental costs to the business units responsible for generating these costs. The basic idea is simple:

- Place all environmentally related costs in well-defined cost pools.

- Develop simple rules and supporting practices to allocate each pool to a product module.

- Ensure that the financial system enforces this accounting system.

Mehoopany's own system for allocating costs to business units is very good:

- The cost of MEG is allocated to product units using simple rules subject to annual revision.

- The plant tracks all waste streams and either charges business modules for the costs the waste imposes, credits the modules for revenues generated from selling waste, or credits the modules for costs displaced by using waste for in-house processes. Fuel displaced is valued at the full cost savings associated with the fuel.

- Allocating the costs of disposing of solid waste can be a problem because it all passes through a single transport point on the way to disposal. To allocate the cost of all this material, Mehoopany simply weighs each container coming from a product module to the transport point and allocates costs in proportion to weight. This does not result in an exact value but is close enough for cost allocation.

- Environmental fines are not an issue. Mehoopany has had only two minor fines in the last 14 years or so.

- Most costs related to the Comprehensive Environmental Response, Compensation, and Liability Act (CERCLA) come from a central corporate fund not allocated to product modules. But CERCLA costs associated with a site remain at that site.

This approach has the strong advantage of translating environmental concerns into a single currency—real cash flows—that is relevant to the core business concerns of each module. Environmental effects are immediately integrated with general business management.

## CONCLUSION

The P&G Mehoopany plant has a strong, well-run, and efficient environmental program. This program is built on a strong corporate EMS philosophy and ethic and uses a TQM-type approach. Mehoopany's EMS tries to take an integrated systems approach to facility issues as much as possible. The plant is effective at integrating environmental issues into the business units, including allocating environmental costs back to business units, and at emphasizing P2 initiatives. Mehoopany effectively uses cross-functional teams to help with this process. Managers base their environmental decisions on strategic thinking about the long-term impacts (potential future regulations, effects on the environment, relationships with stakeholders, etc.), as well as economic rationales. The plant has been effective at reducing its environmental impact and at finding cost savings from environmental initiatives, especially in the solid waste area. Relationships with regulators and community are very good, which feeds into the ability to generate internal management support to be more proactive and innovative in some environmental approaches. Management has invested substantial resources (man-hours, dollars, training, etc.) to develop and maintain this program and has effectively trained and motivated the employees to support it.

# WALT DISNEY WORLD RESORT
# ENVIRONMENTAL MANAGEMENT CASE STUDY

This case study is based primarily on interviews of Walt Disney World Resort (WDWR) staff members that took place in fall 1966. Brochures and written information from the Walt Disney Company were also used when applicable. Please note that case studies are snapshots of a particular organization at a particular time and that WDWR's program has continued to evolve since the interviews. Subsequent communications with WDWR have indicated that, while some specific details may have changed, the message is largely the same.

This appendix gives an overview of WDWR and describes its environmental management system (EMS) implementation, including the facility's environmental policies, organizations, accomplishments, and activities. Issues that are most useful for DoD facilities, such as employee motivation, have been given special attention. The appendix ends with a brief conclusion.

## CASE STUDY OVERVIEW

The large Walt Disney Company theme park and resort complex in central Florida consists of a diverse set of service and entertainment properties spread over more than 30,500 acres. The more than 50,000 employees serve more than 100,000 visitors each day.[1] WDWR's component properties have a large amount of independent

---

[1] Note that Disney refers to employees as *cast members* and to visitors as *guests.*

224 Integrated Facility Environmental Management Approaches

authority and flexibility, and the organization is more distributed than in some more-traditional industries.

WDWR's size, diversity, complexity, employee population, and organization made developing a coordinated and effective EMS challenging. But the resulting EMS has indeed been effective, as the facility's record of environmental accomplishments demonstrates. One key to this success was effective integration of proactive environmental policies and activities throughout this facility. The facility's EMS is less structured and more informal than those of many other facilities. Moreover, many of WDWR's policies and its implementation philosophy tend to fit into the ISO 14001-TQEM framework, in which management policies tend to be proactive, focus on customers, stress continuous improvement, measure results, emphasize training, etc. The cultures of both the company and the facility, which value customers and the company's image highly, are integral to WDWR's environmental policy and activities. The facility's culture is flexible and fosters individual creativity, innovation, and continuous improvement. All these elements have helped create a proactive environmental program across the facility.

Environmental activities are communicated and integrated effectively both across the facility itself and across the corporation. WDWR, for example, uses internal cross-functional teams and cross-functional organizational structures to facilitate and communicate environmental issues. Innovative nonmonetary awards and friendly competition have motivated the staff to carry out environmental activities, even when such activities are not part of someone's primary function. An important contributing factor here is that the cast members themselves have helped to develop these and other innovative motivational programs.

WDWR has been able to justify and thus to make extensive capital investments in such environmental projects as on-site facilities for material recovery, composing, and wastewater treatment.[2] Management has recognized that the benefits of environmental projects often go beyond standard cost calculations. For example, it makes long-term, strategic business sense to have good working relation-

---

[2]These are discussed in more detail below.

ships with regulators and to gain additional control over development operations. WDWR has developed very good relationships with regulators and other stakeholders, which have yielded such benefits for both the facility and the environment as innovative permit processes.

## THE COMPANY AND THE FACILITY

The Walt Disney Company owns and operates theme parks, resorts, movie studios, a cruise line, and television and radio broadcasting stations; makes films and television shows; and produces and sells consumer products. These ventures provided revenues of over $22 billion in 1997 (Disney, 1997).

One major segment of the vast Disney enterprise is WDWR. Because of its size, employee and visitor population, and organization, the facility is in essence a separate community. It therefore deals with its own natural resource, industrial, commercial, and residential environmental issues. The facility thus has much in common with large defense installations. The Reedy Creek Improvement District (RCID) manages the facility much like a city or county, with its own landfill, infrastructure management and maintenance, sewage treatment plant, etc. In fact, the state of Florida has established the RCID as a special tax district.

WDWR is organizationally decentralized, being subdivided into a number of distinct properties. These properties include the four theme parks (Epcot, Magic Kingdom, Disney's Animal Kingdom, and Disney-MGM Studios), the resort hotels (Contemporary Hotel, Grand Floridian, Polynesian, etc.), and various other functional units (All-Star, Blizzard Beach, Bonnet Creek, Caribbean Beach, Casting & Sun Trust, Disney University, Dixie Landings, Epcot Center, Facility Support, Port & Dixie, Pleasure Island, Team Disney, Textile Services, Typhoon Lagoon, Village Marketplace, WDWR Warehouse, Wild Lodge, and Yacht & Beach).

All the properties operate independently, each with its own manager responsible for its own activities and departments. However, facility departments provide functional support to these properties. The functional support departments include such traditional business functions as legal, community relations, public affairs, and facility support.  There are first aid stations at each attraction and two veterinary hospitals on the facility, but no hospitals.

WDWR also leases major building facilities on its property to third parties, such as businesses.  There are less than 10 of these, which include the Swan and Dolphin hotels, the Grosvenor Resort, and Howard Johnson.

WDWR employees have many similarities to those of a large military installation.  The average cast member is in his or her mid-20s, and many are college students.  Turnover is high in certain segments, in part because some of these young people who want to start careers in the entertainment field and others do not want to make a career at WDWR.  All cast members are identified by first name on their name tags.

All this means that the organization is more distributed than a smaller more-traditional industrial organization would be.  As a result, authority, coordination, and commitment issues have made addressing some environmental issues difficult.  Many different parts of the organization have environmental activities, authority, and/or responsibility.  While the ultimate authority is the Disney Corporate Vice President for Environmental Policy, in California, he has little operational authority over WDWR environmental activities because of the distributed organization.  WDWR's specific operational structure will be discussed shortly, after a brief overview of the environmental achievements of the company and the facility.

## ENVIRONMENTAL ACCOMPLISHMENTS

Disney as a corporation and the WDWR site are very proactive in the environmental area.  The Walt Disney Company's environmental accomplishments in 1997, outside WDWR, include the following:

- In California, the company recovered 80,000 tons of waste in 1996.

- In California, Walt Disney Imagineering (WDI) recycled more than 4,000 gallons of water-based paint that was donated and used for graffiti eradication and community cleanup.

- Federal authorities praised the American Broadcasting Corporation (ABC) for improving lighting in at least 90 percent of its upgradable square footage, all part of the Environmental Protection Agency's Green Lights program.

- ABC Television Center has continued to exceed the industry standard for recycling solid waste, such as recovering more than eight tons of videotape reels in just four months.

- Disneyland designed and began using hand-held waste compactors to compress trash in each bin. The new devices, made from recycled plastic collected at the park, are easy to use and cost 75 percent less than the previous compactors.

- The Rivers of America attraction at Disneyland Paris has installed a water-treatment system that relies on microorganisms to keep the water clean. Since early 1996, neither chlorine nor other chemicals have been used, yet the water's appearance has improved noticeably.

- Disney studio sets are now built from North American Douglas fir and veneer instead of Brazilian rain forest products. All set pieces are catalogued by computer and routinely reused (Disney, 1997).

WDWR has a wide range of environmental accomplishments, including such areas as natural resources, integrated pest management (IPM), solid waste reduction, recycling, and energy conservation. WDWR has been especially proactive in managing natural resources. Nearly one-third of the WDWR property remains in its natural state as a wildlife conservation area. South of WDWR, the Disney Wilderness Preserve is home to one of the nation's largest concentrations of bald eagles, as well as such other protected species as sandhill cranes, wood storks, and crested caracaras. WDWR has joined with government agencies and The Nature Conservancy to restore the land, manage it, and establish an on-site environmental learning center.

The IPM program at WDWR has replaced traditional pesticides throughout the facility with environmentally safer biorationals and has increased the use of biological controls, in which good bugs eat bad bugs. The program has reduced the use of traditional insecticides by more than 70 percent.

The tens of millions of guests each year present large challenges for water and energy conservation. Every day, the wastewater treatment facility handles about 10 million gallons of water, reclaiming it for such purposes as irrigation or returning it to the Florida aquifer. Infrared sensors in many of the rest rooms and automatic irrigation controls also reduce the amount of water used, by as much as 250 million gallons annually. The entire WDWR property will soon be irrigated with reclaimed water. WDWR constantly audits energy use and, like other Disney operations participates in the U.S. Environmental Protection Agency's Green Lights program.

The facility encourages recycling wherever possible. The on-site Material Recover Facility (MRF) separates and densifies recyclable materials, including paper, plastic, glass, steel, aluminum, and cardboard. The MRF handles than 45 tons of these recyclables daily, an average of more than 30 percent of these materials used. Such other items as used equipment and excess items are sold to staff or auctioned to the public. The MRF also recycles the rafts and tubes from the water parks. Around 3,000 tons of food waste is used as livestock feed and compost each year. Sewage by-products, landscape waste, paper, degradable construction debris, and ground wooden pallets are combined to produce 50,000 pounds of compost a day, some of which is used as a soil additive along WDWR roadways.

Green purchasing takes place whenever possible. This means buying recycled, recyclable, and otherwise environmentally friendly products and preferring vendors who demonstrate best environmental ethics. The facility purchases in bulk to reduce waste, uses recycled paper for its millions of brochures and other printed materials, and uses a 100-percent recycled and recyclable corrugated product for shipping.

Reuse is another important activity. Leftover and used building supplies, computer components, old costumes, and other items are donated to local nonprofit organizations. Each month, nearly 40,000 pounds of prepared food that was not served is donated to the Second Harvest Food Bank, which serves the hungry in central Florida.[3]

Disney and WDWR have won numerous environmental awards. In 1995, the company received the U.S. Conference of Mayors' National

---

[3]These environmental accomplishments are taken from different company literature including Environmentality Program literature (see http://www.disney.com/DisneyWorld/OtherInfo/inf94.html) and Disney (1996).

Office Recycling Award, the Grand Challenge Award being recognized for such activities as $30 million annual purchase of recycled paper products. In 1995, WDWR received the Trend Setter Award and the International Recycling Excellence Gold Award from the Solid Waste Association of North America. The facility also was awarded the Georgia-Pacific Corporate Excellence Award for workplace recycling.

## ORGANIZATIONAL STRUCTURES

This section briefly describes the main departments and divisions at WDWR that deal with most of the environmental issues. The EMS section, below, describes the ones that have major roles in developing and implementing environmental policy in greater detail and discusses some of their accomplishments.

### Environmental Initiatives (EI)

EI handles the internal and external nonlegal coordination, communication, and awareness for WDWR's environmental activities, as part of Disney's Environmentality philosophy (explained in detail later). This organization helps facilitate many of the environmental activities that are not related to legal or compliance issues. Other program functions include environmental research, promoting waste minimization across the entire site, and promoting habitat and resource conservation.

### Environmental Affairs Division (EAD)

EAD handles most compliance issues. Its staff handles permitting, dealing with regulators, and ensuring that WDWR is in compliance, as well as most of the legal issues related to the environment. This division reports to the company's legal department and often deals with the Risk Management Division (RMD) on issues related to worker health and safety.

### Reedy Creek Improvement District (RCID)

RCID was created in 1968 as a public entity, similar to a county. It was created to manage and provide WDWR's infrastructure—roads, water, and power. RCID is a special taxing district that pays for this

infrastructure by assessing WDWR. RCID also has regulatory authority, for example, it can report drainage problems to the Florida
Department of Environmental Protection (DEP). Reedy Creek
Energy Services Inc. (RCES) provides the operations, maintenance,
and design services to RCID.

## Risk Management Division

The Risk Management Division includes the Industrial Hygiene,
Safety, and Environmental Health Departments, dealing with worker
health and safety, food sanitation, and worker compensation. This
division reports to Disney company administration.

## Epcot Center

This theme park has over 20 different country, technology, and functional pavilions for visitors of all ages. The Land Pavilion does environmental research related to agriculture, such as IPM. The Living
Seas Pavilion does some environmental research as well, and has
worked with the Florida DEP and universities on manatee research.
In 1997, the pavilion had three manatees.

## Walt Disney Imagineering Division

WDI is the research and development part of Disney. The main
location is in California, although there is a large contingent in
Florida. WDI does some environmental research, for instance, on
water quality and minimizing air emissions from fireworks. This
division also handles property development issues, which includes
dealing with significant natural resource issues in Florida. There are
two environmental people in Florida and three in California.

## Disney's Animal Kingdom Theme Park

Disney Animal Kingdom was still being built in 1996 and was completed in April 1998. One objective of the design was to present ani-
mals in their natural surroundings as much as possible. WDWR was
also trying to make this park as environmentally conscientious as
possible, using green materials, using environmentally friendly pest
controls, doing environmentally friendly water management, etc.

## Celebration

Celebration is an entire community near WDWR that Disney built from the ground up, much as any other developer. Disney has been trying to make the community more pedestrian friendly and community friendly for residents. For instance, residents can walk to some local stores, such as the grocery. In 1996, they also planned to include buses or light rail. In creating the community's design, Disney took inspiration from historical construction in communities that people found desirable to live in. The Celebration development had only general environmental impact from road and utilities, not any special species issues.

## CORPORATE CULTURE

In many ways, WDWR's management structure is less formal than those of some more-traditional industry organizations. For example, there have historically been no organization charts. Communication mechanisms and paperwork likewise tend to be more informal than in most companies; for example, everyone calls everyone else by their first names. The resulting relaxed organization is flexible and fosters individual creativity and innovation. Both the corporate and facility cultures are open to new ideas.

Besides promoting creativity and flexibility, Disney's corporate culture is customer-oriented and very concerned about the company's public image. Michael D. Eisner, Disney Chairman and Chief Executive Officer, explains this way:

> Make no mistake about it, as large as our company has become, our single greatest asset is the same as it was at the very beginning—the Disney name. In a world of limitless choice, the value of a brand that consumers trust is inestimable, but that trust must continually be earned. (Disney, 1997.)

Disney's company image is integral to its operations. For example there are specific standards for how employees dress, behave, and even smile at customers. Upper management is very sensitive to potential negative publicity, especially in Florida.

In central Florida, WDWR is very visible in local papers because it is the largest business in town, both in terms of the area it covers and its employee population.  Because it is the largest commercial facility in the area, some in the community view WDWR as the "big bad" corporate facility.  Some local residents have a love-hate relationship with WDWR.  People like to blame Disney for everything, and little issues may get blown out of proportion in local media, especially environmental compliance issues.  Many defense installations face a similar community image problem because of their size, uniqueness, and effects on the community.

## THE EMS

WDWR has a very proactive environmental program and an effective EMS, although it is neither of the standard ISO 14001–TQEM type nor of the traditional formal industry type.  The system tends to be less structured and has fewer documentation and reporting require-ments than if the EMS were more formal.  Despite the relative infor-mality, many of WDWR's policies and its implementation philosophy do fit into the ISO 14001–TQEM framework because they are proac-tive, focus on customers, require continuous improvement, measure results, emphasize training, etc.  But the system also can be complex and confusing to understand.

### Environmental Vision, Mission, and Goals

*Environmentality* is essentially the company's environmental pro-gram.  However, Environmentality is also the company's philosophi-cal, promotional, and motivational approach to environmental issues:

> Environmentality is an attitude and a commitment to our environ-ment, where we, as the Walt Disney organization, actively seek ways to be friendlier to our planet.  We're committed to making smart choices now to preserve our world for the future.  We encourage environmental awareness among our Cast, our Guests, and the community.[4]

WDWR's facility vision for Environmentality is as follows:

---

[4]See WDWR Environmentality Program web site (http://www.disney.com/DisneyWorld/OtherInfo/inf94.html).

> The Walt Disney World Resort is a "Green Property" where Environmentality is communicated to all guests, cast members, and community by what we say and what we do. We strive to be a model for the world. (WDWR, 1996.)

WDWR (1996) has also defined Environmentality in business terms so that all properties and employees understand how it is important to their business:

- going beyond what the law requires
- improving guest service
- meeting cast expectations
- achieving positive operational results
- doing good business
- doing what is right for the environment.

The facility works toward its Environmentality mission of being a green property that sees environmental programs as integral to its business plan by

- ensuring consistency in propertywide environmental initiatives
- initiating experimental pilot programs
- replicating successful model programs
- optimizing cost savings and revenue production
- communicating the message effectively
- practicing Environmentality throughout WDWR
- exceeding guest expectations for environmental responsibility.

Specific long-term Environmentality goals include

- incorporating WDWR Environmental Compelling Business Reasons throughout business planning and operational processes, such as in business plans, action plans, standard operational procedures, etc.
- maintaining a benchmark database of outstanding programs outside WDWR
- providing environmental leadership.

In 1996, the shorter-term goals for the next year included

- achieving an overall recycling rate of 55 percent
- reducing energy use by 5 percent
- reducing insecticide use by 90 percent
- using recycled units for 100 percent of laser printer cartridges.

## Overview of Environmentality Structure

The organization that carries out WDWR's Environmentality mission, policy, and goals has five formal elements:

- The Environmental Initiatives Steering Committee, whose almost 20 members include WDWR cast members; WDI, RCES, and EI staff; theme park directors; and other key facility management and staff. This committee develops WDWR action plans and priorities, establishes accountability guidelines for WDWR's Environmentality program, and provides leadership for all partners in Environmentality. The committee reports to other Disney executive committees annually.

- EI, a cross-functional department that promotes and integrates environmental activities throughout WDWR. This department will be discussed below.

- Environmental Circles of Excellence (ECEs), voluntary environmental organizations of cast members at local properties that help address environmental issues in their areas. Both hourly and salaried employees participate. The ECEs establish priorities and localized action plans and help motivate cast members to implement them. There are over 20 active ECEs throughout WDWR, including the following ECEs: Epcot, Magic Kingdom, Grand Floridian, Contemporary Hotel, Ft. Wilderness, Delivery, WDWR Nursery, Wilderness Lodge, All-Star Resorts, Typhoon Lagoon, and WDI. How they work will be discussed below, in "Training and Motivating People."

- Environmental Technical Advisory Groups (ETAGs), interdisciplinary cross functional groups that provide specialized environmental expertise. They recommend policy for their specialized areas. WDWR has about a dozen ETAGs. ETAGs include

Energy Star Team, The Green Team, Recycling Committee, Waste Prevention Task Force, Alternative Fuels Committees, Wildflower Roundtable, Compost/Organic Fertilizer Committee, Natural Habitat Group, Chemical Usage Review Board, Water Use Committee, and the Pest Management Advisory Committee.

- Departments with environmental responsibility, of which the most important ones are WDWR Community Relations, WDWR publicity, WDWR news and media information, EAD, WDI, the Disney Development Company, RCES, the Disney University, Epcot Science and Technology, and other WDWR operating areas. Many of these are discussed below.

## ORGANIZATIONAL RESPONSIBILITIES, ACTIVITIES, AND RESULTS

### Environmental Initiatives Department

EI is a cross-functional organization that has promoted environmental activities at WDWR since 1994; all its activities are part of the Environmentality program. The department provides educational activities and disseminates information, for the sake of promoting environmental awareness, communication, coordination, and implementation of new and better environmental ideas. The department's specific responsibilities under the WDWR's EMS include

- identifying best practices and encouraging replication
- collecting data and maintaining information
- communicating with all environmental groups
- supporting pilot environmental programs
- serving on the Environmental Initiatives Steering Committee
- maintaining Environmentality phone line for phone inquiries
- publishing articles monthly in the facility newspaper, *Eyes and Ears.*

EI sees everyone as a partner in Disney's Environmentality and promotes the program in all WDWR activities. Therefore, the staff works with and tries to reach out to all WDWR cast members, WDI cast members, and others operating at WDWR, such as contractors, tenants, and vendors. EI Staff members are very proactive about environmental activities because that is their mission, and they are good at promoting innovative and creative ideas. They are environmental champions who help integrate environmental issues throughout the organization. They also effectively motivate and support other WDWR environmental champions, such as the former operations manager of the Contemporary Hotel. Three staff members have personal expertise in the food service area, recycling, and other environmental activities.

EI's actual program consists of four main functions:

1. **Communication and Awareness.** The communication and awareness activities are discussed at more length below, in "Training and Motivating People."

2. **Waste Minimization.** EI helps the various properties implement waste minimization activities. EI helps identify activities, to evaluate the potential savings, and to use these to show the property areas how they can benefit from Environmentality. Some specific activities include the following:

   — Trying to identify products that could be used that are better for the environment.[5] After identifying a new, more environmentally friendly product, EI works with the properties to encourage them to replace the old product with the new one. For example, EI has experimented with kitty litter made from such alternative materials as peanut shells or corn stalks, which can go into a compost pile instead of a landfill. The cost of the landfill is included in the savings comparison for such a product.

   — Tracking quantities of printed material generated and how much is actually used, such as the number of theme park brochures printed and used each week. This allows more accurate ordering of amounts and minimizes what ends up in the waste stream.

   — Providing recycling containers for guest use. Before EI began working with the various properties, especially the theme

---

[5]Other organizations at WDWR, such as RCES, may also help in such efforts.

parks, to provide such containers for guests, WDWR's recycling had taken place backstage. Since guests did not see the recycling, they began asking why WDWR did not recycle. EI wanted one generic container for recycling at all the different properties. Because everything, even trash cans, is themed within the theme parks, the designers wanted different, themed recycling containers for each park. They tried this system, but it did not work very well.

EI then convinced the designers to create a recycling container that would be consistent throughout WDWR. The resulting recycling bins, for cans and bottles only, are strategically located next to regular trash cans. The Magic Kingdom has about 20, and Epcot has six to eight. These bins have been very successful, with very little contamination.

— Providing refillable beverage containers. EI was working with the many different properties to coordinate having a refillable souvenir mug that would be available throughout WDWR at the same price. Trying to reach consensus on the size of the mug, how to refill it (because of health issues), and price was quite a challenge.

3. **Habitat and Resource Conservation.** EI helps the properties implement habitat protection and resource conservation activities, mostly the latter. The properties often deal with other organizations, such as the Horticulture Department, on habitat issues. Also, the properties have flexibility to pursue their own environmental ideas and projects, but EI helps provide support and often facilitates information-sharing. Some other activities include

— Natural resource education and awareness activities. For example, in 1996, one staff member gave presentations about local species, such as endangered manatees and the endangered tortoises at local schools and wrote articles on conservation for *Eyes and Ears* to help raise the awareness of cast members, both on and off the job. She also sent memos to cast members to alert them about natural resource issues on WDWR property. One of these alerted personnel building the Animal Kingdom, who were not aware that wild turkeys nested nearby, to the fact that the baby turkeys tended to cross the back roads.

— Resource conservation. One example of EI's efforts in energy conservation is its participation in the Green Lights program and helping properties see the cost-saving potential. For example, EI might explain to a particular hotel that facing a price tag of $600,000 for retrofitting with "green" lights—$500,000 more than with normal lighting—that the return on investment is $200,000 per year. EI also works with other groups, such as purchasing, on resource conservation. For example, a purchasing buyer once suggested reducing napkin size by 25 percent. With EI's encouragement, purchasing carried out this good suggestion. Such issues usually fall in the domain of purchasing or of the food and beverages group, but EI works with the purchasing group quite a bit. Many cast members in purchasing work enthusiastically on Environmentality and actively participate in EI's environmental awareness days.

4. **Research.** EI staff investigates new products that could be purchased to minimize waste and conserve resources, mainly by talking with people, reading, and surfing the Net. The division also does some research with WDI. However, if the research requires more technical or engineering effort, RCID Environmental Lab conducts it. One research example is WDWR's investigation of compostable food containers, such as those based on starch. The Horticulture Division and the RCID Environmental Lab are working on that particular project, but the Land Pavilion at Epcot Center is also doing some research on food containers. WDWR also works with universities on such issues.

## Environmental Affairs Division

EAD staff handles most compliance issues for WDWR: permitting, dealing with regulators, and ensuring that WDWR is within compliance. These activities include training in operating procedures and compliance. The division's goal is that WDWR will be 100-percent compliant. EAD and the Risk Management Division (RMD) used to be in the same division and still work together on worker health and safety issues.

EAD has a cast of 13, including clerical staff, in three departments. The following subsections describe these departments; note that their names are slightly misleading, given their actual functions.

**Environmental Control Department.** This environmental management department handles air regulation and hazardous waste issues. The department also manages the over 70 underground storage tanks that WDWR has for fuel oil, etc.

*   *Air.* The Environmental Control Department handles air permitting, such as WDWR's Clean Air Act Amendments (CAAA) Title V permit. WDWR is a Title V facility mainly because of its large dry cleaning operation and its two power-generation facilities. Most of the facility's hazardous air pollutant emissions come from painting operations. Some specific points:

    –   The facility once had separate air permits for each source. But because the facility meets specific Title V criteria (contiguous, single ownership, single Standard Industrial Classification code, etc.), it is now classed as a single source. Because of its power plants, WDWR had to meet a deadline to submit its Title V permit on June 16, 1996. The process was tedious and expensive, partly because it was difficult to estimate the emissions of the backup generators. Although Orlando is not a nonattainment area, it is a maintenance area for ozone.

    —   WDWR has installed five new closed-looped machines for dry-cleaning. These machines help cut down the facility's use of perchloroethylene. Use of a carbon absorber process to clean the machines minimizes health risks to the workers from air emissions. Disney's Industrial Hygiene Department required this process for the health and safety reasons.

    —   WDWR does have to submit some Toxic Release Inventory data and had to submit more data starting in 2000 because of expanding operations and evolving regulations.

    —   Under CAAA, vehicle fleets may be required to buy low-emission, alternative-fueled vehicles. EAD staff members are following this issue. WDWR has designated a committee to follow the environmental issues associated with transportation.

- *Hazardous waste issues.* WDWR produces approximately 350 tons of hazardous waste per year, excluding waste oil.[6] These wastes are mainly paint and paint by-products. The facility also generates hazardous waste as a city would. Upper management backs the hazardous waste program strongly because WDWR had a bad experience with a hazardous waste violation in 1988, and this incident is still in their minds (see "Training and Motivating People," below). Some specific points:

  — WDWR often uses high performance paints, given Disney's emphasis on appearance, to achieve extra durability and bright colors. This can make it difficult to minimize the environmental impact because of such specialized points. Also, many of the painting operations are unique and unlike those of factory assembly lines, making it hard to separate and reuse paint wastes. For example, they have unsuccessfully attempted to distill out the paint solvents. WDWR does donate leftover paints and other building materials, such as carpeting pieces, to the Orange County Distribution Center and Habitat for Humanity projects, which helps minimize waste.

  — The facility's fiberglass layout operations have a closed-loop system for acetone recovery that reduces acetone waste by a ratio of 7 to 1.

  — There are no Superfund sites at WDWR. However, the facility is considered a potentially responsible party because of waste sent to a Seaboard Chemical site in North Carolina.

  — WDWR is conducting remediation at several petroleum-contaminated sites on its property, as required by Florida state law.

  — WDWR also handles biohazardous waste from its first aid stations, veterinary facilities, and guest rooms. For example, the resorts collect some syringes from guest rooms (for example, left by a diabetic guest).

  — The facility is trying to enter into a contract with a waste disposal company as the sole contractor for both WDWR and

---

[6]Florida law does not consider oil to be a hazardous waste.

Disneyland. The benefits would include price and liability protection.

**Compliance Department.** This department deals mainly with compliance issues related to construction activities related to water issues, but the main issue is stormwater runoff and U.S. EPA's National Pollutant Discharge Elimination System. They deal with the South Florida Water Management District (SFWMD) and RCID, both of which have regulatory authority.

**Environmental Permits Department.** This department manages the permitting process for new operations requiring sanitary or potable water hookups, working with the Florida DEP, which handles water permitting for the state.

Because of its many construction and other dynamic activities, WDWR has many trailers and other facilities that require sanitary or potable water hookups, many of them small. Regulations require submission and approval of a permit application for each such hookup. WDWR and the Florida DEP thus negotiated an agreement that relieves the facility of having to go through this permitting process for each small hookup. The Environmental Permits Department and RCID developed an intracompany permitting system after DEP gave them the necessary regulatory authority. DEP trusts the Environmental Permits Department to act as the manager and watchdog for the company's small permit sources. The department has developed its own internal permit application process. Besides issuing permits, the department collects and reviews the data to make sure that these small sources remain in compliance. DEP has reserved the right to review WDWR's paperwork and/or to come in at any time to inspect this system. Because the original permitting process was time consuming both for DEP and for WDWR, this change has been a win-win situation for both. WDWR also wins because it can process the permits faster than DEP. The Environmental Permits Department can respond to an application from on site within one-and-one-half days, while DEP took 30 days. This timing can be critical for some projects that need the hookup approvals right away.

Because the Environmental Permits Department has an expert who handles wetlands and endangered species issues, it has not had to hire a contractor. This expert is extremely knowledgeable about wetlands, native flora and fauna, endangered species, etc. She also volunteers on her own time to do environmental work outside of WDWR property and is active in local environmental groups, having been on the boards of the local chapter of The Nature Conservancy and the National Audubon Society, and has won many environmental awards. The regulators trust both her dedication and her technical knowledge. She can explain to them why WDWR is doing things the way they are. She also advises WDI on natural resource issues related to development.

## WDI

One main group within WDI is the Planning and Infrastructure Department (PID), which builds everything on the WDWR property and handles development issues, such as building and development permits. The department also deals with natural resource issues, such as wetlands mitigation and development of an environmental impact statement (EIS), if needed. PID also handles the landscaping issues. The staff consists of about 30, with four in the permitting group. The landscape architects also work for PID.

**Twenty-Year Permit and Wetlands Mitigation.** In 1992, WDWR reached an agreement for a 20-year permit for the development of part of the Disney property regarding wetlands issues. The permit was approved by and incorporated permit requirements of many different regulatory agencies, including the Army Corps or Engineers, Florida DEP state water resources regulators, SFWMD permit, U.S. Fish and Wildlife Service permit, and Florida Freshwater Fish permit. Disney spent over $40 million on the permitting process, including the cost of the Disney Wilderness Preserve, but ended up saving money in the long run. Continuing the previous piecemeal process would have been more time consuming and costly, and the company probably would not have been able to develop as much of the property.

The permit was beneficial for all parties involved, as well as for the environment. In particular, as part of the agreement, Disney purchased the 8,500-acre Walker Ranch and donated it to The Nature Conservancy as a large-scale wetlands mitigation and preserve area, called the Disney Wilderness Preserve. Disney also agreed to fund the preserve's management for 20 years while The Nature Conservancy manages it. The preserve now covers 13,000 acres because other organizations have purchased and donated land. Disney also modified its original planned expansion to affect only 446 acres of wetlands and placed permanent conservation easements on 7,500 acres of WDWR property guarantee that the land will remain in its natural state.

*History.* From 1984 to 1990, WDWR was doing individual permits for each development project. This piecemeal permitting process made it hard to understand the true environmental impacts. Also, it is very hard to get the many different regulators to agree on each permit.

The regulators actually asked Disney to do a comprehensive permit for all its property and development plans. In exchange for revealing its development plans for the next 20 years, Disney would receive a 20-year permit for wetlands and development. The company has had this permit since 1992. New development requires permits, but now the Wilderness Preserve land donation has taken care of the required mitigation of the development's impact. The 20-year permit has made the rest of the permitting process fairly simple.

Disney has to live within its approved development plan because that is the environmental impact that the permit allows. However, the company can make minor adjustments for unexpected site conditions. For example, it can build up to 100 feet away from where the plan says; the plan actually includes general development areas rather than specific details for each building. The permit indicates which wetland areas must be left in the natural state.

*The Permit Development Process.* As part of the planning process for the permit application, WDWR had to map roads, development areas and natural resources. To do this, the facility hired a team of Orlando consultants. They entered data on hydrology, soils, wetlands, flora and fauna, endangered species, existing and proposed roads, etc., for all 31,000 acres into a geographical information system (GIS). The process was expensive and took about six years to complete.

One of the most important parts of the process was dealing with the regulators and environmental groups and showing them the benefits of the plan. From the very beginning, a WDWR staff member met with regulators, beginning at both the highest and local levels within each agency. For example, he began with both the EPA Regional

Administrator and the local EPA regulator, presenting a briefing detailing the benefits for both the regulators and the environment. Thus, the 20-year permit's benefits for the regulators would be saving time and money and fulfilling their request for a comprehensive plan.

Similarly, from the very beginning, the WDWR staff member met with all the local environmental and citizens groups to show them the environmental benefits of the plan. The staff member began with the most anti-Disney organizations. He was open and honest with them and also asked them what they wanted. The Nature Conservancy actually came up with the idea for Disney to purchase Walker Ranch. All the environmental groups accepted the permit deal, and no protests were held. At the time, the state had put a high priority on purchasing Walker Ranch because of its interesting habitats and location; both the ranch and the WDWR property are at the headwaters of the Everglades system. The ranch's former owners had wanted to develop the property, but their application for a permit to conduct a large-scale development was refused. Therefore, the owners were quite willing to sell the property.

Disney's honesty and credibility were important to this process. Disney did not play games. For instance, WDWR honestly pointed out which of its wetlands were of low quality and which were of higher-quality wetlands and tried to ensure that the plans would not affect the higher-quality ones. Then, WDWR took the regulators and environmental groups out to show them all the wetlands that the development would effect to verify that they were of low quality. WDWR proved to these individuals that it was being honest and trying to do as much as possible to minimize the environmental impact. Thus, WDWR won their trust by playing it straight.

At first, it was hard to get state regulators to agree to the idea. However, Carol Browner, head of Florida DEP at the time, was open to the new ideas. Also, WDWR was able to show that the small pieces of wetlands involved in past mitigation efforts were not doing very well. Florida DEP regulators who had been anti-Disney became good friends, because Disney had been honest and "did not play the games." There was also a problem at first with some U.S. EPA headquarters regulators, who almost derailed the effort before they understood the details. Another issue was convincing the regulators to accept a global concept for the permit: general development areas rather than site-specific details. The final plan did include specific details for roads and utility lines, because these had the main impacts on the wetlands, but mapped out only general areas for developments, rather than individual building sites.

The WDWR staff member had also approached Disney management at the very beginning to explain the opportunity to do a long-term permit that would open development entitlements for over 10,000 acres. Because of his explanation that continuing the piecemeal permitting process would be more time consuming and expensive and that WDWR would probably not be able to develop as much of the property otherwise, management agreed to fund the effort. Also, WDWR staff showed management some of the cost savings and net present value (NPV) attributable to all the potential development. The lead staff member continued to keep upper management posted on the process as it progressed making sure that management bought into the plan as it evolved.

WDWR obtained the Disney president's approval throughout the process, first to proceed with the 20-year permit process and then, later, for the Walker Ranch deal. Ultimately, Disney's $40 million investment in the process was justified because of the development advantages the permit provided. The permit deal meant that the revenues per developed acre would be larger than the expenses.

An important part of the success of this permit deal was building consensus both within Disney and with the outside community and regulators and making sure there were "no surprises" for anyone interested in the process.

**Disney Wilderness Preserve.** Disney's funding for the preserve over the next 20 years covers utilities, supplies, the salaries of its staff, etc., at an annual cost of about $420,000. The Nature Conservancy actually manages the property. In the preserve's first year of operation, Disney also provided over $200,000 for capital equipment. The company is also building an environmental center on the preserve, working with The Nature Conservancy.

**Recommendations to Others Pursuing Such Permits.** The WDWR staff member advises others wanting to create such permits to determine the best possible wetlands mitigation in the area. This mitigation area might not be on company-owned property. It is important to hire a good local environmental consultant who knows local issues, concerns, habitats, etc., as well as a good local environmental lawyer. Both of these need to know about local laws and politics. Such local knowledge is more important than the prestige of using a national firm. In this process, it is also important to reach out to the community and to be willing to compromise.

Some corporate Disney staff who had unsuccessfully tried to develop a Disney theme park in Northern Virginia, near the District of Columbia, asked the WDWR lead staff member about how the successful WDWR development process worked.[7] He asked them whether they had talked to the local people in Virginia. They said that they had talked to the governor and the congressmen. The WDWR lead staff member then pointed out that they had been talking with the wrong people. They should have talked with local community members, politicians, and environmental groups, engaging all community members in an honest dialogue. Most importantly, they needed to listen and understand, and their development plans needed to address all the different community concerns.

## Other WDI Environmental Activities

**Species Issues.** In Florida, it is necessary to deal not only with the federal endangered species lists but also the state protected species list. The latter has three categories: endangered species, threatened species, and species of special concern. Before clearing a specific development site, WDWR must review the species living there and address the species regulations.

At the Animal Kingdom development, WDWR found one federal endangered species, a scrub jay family. WDWR successfully relocated the scrub jay family. This site also had some state protected species, including the gopher tortoises and the sand skinks (a skink is a small lizard with no legs). The local regulators had not even known the skinks were there; WDWR staff members found them during the site survey and told the regulators, again demonstrating the facility's

---

[7]The Northern Virginia park effort had been defeated by strong local opposition and negative publicity.

honesty. WDWR got a permit for the gopher tortoise takings.[8] They also captured and donated many of the tortoises, along with money, to a local university for research. WDWR received a permit to relocate the sand skinks to another site on the property. The University of Florida is monitoring and studying these skinks in their new home. Relocating the skinks again demonstrated the benefits of WDWR's permit to the regulators.

**Xeriscape.** Outside the theme parks, such as at the resorts, WDWR tries to use native species, especially drought-tolerant species. For this, the landscaping staff refers to the published list of plant species that SFWMD prefers people use. The theme parks, on the other hand, plant according to their specific themes.

**Green Building.** WDWR hotels already use more green building practices than would a standard hotel. However, sometimes it is difficult to use more environmentally friendly materials in large structures because such materials have been developed for residential construction. WDWR insulates its buildings as much as possible because of weather conditions and air conditioning energy usage. Building construction debris goes to the on-site landfill. The facility reuses a lot of its concrete debris by crushing it for use as gravel, for example.

## Reedy Creek Improvement District (RCID)

RCID resembles a local county government, and although it is unique, it is still subject to the laws that apply to counties. Its boundaries are almost identical with those of WDWR. The district provides utility services to and environmental control for WDWR. RCID has the regulatory authority to issue building, electrical, water, and sewer permits. WDWR pays RCID for its utilities.

**RCES.** RCES was originally known as the Reedy Creek Utility Company; this changed in 1968, when that entity gave or sold its utilities to RCID. Now, RCES is a service organization providing the operations and maintenance and design for RCID. This subsidiary of the Walt Disney Company manages WDWR's on-site MRF, landfill,

---

[8]The term *takings* means that the landowner can destroy the habitat of the wildlife in question, regardless of the ultimate effect on the wildlife.

wastewater treatment facility, and energy operations. RCES is funded through WDWR administrative overhead. RCES helps set the utility rates that RCID charges WDWR. RCES can reward good behavior on WDWR's part and must report all spills to the state agency. An environmental coordinator, who reports to the RCES director, makes sure everyone is in compliance.

RCES has four divisions. The Energy Production division handles electrical production and distribution, natural gas distribution, high temperature hot water, and fuel oil storage. WDWR's energy conservation program is very proactive. For economic reasons, RCID does more in this area than any other county in Florida. The Planning and Engineering Group includes a survey department and an engineering department. The Instrumentation and Control Group handles the computer network, personal computers, instruments, etc.

The fourth division, Water and Waste Resources, is the most relevant for environmental issues. The division has five departments: Solid Waste, Wastewater, Water Supply, Drainage (stormwater utility), and Recycling of Solid Waste. Most environmental concerns fall under solid waste, wastewater, and water supply, as explained in the next several subparagraphs.

*Solid Waste Issues.* The volume of solid waste WDWR generates has gone up 2 to 3 percent per year. But if not for source reduction, the growth rate would be a lot higher because of the growth in WDWR's activities. Such purchasing practices as "buying smart" are one way method of source reduction.

RCES charges by weight for what WDWR sends to the landfills but does not charge for recycling. Each hotel, each theme park, each water park, etc., pays its own utility bills as a customer of RCES, including landfill fees. Thus, the fees provide an incentive for the properties to recycle.

Florida has different landfill types. Class 1, for example, is for household waste, and Class 3 is for construction debris and landscape waste. A Florida state recycling law that went into effect in 1993 basically requires all Florida counties, including RCID, to recycle at least 30 percent of what they generate in solid waste. But this law applies only to Class 1 (household) waste.

WDWR has its own Class 3 landfill site, which is nearly full, but sends Class 1 to a nearby county landfill site because it must be taken off the property. The county Class 1 landfill charges a tipping fee of $35.00 per ton plus $5 per ton for transportation, yielding a total cost of $40 per ton. The tipping fee at WDWR's Class 3 landfill is $40 per load. At the new Class 3 landfill off property, the fee will be $8.50 per ton, plus the cost of transportation.

*Recycling.* WDWR recycled 33.3 percent of its Class 1 waste—glass, aluminum, cardboard, mixed office paper, and food waste—in 1995. For recycling, WDWR looked at a variety of options and chose both conventional and unconventional methods.

About half of the Class 1 recycling credit is from the food waste of WDWR's many kitchens and restaurants. About two-thirds of it is composted on site. The facility pays local farmers to collect the last third; they pelletize the food waste and sell it to other farmers, such as hog farmers. In addition, there are about 70 cardboard bailing machines throughout RCID.

WDWR recycles about 73 percent of its Class 3 waste (by weight), primarily in the form of concrete construction debris. The on-site landfill crushes the concrete, which is then reused for structural fill, roadway bedding, etc. Any extra concrete is dumped at the landfill.

Overall WDWR recycles about 56 percent of its waste. That is about double the rate of most Florida counties, although a few recycle a higher percentage of Class 1 materials than WDWR.

Every month, RCES produces a recycling report card covering Class 1 materials for all of its 45 customers. This report provides three different lists to the customers with the percentage of materials recycled by each customer on it. These lists are alphabetical order, highest percentage of recycled materials, and highest percentage improvement. There is a large amount of peer pressure to do well on this recycling list. Another incentive is the fact that the customers are charged for the waste pickup and the cost of dumping it at a landfill.

RCES has a full-time recycling administrator who educates customers about recycling, including helping them learn how to get the most "bang for the buck," i.e., when they should emphasize recycling efforts because of the potential cost savings. The information came from an RCES waste characterization study that evaluated the volumes, weights, and costs associated with various wastes at WDWR. Recycling plastic is discouraged because there is no real market for it, especially because the plastics at WDWR are mixed and can be contaminated with food wastes.

**Material Recovery Facility (MRF).**   The MRF was built in 1991 at a cost of about $4 million and became functional in 1992.   In 1996, seven employees worked on the sorting floor, and three were support and management staff.   The MRF was primarily built because of the Florida state recycling law.   Although the law itself is weak, with no real penalty for noncompliance, Disney did not want to look bad in the public eye by not complying.   Each county sends a recycling report to the state, and RCID did not want to appear to be one of the worst-performing counties if Florida DEP were to compare them.

As is standard for capital-intensive projects, the MRF had to be justified up through the Disney chain of command.   After that, the project also required RCID approval.   The consultant who recommended that WDWR build and operate the MRF also designed the facility.   The design process included visits to other facilities to help determine what would work best for WDWR.   The facility made money in 1994 because the demand for recycled materials was relatively high, but lost a small amount in 1996 because lower demand meant lower prices.

The MRF has two main functions:  removing contamination from the materials, then densifying them using industrial equipment for compacting and baling.

Customers are required to segregate their recyclables by type:

1. glass
2. aluminum and steel
3. mixed office paper
4. cardboard
5. mixed plastics
6. newspapers.

But these are not always properly sorted.   The MRF uses a machine to remove contamination from steel and aluminum, but paper, cardboard, plastic, and glass must be decontaminated by hand.   The facility must pay to get rid of the glass it sorts out, but the cost is less than it would be to dispose of it at the landfill.

*The Composting Facility.*  After an unsuccessful attempt to use a composting process with a reactor vessel in the late 1980s, the facility hired consultants to evaluate the best method for WDWR.  RCES engineering group oversees such evaluation processes.

Now, this open-air facility uses the aerated static pile method of composting.  Food waste, wastewater treatment residuals, and wood chips are mixed together and allowed to sit in piles for about 4 weeks, with aeration through pipes.  The temperature of the mixture is monitored.  Next, machines process the material by grinding it together.  This material then cures in piles for about another four weeks.  The finished products are a composted fertilizer and a "tea" (liquid fertilizer).

WDWR uses the composted fertilizer along roadways and other places that do not require specialized or heavy amounts of fertilizer.  The excess fertilizer is sold to the citrus industry at $11.00 per ton.  Because the compost tea has antifungal properties, it is applied to certain vegetation at WDWR.  RCES and WDWR's horticulture group are conducting experiments to improve their understanding of these properties, an idea that originally came from one of the horticulturists.

Part of the composting process involves using an industrial grinder to grind up landscape debris and old pallets to create the wood chips for the mixture.  The wood chips help create the right amount of carbon for the composting process.

*Water Supply.*  Everyday, DWR consumes 14 to 15 million gallons of drinking water.  The water comes from the Florida aquifer and is treated only with chlorine.  SFWMD issues permits to businesses that set a specific amount of water they may take from the aquifer.  WDWR periodically applies for and renews its SFWMD water-use permit.

WDWR uses water conservation devices throughout the property and has a water reuse and reclamation system.  Reclaimed wastewater is used for nonpotable purposes, such as irrigation and watering the golf courses.  This reclaimed water is piped throughout the property in purple piping system to clearly distinguish it.  These activities have helped demonstrate to Florida DEP and SFWMD that WDWR is doing the right thing about water conservation.

*Wastewater.* It took WDWR 15 to 20 years to become more proactive about wastewater treatment, but the result is a $100 million on-site wastewater treatment plant, which RCES runs. This is a "no discharge" facility, in which all wastewater is treated and used for other purposes. All the plant's outputs are reused in one of three ways:

1. Sludge is used as input for the composting process.

2. Some of the treated water is reused to recharge the ground water table.

3. The rest of the treated water is reused for irrigation.

This facility is about 10 years ahead of most the rest of the country. However, such advanced facilities are more common in Florida that often has stricter environmental regulations and concerns around water.

## Property Example:  Contemporary Hotel

Individual WDWR properties can have great influence on environmental issues and have the flexibility to develop their own environmental projects. In 1996, the operations manager for the Contemporary Hotel was an innovative, environmentally conscious manager who personally spearheaded many environmental initiatives. The Contemporary Hotel has over 1,050 rooms and 120,000 square feet of meeting space. Hotel areas include custodial, room, food and beverage, and landscape departments.

Management has very effectively motivated cast members to do environmental activities, such as recycling, as will be discussed later. The hotel recycles 59 percent, mostly cardboard, of its waste. The kitchens are very proud of recycling 100 percent of their food waste by weight. The hotel has also been very effective at energy conservation, including being active in the U.S. EPA Green Lights program.

The operations manager is responsible for engineering, the recreation department, capital projects, equipment procurement, and other functions. He reports directly to the hotel's general manager. The operations manager was the environmental point of contact for the Contemporary Hotel and was also the hotel's energy chairman. The manager in 1996 was also the only operator on the WDWR environmental steering committee, most of whose members come from staff positions. He was a very dynamic individual who was concerned about the environment and savvy about ways to help the environment. He was active on WDWR's Demand Side Management committee. He viewed Environmentality as a holistic environmental approach that includes considering suppliers and other things that happen far down the road. He also believed Environmentality has a positive effect not only on the use of resources but also on the guest experience.

**Energy.** Because of seasonal peaks in demand, a single August day costs WDWR millions of extra dollars for energy. In addition, the facility's organizational structure makes it difficult for RCID to offer financial incentives for energy conservation. WDWR has addressed this effectively by offering the resorts awards for improving their energy conservation. Each month, the improvement percentages for all 13 resorts are announced so that resort staffs can compare to their own performance this month against that of the previous month, as well as against the percentages for the others. Thus, the staffs challenge themselves with this program. The Contemporary Hotel tends to be one of the top performers in this friendly energy-conservation competition among the hotels. WDWR has a Demand Side Management committee to help address energy usage.

**Integrated Pest Management.** The Contemporary Hotel has helped WDWR's IPM program in several ways, such as contributing money to raise butterflies. As part of its own IPM program, the hotel releases insects to control other insects. The hotel and WDWR also do a variety of good sanitation procedures to keep insects out of their facilities. For example, concrete curbs inside the walls of the Contemporary Hotel help keep cockroaches out of the building.

**Recycling.** Like the rest of WDWR, the hotel staff had originally done recycling backstage, where the guests did not see it. A test of recycling containers showed that the guests themselves would recycle. There are now recycling containers in different public locations around the resort, as well as recycling bags in the guest rooms. Members of the custodial staff also do some quick recycling in the rooms. In addition, the hotel encourages cast members who do not have curbside recycling at home to bring such items as glass and cans to work for recycling. At the time of our interviews, the hotel was planning to do a flow audit to try to improve is waste reduction and recycling activities. Landscaping also recycles.

**Other Environmental Programs for Guests.** In addition to a brochure about Environmentality, Disney was developing a video about environmental issues for all WDWR's guests.

Another hotel program for guests that works very well is sheet and towel washing minimization. Guests can choose to have clean sheets and towels once every four days, instead of every day. To indicate a desire for clean towels, guests leave them on the floor. A card in each room that explains the savings in chemicals, energy, carbon dioxide emissions, etc., per pound of laundry not washed.

A similar option is available for soap bars. The hotel is considering switching to liquid soap dispensers instead of bar soaps in the guest rooms. However, this would require a WDWR-wide effort—for all 13,000 rooms—because of purchasing procedures. The soap for all WDWR properties comes from a single supplier.

Because the hotel is a four-star resort, the housekeeping staff also places new rolls of toilet paper in each new guest's room. This means that there will be a lot of partially used toilet paper rolls. Instead of discarding them, the staff rerolls them for use backstage.

The Contemporary Hotel also has an Operating Circle of Excellence (a voluntary organization of staff), which deals with all operational issues at the hotel. This circle also addresses some environmental issues. The operations manager tries to solve as many problems as possible either in the cast Safety, Environment, Energy and Security Committee (SEES) circle (a voluntary organization of staff who work on environmental, energy, safety, and security issues) or in the Operating Circle of Excellence.

## Other Environmental Activities

**IPM.** At WDWR, the objective of IPM is to control pests in an environmentally responsible way. The horticulture group has handled the IPM activities. WDWR's pest management group manages chemicals and pesticides and helps with IPM, as well as doing some research and development. A designated pest manager helps handle IPM at WDWR. WDWR tries to use environmentally responsible chemicals when necessary and as little as possible of those. Not using chemicals is cheaper in the long run because of regulation and associated training, handling, use, and disposal costs. Thus, 98 percent of lawn and garden care on WDWR grounds uses IPM.

As part of the IPM program, the pest management group raises lady-bugs, butterflies, and other insects. The Land Pavilion at Epcot Center helps raise these insects and does IPM-related research. In 1996, WDWR was planning to start raising and releasing praying mantises and to build an insectarium to raise such insects.

**Ecosystem Management.** WDWR has set aside about one-third of its property, including 8,300 acres of wetland, to be kept in its natural and not be developed. Although the facility does not really manage these areas for conservation, except for water issues, it has started an initiative for ecosystem management. This initiative includes examination of possible ways to enhance the species' habitats within the open and conservation areas.

**Purchasing.** In 1996, the purchasing department was also exploring different environmental options. Purchasing has a partnering agreement with Eco-Lab to develop more environmentally responsible cleaning materials. Because WDWR is such a large customer, it has a certain amount of purchasing clout. For example, this allowed purchasing to tell vendors how to package items to minimize waste. Purchasing's materials acquisition team also looks at environmentally responsible issues with respect to packaging, products, etc.

## ASSESSMENT AND PRIORITY SETTING

WDWR's divisions use many different methods of budgeting, monitoring, assessing, and prioritizing environmental activities. We have already discussed some of these in reviewing individual environmental activities. This section discusses some of these costing and assessment activities in more detail.

### EI's Budgeting, Assessment, and Justification Process

EI's annual budget pays for travel, newsletters, flyers, pilot project funds, environmental pins, displays, etc., but special ideas often receive additional funding. The group prioritizes its activities through an annual planning process. To receive additional money, the staff must either demonstrate a return on the investment or have some other justification. For example, the company is strong on rewarding employees for good work, so this is a possible justification.

Showing cost savings is an important part of the Environmentality program, and one of EI's jobs is to show properties how environmental activities can save them money.  Staff members meet with the property managers and explain all the benefits, both financial and nonfinancial.  To get the managers' attention, EI staff begin by asking: "How would you like to save some money?"  Staff members then explain ways to do so.  Of course, not all projects have financial advantages.  When one does not, but does have a dollar equivalent, EI explains the environmental benefits, and most managers will implement the idea that is better for the environment.  EI personnel also make a point of talking with property staff members, because they believe that a project will not work nine times out of ten if they talk only with management.

EI's presentation for properties on the cost savings covers "Business Reasons for Environmentality."  The presentation includes cost comparisons of traditional versus environmentally friendly alternatives for such items as laser printer cartridges, mulch, copying, food waste, and energy use.  For example, hardwood mulch is both better for the environment and cheaper than cypress, making double-sided copies uses less paper, composting food waste is preferable to sending it to a landfill, and the Green Lights program saves energy.  Table B.1 presents one of the comparisons, the annual cost for using new laser printer cartridges versus that for using recycled ones.  Such specific money-saving examples are very effective at convincing property managers to become more active in the Environmentality program.

The presentation also includes summary statistics that compare revenues from current practices with other potential environmental practices, such as recycling and energy savings, by property area.  Table B.2 displays one of these summary tables, representing recycling in 1995.  Such data help motivate properties to engage in these activities for business reasons and also because they encourage friendly competition with other properties.  If the employees at one property see that it is doing worse than some others in this area, this helps motivate them to do better.

One potential problem is that, while the savings from a property's environmental activities are returned to it, the savings do not necessarily go back to the specific area that really earned the savings.  For

Table B.1

Compelling Business Reasons for Environmentality at WDWR—
Laser Printer Cartridges, 1995

| | Quantity Using | | | |
| --- | --- | --- | --- | --- |
| | Traditional Methods (New Units) | Environmental Strategy (Recycled Units) | Cost per Unit ($) | Cost per Year ($) |
| Traditional methods only new units purchased | 8,803 | 0 | 72.22 | 670,695 |
| 75% recycled units purchased | 2,201 | 6,602 | 48.47 | 426,733 |
| 100% recycled units purchased | 0 | 8,803 | 40.56 | 357,050 |

example, at a theme park, an individual restaurant that saved money through recycling would not directly realize the savings. This results partly from monitoring and accounting limitations, which EI is trying to change. For example, utility costs at Epcot are not broken out by pavilion; changing the accounting procedures to separate these costs would allow the savings to go to the pavilions that earned them.

## EAD Assessment and Priority Setting

**Costing and Justification Issues.** Competition makes acquiring funding difficult at WDWR. The hazardous waste budget, which covers equipment, maintenance, permit fees, consultants, etc., has strong support. EAD has justified its funding requests for these items simply by the need for compliance. Upper management is well aware that it needs to be proactive about environmental compliance, because it is more costly to receive a violation. This is not just an issue of possible fines and penalties but also of potential damage to the company image. Avoiding bad publicity is thus an important justification in and of itself.

EAD's internal rate of return requires payback in about 18 months, or longer for larger equipment purchases. For instance, approval of a latex paint evaporator came with an 18-month payback period. The

Table B.2

Compelling Business Reasons for Environmentality at WDWR—
Recycling Summary by Area, 1995

|  | Currently Generated (tons) | Currently Recycled (tons) | Currently Recycled (%) | Other Potential Opportunity | Other Potential Revenue ($) |
|---|---|---|---|---|---|
| All Star Resorts | 2,390 | 585 | 24 | 785 | 77,014 |
| Blizzard Beach | 445 | 103 | 23 | 152 | 14,942 |
| Caribbean Beach | 1,696 | 381 | 22 | 591 | 57,920 |
| Casting and Sun Trust | 198 | 60 | 30 | 52 | 5,101 |
| Contemporary | 2,774 | 1265 | 46 | 325 | 31,908 |
| Disney University | 118 | 46 | 39 | 27 | 2,662 |
| Epcot | 8,742 | 1972 | 23 | 3,040 | 298,120 |
| Facilities Support | 278 | 97 | 35 | 68 | 6,691 |
| Ft. Wilderness | 1,922 | 501 | 26 | 601 | 58,904 |
| Golf Operations | 142 | 40 | 28 | 38 | 3,771 |
| Grand Floridian | 3,154 | 1452 | 46 | 356 | 34,912 |
| Magic Kingdom | 8,154 | 1812 | 22 | 2,862 | 280,736 |
| Old Key West | 765 | 65 | 80 | 374 | 36,689 |
| Pleasure Island | 2,070 | 402 | 19 | 629 | 61,659 |
| Polynesian | 2,579 | 549 | 21 | 929 | 91,147 |
| Port & Dixie | 2,960 | 1003 | 34 | 694 | 68,070 |
| Studio | 5,008 | 1338 | 27 | 1,533 | 150,376 |
| Team Disney | 517 | 244 | 47 | 52 | 5,114 |

**Table B.2—Continued**

|  | Currently Generated (tons) | Currently Recycled (tons) | Currently Recycled (%) | Other Potential Opportunity | Other Potential Revenue ($) |
|---|---|---|---|---|---|
| Textile Services | 869 | 629 | 72 | 90 | 8,872 |
| Typhoon Lagoon | 419 | 73 | 17 | 167 | 16,406 |
| Village/Disney Inst. | 374 | 134 | 36 | 80 | 7,883 |
| Village Marketplace | 2,327 | 462 | 20 | 703 | 68,942 |
| W. D. W. Warehouses | 874 | 525 | 60 | 132 | 12,901 |
| Wilderness Lodge | 1,492 | 577 | 39 | 278 | 27,312 |
| Yacht & Beach | 2,828 | 859 | 30 | 763 | 74,808 |
| Others |  |  |  |  | 137,026 |
| Total |  |  |  |  | 1,639,836 |

SOURCE: WDWR.

division is trying to get the paint company to buy it, and the division would then rent it. If the company will not buy it, EAD will. Funding can be approved without the given rate of return if it is justified for compliance reasons. For instance, this was the justification for improvements to the roof over the hazardous waste–management area.

**P2.** P2 projects have to be justified by their savings. EAD is trying to be more proactive and is doing more P2. However, funding is not so much of a bottleneck as identifying the right projects. P2 has been somewhat frustrating at times, especially in the area of hazardous chemicals and waste. P2 projects can be hard to identify. EAD has not made many inroads in minimizing hazardous waste.

An attempt to switch to water-based paints at the theme parks was unsuccessful because the parks need to use high-performance paints. For example, the paints must have a certain level of shine, ultraviolet protection, weather resistance, etc. These requirements make product substitution difficult. It is also hard for WDWR to do "pharmacy concepts" because the catalysts must be mixed with the paints in certain set amounts. WDWR is exploring a supply agreement with a major paint company. If the paint company receives sole-supplier status, it can create a more-precise paint catalyst process that can minimize paint use. The facility did switch to some high-solid paints that do not use as much solvent, thereby reducing both hazardous air and solid waste emissions. This just required switching spraying equipment and slightly revising application procedures. However, this activity had minimal effect on the overall waste supply.

EAD has been able to be more proactive about solid waste and recycling activities. For instance, the division recycles wood products and uses the waste in its composting operations.

**Tracking Compliance.** For air emissions, employees fill out log sheets as they use paint and adhesive booths, perchloroethylene machines, etc. EAD also monitors boilers. The division has a computer program that estimates when the facility will exceed permit emission levels for volatile organic compounds, based on current usage. The staff makes adjustments accordingly, either changing the emission rate or readjusting the permits with the regulators accordingly.

There is one water treatment permit for the treatment system at Discovery Island. EAD makes sure that the treatment system is working properly.

There are no official forms or reports for tracking compliance. Instead, the staff keeps the legal vice president apprised of compliance issues via a weekly meeting.

## WDI Assessment Process

In developing the 20-year development permit, WDI had to convince management that it would be worth the $40 million expense. WDI staff members were able to show management the cost savings and net present value this project would yield because of all the property development the permit would allow. More importantly, they showed management the business advantage of this innovative permit: the ability to develop more of the site and do it more efficiently than the traditional piecemeal approaches to development would allow. WDWR also received numerous public relations benefits from this deal with the regulators, environmental groups, and community.

WDWR is now using or plans to apply its GIS tool for a wide variety of uses, such as land management. For instance, there is a GIS layer for areas to be mowed, which allows more-accurate management of the mowing, thus saving money. The facility could also use this system for tracking road surfaces and mapping utilities. WDI Planning and Infrastructure has a centralized database within WDWR's GIS.

## RCES Budget and Finance Issues

RCES has been very effective at investing in capital-intensive environmental projects, such as the MRF and wastewater treatment plant discussed earlier. RCES's overall budget has three main parts:

1. basic operating expenses (such as supplies)
2. labor
3. planned work (includes capital, return on investment, safety, and regulatory items).

The criteria for prioritizing projects in the areas of wastewater, recycling, and solid waste are return on investment, safety, and regulatory justification. If there is no regulatory reason for an item, it must make good economic sense. Also, RCES may justify an item by potential future regulatory concerns.

RCES just received $1.3 million to extend the reclaimed water distribution system. The justification was that this system could provide more reclaimed water and that this would look good in negotiations with SFWMD over the renewal of the water use permit. A financing official wanted RCES to share information about this project later, so it could be a bargaining chip. RCES, however, did not want to play games, preferring to be up front about all its plans from the beginning of negotiations. RCES also justified the timing of this investment because the work could be done concurrently with a road-widening project. Thus, the project would cost less now than it would later.

WDWR's finance group wants a return on investment in five years or less, as does Disney upper management. This is important in part because Disney subsidiaries compete for funding.

## Environmental Financing and Assessment at the Contemporary Hotel

According to the hotel's operations manager, its environmental activities do not create much of an expense. Within a service organization, such as this hotel, 70 percent of the costs are due to the labor involved.

For larger investments, the manager uses an internal rate of return of 20 percent to justify projects to WDWR management. This figure may vary somewhat, however. For example, the initial rate that lighting projects must meet at WDWR is a 20-percent return; this decreases to 12 percent until the properties run out of lighting projects. WDWR's various Green Lights projects saved enough money to power the new Wild Animal Kingdom Park. The hotel operations manager also mentioned that rates of return include more than money and must take other benefits into account.

In his position, the operations manager also tries to make capital purchases and implement hotel projects that are better for the environment. For example, he has made improvements in facility energy management. Each guest room now has a Direct Digital Control unit, which allows individual control of the room's heating, cooling, and humidity, as well as the actual temperature. This unit cost $25.00 extra per room. The guests like this control, and it enables the hotel to reduce temperature in unoccupied rooms to save energy. The manager did not have to compute an internal rate of return for this activity because it provided a large amount of functionality at a minimal cost.

**Energy Cost Issues.** The rate justification issue can be confusing with respect to energy usage. The operations manager pays RCID 6 cents per kilowatt-hour for energy usage, but this is essentially "funny" money because it is internal to Disney. RCID buys at 2 cents per kilowatt-hour, so the manager's justification must be based on the 2-cent rate.

The Green Lights program yield a net present value of better than 20 percent, so it was easy to justify from a cost standpoint. The quality of the lighting was a bigger issue. The operations manager was able to show that the hotel could purchase good quality lighting even with Green Light products.

As mentioned earlier, WDWR has developed an effective tracking and awards program for energy conservation at the different resorts. This program allows each resort to track its own success and compare itself to the others. WDWR energy group provided this tool, which is not only good for monitoring performance but has also been used to demonstrate energy savings and motivate staff members. The Contemporary Hotel's operations manager has also explained how this energy saving converts into issues that are more meaningful to cast members, for example, how much it saves on carbon dioxide emissions and how many houses the savings could power.

## PROMOTING EFFECTIVE RELATIONSHIPS WITH RELEVANT STAKEHOLDERS

Given its size, complex operations, and decentralized management structure, WDWR has found internal communications to be very important for developing an effective environmental management program. Because company image is so important to Disney and because of the need for an effective EMS, the facility has also developed effective ways to communicate with its stakeholders, especially the regulators, community groups, and customers.

## Relationships Internal to Disney

Disney's decentralized management structure can make it hard to coordinate and communicate about environmental issues, which is part of the reason EI was created. Also, WDWR property managers have a lot of independence in how they operate. WDWR has a series of formal and informal mechanisms to communicate both within the facility and with other parts of the company on environmental issues.

Cross-functional teams are used extensively for environmental communications in several different ways. First, as discussed earlier, WDWR's Environmental Initiatives Steering Committee, consisting of the Environmental Vice President and WDWR's executive directors, meets once a month. This meeting keeps all the resort and corporate top management aware of environmental activities and helps cross-pollinate functional areas. Similarly, the ETAGs are interdisciplinary cross-functional groups that provide specialized environmental expertise and communications; the Demand Side Management Team's communications about energy conservation are an example. The more than 20 ECEs help address environmental issues in their areas, effectively helping to establish environmental priorities, develop localized action plans, and motivate cast to implement them. Finally, EI is the facilitywide environmental communication organization.

To better illustrate some of the communication channels, this subsection briefly discusses some of the different departments environmental iterations.

Because EI is a catalyst and facilitator for environmental activities, its staff actively and constantly communicates with others throughout WDWR. For example, one member of the EI staff regularly deals with four people in environmental control and two to three people at RCES. The contact with RCES is mainly about recycling issues.

EI interacts with corporate headquarters basically to keep upper management—specifically, the Disney Corporate Vice President for Environmental Policy—informed about what is going on at WDWR and vice versa. EI staff members also exchange quite a lot of program information directly with Disneyland.

EI benchmarks with other companies and talks with other studios. For example, one staff member talks with the San Diego Zoo and is also familiar with the use of plastic boats for food service at Busch Gardens.

EAD staff members talk frequently with Disneyland compliance staff, sharing problems, solutions, and proactive ideas. Most of EAD's contact with Disney's corporate headquarters is with the legal organization, once or twice a month, as needed. As discussed earlier, EAD also collaborates with WDI in some areas, such as in species and development issues.

RCES regularly provides recycling statistics and news of other accomplishments to the Disney Corporate Vice President for Environmental Policy. This group does not interact much with Disneyland because Disneyland buys its utilities locally.

The operations manager at the Contemporary Hotel networks and shares his environmental information wherever it is needed. He acts as an environmental resource for anyone at WDWR who asks and also shares information with third parties. He has several ways of sharing information with other WDWR properties: the environmental bulletin board, e-mail, and meetings. For example, representatives of the theme parks visit the hotel to see what the manager has done and to exchange ideas.

WDWR is planning a Florida-based information-sharing session, the WDWR Environmental Conference, also inviting Disneyland staff. If this event is successful, the WDWR staff hopes to have other parts of Disney attend so that it evolves into a "Disney Environmental Summit."

## Relationships with Regulators

WDWR has been very effective at developing good working relationships with local, state, and federal regulators. WDWR staff members have been honest and open in dealing with regulators and have earned their respect and trust, one example being informing the regulators about the sand skinks on the property. The staff also collaborates with regulators on new and innovative approaches, such as the Walker Ranch purchase and the 20-year development permit effort.

Many different organizations at WDWR deal with regulators. EAD handles most of these issues. WDI deals with regulators on issues related to development. While RCES also deals with regulators, EI does not because it has no legal authority. We have already described WRI's relationships with regulators, so this subsection will focus on some of the experiences of EAD and RCES.

**EAD's Relationship with Regulators.** EAD has a very good working relationship with the state regulators. For example, as discussed earlier, EAD's Environmental Permits Department has negotiated with Florida DEP so that the facility not have to go through the state water permitting process for each small hookup, but instead has an intracompany permitting system. EAD has the regulatory to do this because Florida DEP trusts the group.

This type of trust has not always existed. In 1988, the facility was fined because of a hazardous waste violation (for labeling), a story that even appeared on CNN. WDWR then hired special staff members to deal with hazardous waste compliance, and there have been no hazardous waste violations since. The facility also changed its relationship with the regulators by building trust and credibility. For example, Florida DEP once automatically came out for an inspection if an employee called with a complaint. Now, the DEP regulator calls EAD staff first to ask about the issue. The relationship with the state water regulators is similar.

This trust was built, in part, by being honest and open with regulators. For instance, rather than trying to hide a mistake, staff members will now call the regulators to report it. The staff has been very open about what it is doing, talking regularly with the regulators and inviting them out to see what is going on in person. Such visits are especially important because WDWR's operations are unique for the area; the facility is not like the surrounding orange plants. WDWR has learned how important it is to educate the regulators, a philosophy the facility has acted on since 1988. The staff had tried it the other way, which did not work. Now the staff helps the regulators understand the unique circumstances of the situation and helps them view issues from the middle ground, rather than as extremes.

The state conducts regular inspections for different media. The facility had not had an air or water violation for about five years prior to the 1996 visit. The hazardous waste inspections are usually annual; there had not been one in two years at the time of the interviews. Water inspections are also conducted regularly.

In 1996, the cogeneration facility had some minor problems with air regulations, but these were actually paperwork problems. The facility had not been fined in the previous three years.

**RCES's Relationship with Regulators.** RCES and WDWR have completely changed their relationships with the regulators, after U.S. EPA had levied fines in the late 1980s over wastewater treatment. RCES and WDWR are now partners with the regulators. WDWR is now more proactive in environmental areas and has earned the regulators' trust by being as open and honest as possible and by being proactive. WDWR created organizations to help make this change happen, such as EI.

## Relationships with Community and Other Stakeholders

WDWR also effectively communicates with the community, general public, and other stakeholders about the facility and its environmental activities. Good relationships with the public are important both for the facility's image and for its customers. WDWR's culture facilitates efforts to protect and enhance the Disney brand name in the environmental area. We have already provided a number of examples of how Disney effectively interacts with the public; this subsection adds to this by discussing other specific organizational community interactions and outreach efforts.

EI has primary responsibility for interaction with the community, customers, and other general-public stakeholders about environmental issues. Public affairs, which deals with the media, also gets involved in environmental outreach if there is any potential for controversy from community groups. EAD and RCES do not interact with the general public. Individual properties, such as the hotels, interaction with the general public through their customers, often on recycling issues.

**EI's General Public and Community Interactions.** EI staff members give talks about Environmentality at local schools. They also may set up displays at a local parks or special community events. The staff developed the Environmentality brochure because so many people from the general public contacted them about their environmental efforts. For example, many school children do environmental projects and often choose WDWR as a topic.

EI's slide show presentation on Environmentality talks about both successes and failures. This is important for the facility's credibility, because it shows that WDWR is not perfect but does learn from its mistakes.

The media relations staff at WDWR handles any sort of controversy from community groups, such as animal rights groups protesting development of Disney Animal Kingdom. The conservation manager and media relations staff also meet with many different environmental and community groups to explain the facility's environmental activities and its other activities that might have an environmental impact, and why. The executive vice president also sits on the boards of The Nature Conservancy and other environmental groups, which helps foster a good relationship with such groups. The local chapter of the National Audubon Society is a big supporter of WDWR's environmental activities.

**WDWR's Creative Approaches.** The Contemporary Hotel releases ladybugs to help control aphids. The staff has made this process into a fun and educational experience for guests. A costumed cast member, Dr. L. Bug, gathers the children in the back of the hotel, then gives each child a small container of ladybugs. They then release the insects while the parents take pictures. During this process, Dr. L. Bug explains to the children and parents how the ladybugs help the environment. The public loves this event.

If RCES can find a mutually attractive economic situation, it tries to work with groups outside of WDWR. For example, RCES has tried to work with the City of Kissimee by treating their wastewater at the WDWR facility, but the price was not good enough for the city. Such cooperative efforts have been more successful with energy.

## TRAINING AND MOTIVATING PEOPLE

WDWR has been very effective at motivating and training the cast members about environmental issues. This is not an easy task, given that there are over 50,000 employees, many in low-paying service jobs; a high turnover rate; and many young employees who are neither highly educated nor technical. Staff members have been empowered to be creative and innovative in developing motivational mechanisms that work best for them. WDWR has used a series of creative and fun nonmonetary awards, recognition, and friendly competitive and peer pressure–type games to motivate staff.

Many different parts of WDWR help to motivate and train cast members about environmental issues. Because of its mission, EI takes the lead on most of these, although, EAD and RCID also provide technical training for their staffs. Also, such individuals as the operations manager at the Contemporary Hotel can take the lead in creating innovative new programs, often with EI's help and encouragement. This section explains EI's many activities, some of EAD's training, and some of the innovative activities that the operations manager helped initiate at the Contemporary Hotel.

## EI's Communication and Awareness Activities

**ECEs.** The circle program was established in 1994. Not every property has these voluntary environmental organization of cast members, although over 20 do. Circles are voluntary grassroots groups that EI helps set up to help implement Environmentality at the local level. They help increase environmental awareness, reinforce training, generate new ideas, and implement day-to-day operational environmental projects. ECEs also motivate other cast members to do Environmentality and are effective at generating some new environmental project ideas and activities. Cast members run the circles themselves, although an EI staff member tries to attend every meeting. The meetings last about an hour and take place every two weeks or once a month. The activities the circles engage in and how often they meet varies from property to property. For example, the Magic Kingdom has a very active circle that meets every two weeks. Epcot's circle meets once a month.

Employees participate in the circles because they care. The majority of participants attend the circle meetings on company time, although some circles meet during the lunch hour. Meetings are limited to one hour. Each circle has 6 to 25 members, but some properties, such as the Magic Kingdom, have a number of minicircles because so many cast members wanted to participate. Because of the limitations on meeting size, cast members who attend represent others who are active but who do not attend the meetings. These representatives may hold other meetings for the other volunteers.

Many groups note whether fellow cast members are doing the right thing for the environment and will help motivate the cast to do environmental activities. For example, one cast member may notice that another is washing food containers out in a storm drain rather than a sanitary drain, a violation of WDWR procedures. A circle member would point this out to EI staff members. EI staff would then try to teach the employee the proper procedure. Another example would be a cast member noticing that his or her area needs more recycling containers. The circle would inform EI, which would arrange for more containers.

If a circle needs money for an activity, EI may be able to provide the funds out of its own annual budget. If not, EI may make a special request to the vice president of WDWR on behalf of the activity. EI may reward a particularly good circle with a pizza party, and upper management will provide extra money for such events. Finally, EI tries to transfer effective ideas on circle comes up with to other circles.

**Environmental Awareness Days.** About once a year, EI helps organize an environmental fair at each property to educate cast members about environmental activities. Such activities include the ECEs and other parts of the Environmentality program. Employees used to receive a gift for participating—a clock in 1996, a radio in 1997, and a watch in 1998.[9] However, to receive the gift, the cast member had to fill out an Environmentality survey that asked how the individual had learned about Environmentality, what he or she thinks WDWR should do, etc.

**Pins.** Another incentive for cast circle participation and Environmentality activities is pins. Active members of the ECEs automatically receive Jiminy Cricket character pins after they have attended at least two meetings.[10] Although some cast members have tried to earn the pins by coming to only one meeting, most participate

---

[9]Since then, WDWR has stopped the widespread distribution of such gifts.

[10]Here, we describe what was being done in 1996. WDWR has since changed this award system.

because they want to help, not simply for the award. But cast members do not have to be circle members to win pins.

There are also the Environmental Excellence (EE) pins, which reward individuals who have done outstanding work for the environment. The Contemporary Hotel's cast member's circle, SEES, came up with this idea. Cast members wear EE pins on their name tags, which required special permission from the Walt Disney Company, and guests often ask about the pins. This sometimes leads the guests to offer environmental ideas.

There are two type of EE pins: silver and gold. As of fall 1996, EI had given out 200 silver EE and about 10 gold EE pins. The silver pin denotes a cast member who has demonstrated his or her commitment to the environment. The gold pin indicates that the cast member has demonstrated outstanding commitment to the environment. For example, Jen, a cast member at the Magic Kingdom, found out that no recycling was planned for the theme park's Indy 5000 race in 1996. On her own time, she worked with the contractor to get permission to and to make sure that bins were set up and that the materials were recycled. A large amount of recycling occurred at the event. Because of the time effort and energy she spent making this successful recycling happen, Jen received a gold EE pin.

*Eyes and Ears.* WDWR's internal monthly newspaper includes a full-page spread on Environmentality.[11] This page, written by EI staff, mainly highlights program successes and new activities and describes how cast members can become more involved. In 1996, EI staff members also contributed a column to *Eyes and Ears* called "Conservation Corner," which provided information on such native Florida species as manatees. The staff believes this helps motivate and educate cast members about local wildlife issues, helping them be more environmentally responsible both on and off site.

**Earth Day.** Each Earth Day, many of the properties, such as the theme parks, have Earth Day fairs, which EI helps organize. EI sets up displays at these fairs and hands out brochures, stickers, and buttons. Such local outside organizations as the local chapter of the

---

[11]Other parts of Disney have their own versions of *Eyes and Ears*.

Audubon Society also have booths. The first gold EE pins were awarded at Earth Day celebrations in 1996.

**Other.** Other awareness activities include a computer bulletin board, the Environmentality brochure, and environmental displays. In 1996, an Environmentality display was in development for the Magic Kingdom for guest education.

The trainers at Disney University, which new employees must attend, give a two-minute talk about Environmentality and the circles. But many of the properties also have orientations for new employees, some of which incorporate information about environmental issues. A custodian on the Magic Kingdom is assigned full time to explain such environmental issues as recycling and waste minimization to other cast members. For example, he has convinced cast members to order fewer park maps (these have to be printed weekly because of special events), which decreases the number of unused maps that must be thrown away. The money the Magic Kingdom makes on recycling and saves on landfill fees have justified the custodian's salary. Some properties, Discovery Island and Epcot's Land Pavilion, also include environmental educational experiences for guests.

According to one EI staff member, lines of communication are key with everyone—cast members, the public, environmental groups, and regulators. This staff member has a policy of returning phone calls within two days. The director of EI mentioned how important, yet often difficult, communication is. He said it can be hard to reach 50,000 staff members, especially given the relatively high turnover among cast members but also because they are there for many different reasons. No single mechanism works to reach everyone. For example, many do not even read *Eyes and Ears*. The director noted that about 75 to 80 percent of the cast members will change their behavior if shown the advantages, and about 20 to 25 percent will not.

WDWR has no salary or monetary incentives related to the environment, because monetary incentives are not really part of the Disney culture. An employee who saves the company a large amount of money may receive a financial award, but this is an incentive more for management. An EI staff member has won one.

## EAD Training and Incentives

EAD does some training on compliance issues, especially hazardous waste. The staff trained over 300 people in hazardous waste issues in 1995. Memories of the violations back in 1988 have made EAD's hazardous waste training easier than some other areas. However, training and retraining can still be difficult. For instance, it is hard to train resort housekeeping staff, especially because many of them speak only Spanish. For example, housekeeping staff sometimes put bed linens and shirts stained with blood in biohazardous waste, when such items should go to the laundry. Health Services trains staff about biohazardous waste; for example, a housekeeper who finds a syringe in a guest's trash is trained to tell a supervisor, who then removes it.

EAD does not use incentives and punishments for environmental issues, instead handling motivation through personal interaction. If someone does something wrong, EAD staff members point this out and explain the proper procedures.

## Motivating Employees: Contemporary Hotel Experience

It can be difficult to motivate cast members to be interested in and become involved in environmental issues. The operations manager motivates staff members by helping them see that the environmental activities are done for them, their children, and their grandchildren. He shows how things are linked and presents simple facts to make the importance of the issues clear. He makes the impacts seem real using such examples as the fact that it takes 352 years for a Styrofoam cup to degrade.

The operations manager also uses the "shock factor" to educate and motivate, presenting statistics that show the significance of the impact. The shock factor uses large numbers to capture attention and interest; then, the manager encourages the staff to become actively involved in creating positive environmental actions through SEES. These actions begin as the ideas of cast members, not management, and the operations manager provides the resources to carry them out. The manager says that this direct creative involvement is an important means of motivation, as is consistent ongoing support.

The manager also uses educational resources from a local elementary school, because they explain things simply and quickly and include interesting game ideas; he also finds such resources very useful for working with his own staff members. Positive reinforcement is also an important motivator. Recognition is another, and is an important part of the fun and competitive games created to help motivate cast members.

**Motivating Employees: SEES.** The hotel's ECE, started by the operations manager, addresses energy, safety, and security issues, as well as environmental issues. The circle meets monthly and includes a representative from each area of the hotel. A representative of WDWR's hazardous waste group also attends. At these meetings, cast members generate activity ideas, discuss them, and prioritize them. SEES provides the resources to carry out these activities. Because of the way they have taken charge of this group, the members have become more active and have motivated other cast members to act. For example, a kitchen steward motivated to pursue an environmental activity will engage the assistance of the entire kitchen staff.

The SEES cast members have created a vision and goal for each of the four SEES focus areas (environment, energy, security, and safety). Each area has a champion, who monitors its activities. To keep interest at a peak, the group rotates champions, emphasized activities, and individual responsibilities.

Circle members prioritize their ideas and choose the environmental activities on their own, with only a little input and guidance from the operations manager. In prioritizing activities, the manager and the group try to determine how they can get the "biggest bang for the buck," looking at the benefits to the guests, cast members, and stockholders.[12] The operations manager also keeps the group informed about his other environmental activities.

SEES decided to implement two-sided copy machines and copying practices to minimize the hotel's use of paper. The operations manager helped explain how many trees this saves. Also to save paper, the group no longer distributes meeting minutes but posts one copy where everyone can read it.

---

[12]Many of the cast members are stockholders.

**Recognition.** SEES members have developed a series of recognition activities. According to the operations manager, this recognition program has been very successful. The hotel's recycling rate went from 11 to 58 percent in nine months because the mentality about recycling changed. Many employees turned completely around in how they viewed such activities.

It can be hard to get cast members to support an activity, yet it is very important to get them involved. The operations manager stressed over and over again how important it is to give local recognition to employees, to stress that they are accountable for their actions. He said that he could not "say enough about" the point that, if you take the time to explain things to your employees and show them what the savings are, they will understand.

*Pins.* At the simplest level, SEES members receive Jiminy Cricket pins, which had a new, unique pose, for attending meetings. In part because this pin cannot be bought anywhere, it has been very popular. It even became a fad for a while—everyone wanted one.

SEES wanted to develop a special recognition for people who had actually accomplished things. The operations manager challenged the circle to create an award for verified accomplishments that was unique to WDWR or to the Disney Company. The group again chose a pin, the EE pin discussed above. Volunteers designed the pin, and the group decided to have both silver and gold versions and determined the criteria for them. A silver pin means the cast member has demonstrated a commitment to the environment by routinely attending SEES meetings and participating in such activities as recycling. A gold pin means the cast member has demonstrated an environmental accomplishment.

Silver pins can be awarded at any time; the gold pins are awarded once a year at the Earth Day ceremonies at Epcot Center. The Disney Corporate Vice President for Environmental Policy presents the award, after announcing the accomplishments of each individual. This ceremonial presentation enhances the uniqueness, significance, and desirability of the award. Gold pin winners are also mentioned in *Eyes and Ears.* At the Earth Day celebration in April 1996, about 10 gold pins were awarded. About 30 silver pins were issued between January 1995 and fall 1996. The operations manager himself received a gold pin for helping the gold pin become a reality at the Disney Company.

Pins are a very significant part of the Disney culture.  Disney allows cast members to wear only three pins on their name tags: the service pin (1, 5, 10, etc., years), the Partners in Excellence Pin, and the EE pin.  Receiving official Disney approval for the EE pin to exist and to be worn on the name tag was difficult and took 9 to 10 months.  First, the SEES group designed the pin.  Then, EI supported and encouraged the idea, based on the operations manager's suggestions, then the rest of WDWR supported it, including the energy manager from RCID and the WDWR Environmental Steering Committee.  The operations manager obtained the support of the Disney Corporate Vice President for Environmental Policy in Los Angeles, who in turn worked to convince other parts of the Disney Company to accept the award.  In fact, this vice president recognized the importance of the EE pin and thought it should be companywide, not just for WDWR.  Finally, Costuming, which receives 30 to 40 requests per month for new pins, had to accept and approve the EE pin before it could become official policy.  The vice president convinced the department to approve the pin.

*Competition.*  The SEES group also has created a fun competition for Contemporary Hotel cast members.  Every month, SEES hands out a department award to the best-performing department and a "nonaward" to the least, for each SEES issue.[13]  The awards are statues that the winning departments get to display for the next month.  The general manager has made sure that the awards are promptly displayed in the department managers' offices.  The next month, the award moves to the new winner.  The department winning the nonaward has five days to improve.  If it succeeds, the nonaward is taken away so the department does not have to display it for the entire month.

For energy, the positive award is a 9-inch statue of Sorcerer Mickey.  The nonaward is a statue of a burnt-out lightbulb.  For safety and security, the positive award is a statue of Ludwig Von Drake, while the nonaward depicts a miniature broken crutch.  For the environ-

---

[13]Safety and security have been combined in this award system, for a total of six awards.

ment, the positive award is a Jiminy Cricket statue, and the non-award is a clear plastic case containing a hangman's rope with a dead rubber chicken. No one wants to have the rubber chicken nonaward in his or her office; as a result, this award had not been given out in the last four months before our interviews.

The hotel used this award system from 1995 through 1996. The operations manager found that this game to be a fun way to keep people motivated and keeps the program from becoming monotonous.

*Other.* The hotel also hands out Jiminy Cricket certificates for recycling activities. There are no financial rewards for environmental activities, because it is too hard to give bonuses given the corporate culture and because it does not work here. Recognition is instead linked to feeling valued and feeling worth.

## CONCLUSION

Given the physical size, complexity of operations, number of employees, and organizational structure of WDWR, developing a coordinated and effective EMS was challenging. Management has addressed some of the challenges through the use of cross-functional groups and by establishing a department, EI, to facilitate and communicate about environmental issues. The cross-functional organization and teams, along with the other functional departments, have helped WDWR achieve an EMS with impressive environmental results.

The facility has developed very good relationships with regulators and other stakeholders, with benefits not only for the facility but also the regulators themselves and for the environment. The facility has been able to motivate its cast members to take environmental action, despite their typically young ages, lower level of education, and unrelated primary duties and despite relatively high employee turnover. One important element in this success has been employee involvement in developing innovative programs, which include recognition and friendly competition. WDWR has also been able to justify expensive capital environmental projects, including facilities for separating and densifying recyclables ($40 million), composting, and wastewater treatment ($100 million).

Concern about company image and the Environmentality philoso-phy, management support and a system that fosters creativity, inno-vation, and continuous improvement have contributed to WDWR's ability to create an effective EMS. Another major contributor has been the recognition that benefits from environmental projects often go beyond standard cost calculations and often make long-term strategic business sense. Some examples are the development of good working relationships with regulators and gaining additional control over development operations. All these things have helped this large, diverse, and complex business entity integrate proactive environmental policy and activities effectively across its entire facil-ity.

# BIBLIOGRAPHY

Aderson, Steve, and Jeanne Herb, "Building Pollution Prevention into Facilitywide Permitting," *Pollution Prevention Review*, Autumn 1992.

American Productivity and Quality Center, International Benchmarking Clearinghouse links at http://www.apqc.org (last accessed January 23, 2001).

Arnold, Matthew B., and Robert M. Day, *The Next Bottom Line: Making Sustainable Development Tangible*, Washington, D.C.: World Resources Institute, 1998.

Arthur Andersen, http://www.arthurandersen.com (last accessed January 23, 2001).

Aspen Institute, *The Alternative Path*, Washington, D.C., 1996.

Bailey, Paul E., and Peter A. Soyka, "Making Sense of Environmental Accounting," *Total Quality Environmental Management*, Spring 1996.

Barwick, Kathryn, et al., "Facility Pollution Prevention Planning Requirement: An Overview of State Program Evaluations," presented at the National Pollution Prevention Roundtable Facility Planning Workgroup, Washington, D.C., August 1997.

Beardsley, Daniel P., *Incentives for Environmental Improvement: An Assessment of Selected Innovative Programs in the States and Europe*, Washington, D.C.: Global Environmental Management Initiative, 1996.

Begley, Ronald, "ISO 14000 a Step Toward Industry Self-Regulation," *Environmental Science and Technology News*, Vol. 30, No. 7, 1996.

Berube, Michael, et al., "From Pollution Control to Zero Discharge: How the Robbins Company Overcame the Obstacles," *Pollution Prevention Review*, Spring 1992, pp. 189–207.

Blumenfeld, Karen, and Anthony Montrone, "Environmental Strategy—Stepping Up to Business Demands," *Prism*, 4th Quarter 1995.

Boyd, James, Alan J. Krupnick, and Janice Mazurek, "Intel's XL Permit:  A Framework for Evaluation," Washington, D.C.: Resources for the Future, Discussion Paper 98-11, January 1998.

Brown, Howard, and Jim Dray, "Where the Rubber Meets the Road: Measuring the Success of Environmental Programs," *Total Quality Environmental Management*, Spring 1996, pp. 71–80.

Brown, Howard, and Timothy Larson, "Making Business Integration Work:  A Survival Strategy for EHS Managers," *Environmental Quality Management*, Spring 1998.

BRT—*See* the Business Roundtable.

The Business Roundtable, *Facility Level P2 Benchmarking Study*, Washington, D.C., November 1993.

_____, *A Benchmarking Study of Pollution Prevention Planning*, Washington, D.C., August 1998.

Butner, Scott, "ISO 14000—Policy and Regulatory Implication for State Agencies," *National Pollution Prevention Roundtable Spring National Meeting Proceedings*, Washington, D.C., April 10–12, 1996.

"California Tests Replacing Permits with Compliance Plans," *State Environmental Monitor*, Vol. 1, No. 1, March 4, 1996.

Camm, Frank, *Environmental Management in Proactive Commercial Firms:  Lessons for Central Logistics Activites in the Department of Defense*, Santa Monica, Calif.: RAND, MR-1308-OSD, 2001.

Camm, Frank, Jeffrey Drezner, Beth E. Lachman, and Susan Resetar, *Implementing Proactive Environmental Management: Lesons Learned from Best Commercial Practice*, Santa Monica, Calif.: RAND, MR-1371-OSD, 2001.

Cascio, Joe, and Gregory J. Hale, "ISO 14000: A Status Report," *Quality Digest*, February 1998.

Chemical Manufacturers Association, *Responsible Care in Action: 1993–94 Progress Report*, Washington, D.C., 1995.

Council of State Governments, *Ecosystem Connections: Results of CSG Ecosystem Protection Questionnaire*, Washington, D.C., 1995.

Diamond, Craig P., *Environmental Management System Demonstration Project: Final Report*, Ann Arbor, Mich.: NSF International, December 1996.

Dierks, Angie, Allen White, and Karen Shapiro, *New Jersey's Planning Process: Shaping a New Vision of Pollution Prevention*, Boston, Mass.: Tellus Institute, June 1996.

Disney—*See* Walt Disney Company.

Ditz, Daryl, et al., *Green Ledgers: Case Studies in Corporate Environmental Accounting*, Washington, D.C.: World Resources Institute, May 1995.

Drezner, Jeffrey A., and Frank Camm, *Using Process Redesign to Improve DoD's Environmental Security Program: Management of Remediation Programs*, Santa Monica, Calif.: RAND, MR-1024-OSD, 1999.

DuPont—*See* E. I. du Pont de Nemours and Company.

Eagan, Patrick, John Koning Jr., and William Hoffman III, "Developing an Environmental Education Program, Case Study: Motorola," Madison, Wisc.: University of Wisconsin and Schaumburg, Ill.: Motorola, Inc., undated.

Eberhardt, W. A., and J. W. Plageman, "Realizing the Total Value from Waste Prevention and Beneficial Use During Manufacturing," The Procter & Gamble Paper Products Company, unpublished, November 1989.

E. I. du Pont de Nemours and Company, *Sustainable Growth 1998 Progress Report*, Wilmington, Del., 1999.

Ferrone, Bob, "Environmental Life-Cycle Management Emerges," *Total Quality Environmental Management*, Spring 1996, pp. 107–112.

Florida Department of Environmental Protection, *Ecosystem Management Implementation Strategy: Action Plan*, September 1995.

Freeman, H., et al., "Industrial Pollution Prevention: A Critical Overview," *Journal of the Air and Waste Management Association*, Vol. 42, 1992, pp. 618–639.

Gade, Mary A., "The Devolution Revolution Has Already Occurred," *State Environmental Monitor*, Vol. 1, No. 1, March 4, 1996.

Geehan, Nancy, and John Jenkins, *Private Voluntary Options for Open Land Protection*, Wyoming Open Lands Project, briefing slides, September 16, 1996.

Georgia Department of Natural Resources, P2 Assistance Division, "Pollution Prevention Case Study: Pollution Prevention through Team Work at the Southwire Company Starville Plant," 1997.

Georgia-Pacific Corporation, *Making Progress: Environmental and Safety Report 1996*, Atlanta, Ga., 1996.

_____, *Georgia-Pacific 1996 Annual Report*, Atlanta, Ga., 1997a.

_____, "Green Places on Proterra: Unique Sites Within Our Forests," brochure, Atlanta, Ga., 1997b.

Global Environmental Management Initiative, *Benchmarking, the Primer: Benchmarking for Continuous Environmental Improvement*, Washington, D.C., 1994.

Graff, Robert G., et al., *Snapshots of Environmental Cost Accounting*, Washington, D.C.: U.S. Environmental Protection Agency, Environmental Accounting Project, EPA 742-R-98-006, May 1998.

"The Green Machine: Environmental Regulations and Responsibilities Becoming More Important," *Quality Progress*, March 1995, pp. 17–18.

Grumbine, R. Edward, "What is Ecosystem Management," *Conservation Biology*, Vol. 8, No. 1, March 1994.

Hardesty, Jeffrey, et al., *Monitoring Ecological Condition in a Northwest Florida Sandhill Matrix Ecosystem*, Gainesville, Fla.: The Nature Conservancy, October 13, 1997.

Hoffman, Andrew, "Teaching Old Dogs New Tricks: Creating Incentives for Industry to Adopt Pollution Prevention," *Pollution Prevention Review*, Winter 1992–93, pp. 1–11.

IBM—*See* International Business Machines Corporation.

Illinois Hazardous Waste Research and Information Center, *Pollution Prevention: A Guide to Program Implementation*, Champaign, Ill., 1993.

Illinois Environmental Protection Agency, "Program Guidance Document for Participation in Pilot Program for EMS Agreements," October 1996.

Indiana Department of Environmental Management, Office of Pollution Prevention and Technical Assistance, "IDEM 1995 Annual Report on Pollution Prevention in Indiana," 1995.

Intel Corporation, *Environmental, Health and Safety Performance Report: Designing for Safety and the Environment*, Chandler, Ariz., Spring 1998.

_____, *Intel Environmental Health and Safety Performance Report 1998: Designing for the Future*, Chandler, Ariz., 1999. Online at http://www.intel.com/intel/other/ehs/index.htm (last accessed January 17, 2001).

International Business Machines Corporation, *IBM & the Environment: A Progress Report*, Somers, N.Y., 1997a.

_____, *IBM Personal Systems Group Environmental Report*, Somers, N.Y., 1997b.

International Standards Organization, "ISO14000—Meet the Whole Family!" brochure, Geneva, Switzerland: ISO Central Secretariat, 1998.

_____, ISO14000 Web page, 2001. Online at http://www.iso.org /iso/en/iso9000-14000/iso14000/iso14000 index.html (last accessed September 19, 2001).

ISO—*See* International Standards Organization.

Jackson, Suzan L., "Certification of Environmental Management Systems--for ISO 9000 and Competitive Advantage," in Willig (1994).

_____, *The ISO 14001 Implementation Guide: Creating an Integrated Management System*, New York: John Wiley and Sons, 1997.

Johnson, Perry L., *ISO 9000: Meeting the New International Standards*, New York: McGraw-Hill, Inc., 1993.

Johnson, Perry, Inc., "QS-9000—Quality," *Automotive Engineering*, June 1995, pp. 61–65.

Kaplan, Robert S., ed., *Measures for Manufacturing Excellence*, Boston: Harvard Business School Press, 1990.

Kaplan, Robert S., and David P. Norton, *The Balanced Scorecard: Translating Strategy into Action*, Boston: Harvard Business School Press, 1996.

Kennedy, Mitchell, "Critical Issues of Total Cost Assessment: Gathering Environmental Cost Data for P2," *Pollution Prevention Review*, Spring 1998.

Kentucky Pollution Prevention Center, "Creative Solutions to Preventing Pollution at Dow Chemical," *The Bottom Line: A Pollution Prevention Newsletter*, Spring 1998.

Kirchenstein, John J., and Rodger A. Jump, "The European Eco-label and Audit Scheme: New Environmental Standards for Competing Abroad," in Willig (1994).

Kotter, John P., *Leading Change*, Boston: Harvard Business School Press, 1996.

Krueger, Dawn J., "Project XL a Imation Corp., Camarillo, California," paper presented at the Air & Waste Management Association's 90th Annual Meeting & Exhibition, Toronto, Ontario, Canada, June 8–13, 1997.

Lachman, Beth E., "Beyond Command and Control: An Evolution is Occurring in State and Local Government Environmental Activities," paper presented at the Air & Waste Management Association's 90th Annual Meeting & Exhibition, June 8–13, 1997, Toronto, Ontario, Canada, 1997a. Also available as RAND reprint RP-642.

_____, *Linking Sustainable Community Activities to Pollution Prevention: A Sourcebook*, Santa Monica, Calif.: RAND, MR-855-OSTP, 1997b.

Lau, Sabrina M., *Investigating Eco-Industrial Park Development: Final Report & Recommendations for Future Consideration*, The Green Institute, October 1996.

Leonard-Barton, Dorothy, *Wellsprings of Knowledge*, Boston: Harvard Business School Press, 1996.

Levine, Arnold, and Jeffrey Luck, *The New Management Paradigm: A Review of Principles and Practices*, Santa Monica, Calif.: RAND, MR-458-AF, 1994.

Levinson, Jonathan, "A Forest and Paper Industry Report Comparing Leading Companies' Key Policy and Expenditure Issues," *Environmental Quality Management*, Spring 1998, pp. 79–102.

Lockheed Martin Corporation, *What Every Company President Needs to Know About Environment, Safety & Health Management Systems*, brochure, undated.

_____, "Lockheed Martin ESH Report," Spring 1999.

Marsh, Langdon, "Oregon's P2 Vision," *Pollution Prevention Northwest*, the Pacific Northwest Pollution Prevention Research Center, June–August 1996.

McLaughlin, Susan, and Holly Elwood, "Environmental Accounting and EMSs," *Pollution Prevention Review*, Spring 1996

Metro-Dade County, Department of Environmental Resources Management, "Guide to Establishing a Pollution Prevention Assistance Program at the Local Government Level," undated.

Minard, Richard A., Jr., "Transforming Environmental Regulation," *Issues in Science and Technology*, Spring 2001, p. 61ff.

National Academy of Public Administration, *Setting Priorities, Getting Results: A New Direction for EPA*, Washington, D.C., April 1995.

National Association of Local Government Environmental Professionals, *Profiles of Business Leadership on Smart Growth*, Washington, D.C., 1999.

National Institute of Standards and Technology, Multistate Working Group on Environmental Management Systems, *Environmental Management Systems: Voluntary Project Evaluation Guidance*, Gaithersburg, Md., NISTIR 6120, February 1998.

_____, Baldridge National Quality Program, July 19, 2001. Online at http://www.quality.nist.gov (last accessed August 15, 2001).

National Pollution Prevention Roundtable, *Preventing Pollution in Our Cities and Counties: A Compendium of Case Studies*, Washington, D.C., Fall 1995a.

_____, *The National Pollution Prevention Roundtable P2 Yellow Pages (The Green Yellow Pages)*, Washington, D.C., November 1995b.

_____, *The Source: The Ultimate Guide to State Pollution Prevention Legislation*, Washington, D.C., July 1996.

_____, NPPR Yellow Pages July 2000. Online at http://www.p2.org/inforesources/nppr_yps.html (last accessed July 16, 2001).

The Nature Conservancy, *Walker Ranch (The Disney Wilderness Preserve): A Management Plan, Executive Summary*, undated.

New Jersey Department of Environmental Protection, "Facility-wide Permitting," fact sheet, Trenton, N.J., undated.

NIST—*See* National Institute of Standards and Technology.

NPPR—*See* National Pollution Prevention Roundtable.

Ochsner, Michele, Caron Chess, and Michael Greenberg, "Case Study: DuPont's Edge Moore Facility," *Pollution Prevention Review*, Winter 1995–96.

Ohio Environmental Protection Agency, Office of Pollution Prevention, "Governor's Pollution Prevention Award, 1996 Recipient: Wright-Patterson Air Force Base," Columbus, Ohio, June 1997.

_____, "Governor's Pollution Prevention Award, 1997 Recipient: Ford Motor Company, Ohio Assembly Plant," Columbus, Ohio, March 1998.

Oregon Department of Environmental Quality, "Benefiting from Toxic Substance and Hazardous Waste Reduction: A Planning Guide for Oregon Businesses," Portland, Oreg., March 1993.

_____, "Oregon Department of Environmental Quality Pollution Prevention Program: Environmental Stewardship Project and Green Permits Project," Portland, Oreg., November 1996.

_____, "Green Permits and the Environmental Management Incentives Project: April 1998 Update," Portland, Oreg., April 1998.

Pacific Northwest Pollution Prevention Resource Center, "Incorporating P2 into Title V Permits," *Pollution Prevention Northwest*, November–December 1994.

_____, "The P4 Project: A Look Back, A Look Ahead," *Pollution Prevention Northwest*, Spring 1999.

PCSD—*See* The President's Council on Sustainable Development.

Pennsylvania 21st Century Environment Commission, *Report of the Pennsylvania 21st Century Environment Commission*, Harrisburg, Pa., September 1998.

Pennsylvania Department of Environmental Protection, *Strategic Environmental Management in Pennsylvania: New Tools for Moving Beyond Compliance*, October 30, 1996.

_____, *Strategic Environmental Management in Pennsylvania: New Tools for Gaining Environmental and Economic Efficiencies*, September 12, 1997.

_____, Office of Pollution Prevention and Compliance Assistance, Strategic Environmental Management Web Page, August 7, 2001. Online at http://www.dep.state.pa.us/dep/deputate/pollprev/ tech_assistance/zero_emissions/sem/semhp.htm (last accessed September 19, 2001.

Poltorzycki, Steven, *Bringing Sustainable Development Down to Earth*, New York: Arthur D. Little, Inc., 1998.

Porter, Douglas R., *Managing Growth in America's Communities*, Washington, D.C.: Island Press, 1997.

The President's Council on Sustainable Development, *Eco-Efficiency Task Force Report*, Washington, D.C., 1996a.

_____, *Sustainable America: A New Consensus for Prosperity, Opportunity, and a Healthy Environment for the Future*, Washington, D.C., February 1996b.

_____, *Materials: A Report of the Interagency Workgroup on Industrial Ecology, Material and Energy Flows*, Washington, D.C., July 1998.

The Procter & Gamble Co., Core Values and Principles, brochure, undated a.

_____, Environmental Quality Policy, brochure, undated b.

_____, "Procter & Gamble's Environmental Management System (EMS)," company brochure, Cincinnati, Ohio, June 1997.

_____, "Procter & Gamble 1998 Annual Report," 1998. Online at http://www.pg.com/content/pdf/02_investor/financial_reports/ annual_report/annual_report_1998.pdf (last accessed August 15, 2001).

Procter & Gamble Mehoopany, "Procter & Gamble Mehoopany: 25 Years Treating Nature as a Customer," facility brochure, Mehoopany, Pa., undated a.

_____, "Solid Waste Utilization Handbook: Procter & Gamble Paper Products Company, Mehoopany Site," facility pamphlet, Mehoopany, Pa., undated b.

_____, Environmental Summary Information, handout, undated c.

_____, Mehoopany Environmental Group, "Mehoopany Environmental Vision," Procter & Gamble Mehoopany fact sheet, November 1995.

_____, "Procter & Gamble Mehoopany News," facility newspaper, Mehoopany, Pa., February 1997a.

_____, "Procter & Gamble Paper Products Co.—Mehoopany Site Environmental Overview," facility fact sheet, October 1, 1997b.

_____, "Environmental Product Team Mission," facility fact sheet, 1997c.

_____, "Procter & Gamble Mehoopany Environmental Update 1997," facility brochure, Mehoopany, Pa., 1997d.

Renew America, "TODAY: America's Forces Protect the Environment," DoD Legacy Resource Management Program Cooperative Agreement Number DAC87-94-H-0006, 1995.

Resetar, Susan, et al., *Environmental Management and Design: Lessons from Volvo and Hewlett-Packard for the Department of Defense*, Santa Monica, Calif.: RAND, MR-1009-OSD, 1998.

_____, *Technology Forces at Work: Profiles of Environmental Research and Development at DuPont, Intel, Monsanto, and Xerox*, Santa Monica, Calif.: RAND, MR-1068-OSTP, 1999.

Risner, Gary, "Flint River Project XL," Weyerhaeuser Company, presentation at Georgia Governor's Conference on Pollution Prevention and the Environment, October 31, 1997.

Ross & Associates, "Integrating Pollution Prevention into Environmental Agency Day-to-Day Activities: A Pacific Northwest Regional Strategy," prepared for Alaska Department of Conservation, Idaho Division of Environmental Quality, Oregon Department of Environmental Quality, Washington Department of Ecology, and Region 10 of the U.S. EPA, April 1996.

Stromberg, Janet P., "Rulemaking by Permit: The Silver Lining in Title V," presented at the Air & Waste Management Association 89th Annual Meeting, Nashville, Tennessee, June 1996.

3M, "3M Environmental Progress Report," 1998. Online at http://www.mmm.com/profile/envt/epr/index.htm (last accessed January 17, 2001).

Texas Natural Resources Conservation Commission, Office of Pollution Prevention and Recycling, "A Report to 74th Texas Legislature: P2 and Waste Reduction in Texas," March 1, 1995.

U.S.–Asia Environmental Partnership, *Global Environmental Management: Candid Views of Fortune 500 Companies*, Washington, D.C. October 1997.

U.S. Environmental Protection Agency, "Beyond the Horizon: Using Foresight to Protect the Environmental Future," EPA-SAB-EC-95-007, January 1995a.

_____, "ISO 14000: International Environmental Management Standards," fact sheet, EPA/742-F-95-006, May 1995b.

_____, *Partnerships in Preventing Pollution: A Catalogue of the Agency's Partnership Programs*, EPA 100-B-96-001, Spring 1996.

_____, *Managing for Better Environmental Results*, EPA100-R-97-004, March 1997.

_____, *XL Project Progress Report: Weyerhaeuser Flint River Operations*, 1998a.

_____, *Partners for the Environment: A Catalogue of the Agency's Partnership Programs*, EPA 100-B-97-003, Spring 1998b.

_____, *Reinventing Environmental Protection*, EPA 100-R-99-002, March 1999.

_____, Environmental Accounting Project, "10 Ways Environmental Accounting Can Help Your Small Business," undated.

_____, Environmental Accounting Project, Web site, October 23, 2000. See www.epa.gov/opptintr/acctg (last viewed January 23, 2001).

_____, Project XL Web site, http://www.epa.gov/projectxl/ (August 13, 2001 update; last accessed August 15, 2001)

_____, Project XL at a Glance, http://yosemite.epa.gov/xl/xl_home.nsf/all/xl_glance (June 1999). See current Project XL Web site for updated information.

_____, Project XL Information, http://yosemite.epa.gov/xl/xl_home.nsf/all/xl_info (June 1999). See current Project XL Web site for updated information.

_____, Project XL page for Intel Corporation, http://yosemite.epa.gov/xl/xl_home.nsf/all/intel.html (undated). See December 2, 1999 update at http://www.epa.gov/projectxl/intel/ (last accessed August 15, 2001).

_____, Project XL page for Weyerhauser Company, http://yosemite.epa.gov/xl/xl_home.nsf/all/weyer.html (undated). See August 1, 2000 update at http://www.epa.gov/projectxl/weyer/ (last accessed August 15, 2001).

_____, Project XL page for Imation, http://yosemite.epa.gov/xl/xl_home.nsf/all/Imation.html. See October 18, 2000 update at http://www.epa.gov/projectxl/imation/ (last accessed August 15, 2001).

_____, Inactive XL Projects, http://www.epa.gov/projectxl/inactive.htm (last accessed January 26, 2001). See June 15, 2001 update at http://www.epa.gov/projectxl/inactive.htm (last accessed August 15, 2001).

U.S. Air Force, Air Force Materiel Command, Air Force Development Test Center, Office of Public Affairs, Classes of Ecosystems, fact sheet, August 1996. See http://www.eglin.af.mil/46tw/46xp/46xpe/fact/ecosys.htm (last accessed August 10, 2001).

U.S. EPA—See U.S. Environmental Protection Agency.

U.S. General Accounting Office, *Environmental Management: An Integrated Approach Could Reduce Pollution and Increase Regulatory Efficiency*, Washington, D.C., GAO/RCED-96-41, January 1996.

The Walt Disney Company, *1997 Annual Report*, undated. Online at http://www.disney.com/investors/annual97/index.htm (last accessed January 23, 2001).

_____, "Disney and the Environment," brochure, undated.

_____, "Disney's Enviroport,"brochure, April 1996.

Walt Disney World Resort, "Environmentality," brochure, undated.

_____, "The Business of Environmentality at the Walt Disney World Resort," briefing, Orlando, Fla., 1996.

_____, Questions & Answers, undated, p. 5.   Online at http://asp. disney.go.com/disneyworld/db/seetheworld/questionandanswer /index.asp (1/26/01).

WDWR—*See* Walt Disney World Resort.

Wever, Grace H., *Strategic Environment Management:  Using TQEM and ISO 14000 for Competitive Advantage*, New York:  John Wiley and Sons, 1996.

Wever, Grace H., and George F. Vorhauer, "Kodak's Framework and Assessment Tool for Implementing TQEM," *Total Quality Environmental Management*, Autumn 1993, pp. 19–30.

White House Office of Science and Technology Policy, Environmental Technology Strategy Staff, *Technology for a Sustainable Future: A Framework for Action*, Washington, D.C.:  U.S. Government Printing Office, July 1994.

Willig, John T., *Environmental TQM*, 2nd ed., New York:  McGraw-Hill, 1994.

_____, *Auditing for Environmental Quality Leadership*, New York: John Wiley and Sons, 1995.

Womack, James P., and Daniel T. Jones, *Lean Thinking*, New York: Simon and Schuster, 1996.

World Business Council for Sustainable Development, "Information and Publications," brochure, Geneva, Switzerland, undated. Online at http://www.wbcsd.ch/ (last accessed january 26, 2001).

_____, Web site, http://www.wbcsd.ch/ (last accessed January 23, 2001).

_____, http://www.wbcsd.ch/aboutus/members.htm.

The World Commission on Environment and Development (the Bruntland Commission), *Our Common Future*, Oxford: Oxford University Press, 1987.

Yaffee, Steven L., et al., *Ecosystem Management in the United States: An Assessment of Current Experience*, Washington, D.C.: Island Press, 1996.